THE RETURNED

THE RETURNED

FORMER U.S. MIGRANTS' LIVES IN MEXICO CITY

Claudia Masferrer, Erin R. Hamilton, and Nicole Denier

Russell Sage Foundation NEW YORK

ROR: https://ror.org/02yh9se80
DOI: https://doi.org/10.7758/kokl2957

LIBRARY OF CONGRESS CATALOGING-IN-PUBLICATION DATA

Names: Masferrer, Claudia, author. | Hamilton, Erin R., 1979- author. | Denier, Nicole, author.
Title: The returned : former U.S. migrants' lives in Mexico City / Claudia Masferrer, Erin R. Hamilton, and Nicole Denier.
Other titles: Former United States migrants' lives in Mexico City
Description: New York : Russell Sage Foundation, [2025] | Includes bibliographical references and index. | Summary: "More than two million Mexican migrants returned to Mexico from the United States in the first two decades of the twenty-first century. In this book, Claudia Masferrer, Erin R. Hamilton, and Nicole Denier present the lives of thirty-four people who returned to Mexico City from the United States in the 1990s and 2000s, a period in which U.S. immigration policy became increasingly focused on restriction and enforcement. The authors find that the experience of return migration to Mexico City during this period, after a relatively long time in non-citizen, mostly undocumented status as an immigrant in the United States, leaves the return migrant norteado, "disoriented or lost." Return migrants have trouble finding health care and social services, family life is upended, and economic mobility is limited. The authors discuss what can be done about the hardships of return migration to Mexico City, exploring how existing policies could be expanded and new policies or programs created to better serve the needs of return migrants in Mexico City and beyond"—Provided by publisher.
Identifiers: LCCN 2024027814 (print) | LCCN 2024027815 (ebook) | ISBN 9780871549136 (paperback ; acid-free paper) | ISBN 9781610449342 (ebook)
Subjects: LCSH: Return migrants—Social aspects—Mexico—21st century. | Return migration—Mexico—Mexico City. | United States—Emigration and immigration—Social aspects.
Classification: LCC JV7406 .M374 2025 (print) | LCC JV7406 (ebook) | DDC 305.9/06912097253—dc23/eng/20241216
LC record available at https://lccn.loc.gov/2024027814
LC ebook record available at https://lccn.loc.gov/2024027815

Text design by Matthew T. Avery. Front matter DOI: https://doi.org/10.7758/kokl2957.8361

RUSSELL SAGE FOUNDATION
112 East 64th Street
New York, New York 10065
10 9 8 7 6 5 4 3 2 1

CONTENTS

ILLUSTRATIONS

Figures

Tables

ABOUT THE AUTHORS

CLAUDIA MASFERRER ⦿ is associate professor of demography at El Colegio de México.

ERIN R. HAMILTON ⦿ is professor of sociology at the University of California, Davis.

NICOLE DENIER ⦿ is associate professor of sociology at the University of Alberta.

ACKNOWLEDGMENTS

Our deepest thanks to Francisco Flores Peña, Gabriela Pinillos, Anilú Tomas, and Agnieszka Wieczorek, who worked with us to collect, transcribe, and analyze the interviews for this project.

Many people helped us with the data collection process. We are especially grateful to Silvia Giorguli, president of El Colegio de México (COLMEX), for her support. At COLMEX, the Centre for Demographic, Urban, and Environmental Studies (CEDUA-COLMEX) and Luis Jaime Sobrino, former chair of CEDUA, were generous in hosting Erin, Nicole, and Agniezcka in Mexico City. The grants office at COLMEX (Oficina de Proyectos Especiales) provided administrative support. For their support during our fieldwork, we also thank Luis Ángel Gallegos, Ana Saiz Valenzuela, Allert Brown, Fernando Lozano, Luciana Gandini, Robert Irwin, James Wolfe, Gretchen Kuhner, and Jill Anderson.

Bryan R. Roberts, Fernando Riosmena, Martha Schteingart, Maryann Bylander, Valerie Lima, Caitlin Patler, Yulissa Peñaloza, and Agnieszka Wieczorek gave us expert comments on drafts of parts of the book. Frank Bean, Susan Brown, Leisy Abrego, and Javier Auyero offered helpful advice on publishing the manuscript. Thanks to Yao Lu, Valerie Lima, and Erick Serna for their assistance with different aspects of the project, as well as to Sebastián Estremo for producing the maps.

We appreciate the support for this project provided by the 2018 UC MEXUS-CONACYT Collaborative Grants via the University of California and the Consejo Nacional de Ciencia y Tecnología (CONACYT); a Fulbright Garcia-Robles Scholarship; and the 2018 Program of Postdoctoral Researchers and the Seminar Migration,

Inequality, and Public Policies (MIGDEP) at COLMEX. We also appreciate support for related projects from a grant from the Sectoral Fund for Research for Social Development (#292077); a grant from the UC Davis Academic Senate Committee on Research; the UC Davis Chancellor's Fellowship; the Russell Sage Foundation Presidential Grant (#2011-29160); and a grant from the Eunice Kennedy Shriver National Institute of Child Health and Human Development (1R03HD107298).

We presented this and related work at the symposium "La migración actual en América del Norte: Detención, deportación, retorno" at Casa de la Universidad de California in Mexico City; the Department of Sociology at the University of North Carolina at Chapel Hill; the Center for Family and Demographic Research at Bowling Green State University; the Cornell Population Center's "New Demography of Migration and Mobility" conference; the University of Chicago Immigration Workshop; the Center for Demography and Social Analysis Seminar Series at UC Irvine; the Social Statistics Study Group at the Centre Urbanisation Culture Société at the Institut national de la recherche scientifique; the Penn State Family Symposium at Pennsylvania State University; and "The Deportation System and Its Aftermath," a journal conference at the Russell Sage Foundation. We appreciate the comments and questions from the audience and fellow participants at these events.

Thanks to Michelle Niemann, who gave us crucial writing support and encouragement. We highly recommend her writing coach services!

It was wonderful to work with Suzanne Nichols at the Russell Sage Foundation. We appreciate her enthusiasm, patience, and guidance, as well as the work and ideas of the anonymous reviewers, whose comments helped improve our manuscript. We also thank the rest of the team at Russell Sage Foundation for copyediting, producing, and marketing our work.

We thank our families for their interest in and support of the project. Claudia thanks Víctor, Valentina, Bertha, Elio, Cristina, Ilimani, and Alejandro. Erin thanks Dave, Kai, Annie, John, Donna, Kathryn, Jim, Robins, and Leslie. Nicole thanks Steve, Greg, Allison, and Vanessa. We also appreciate the friends and colleagues—too many to name—who supported us through this process.

We are very grateful to the people we interviewed for this book, who generously shared their time and experiences and opened their homes to us. *Gracias.* Thank you. We dedicate this book to them.

CHAPTER ONE

INTRODUCTION

In a small barbershop in Valle de Chalco, an area in the southeast of the Mexico City metropolitan area in the State of Mexico, Paolo cut a client's hair while his mother, Rocío, showed us pictures of her daughter. "Isn't she just beautiful?" she asked us. "She could have been a movie star." "Or in telenovelas," Paolo yelled to us from the other room. Rocío nodded in agreement. She looked around the room. "This is where I watch my grandchildren while Paolo works. This way we are all together."

Yazmín led us through the street market in Cuautepec, in northern Mexico City. She knew all the vendors by name, and she also knew which ones had the best produce. "No, no, no, don't buy from there!" she scolded under her breath playfully, as one of us took a closer look at some tomatoes. Just a little farther down was her brother-in-law's stall. "He has the best in all of Mexico City!"

Evaristo gave us a ride to the Revolución metro station from the café where we met in Santa María la Rivera, in central Mexico City. "Driving for Uber is better than driving a cab. Safer. But you can't use the Uber app for directions. You have to use Waze," he told us. He made a last-minute turn onto a side street to avoid an approaching traffic jam. "But even with Waze," he said, "you have to know how to navigate the city!"

Olivia lived close to the metro in Ecatepec, in northeastern Mexico City. She rented a room rather than an apartment, in order to save money to purchase her own home. When she had worked long enough, she would apply for a mortgage through the national home loans program

https://doi.org/10.7758/kokl2957.8437

for workers. That way she would have a place in the city where all of her children could gather together.

Mario told us that he was not a big fan of dogs or cats. He didn't hate them, but he didn't love them either. It wasn't the dogs' fault, he told us, but it made him angry when he walked through Cuauhtémoc, in central Mexico City, and saw dog owners who showed off their dogs but didn't pick up after them on the sidewalks of the city. He loved Mexico City, but he hated stepping in dog poop.

Osmundo showed us his family's artwork—bright images of mythical creatures, animals, towns, and fruit—at the art fair in Coyoacán, in south-central Mexico City. Although most tourists were happy to buy the work that the younger generation in his family produced, it was his parents' art that was special. Osmundo took some examples out of a bag to show us. The lines were less precise, the colors more nuanced. "They cost more," he said, "but they are worth it because there are only a few left."

Paolo, Rocío, Yazmín, Evaristo, Olivia, Mario, and Osmundo blend into the landscape of contemporary Mexico City. They walk its streets, shop in its markets, meet their friends for lunch, read local newspapers, and go to church. They rent rooms and own houses there. They provide essential services in travel, cleaning, restaurants, and retail to customers in the city. They vote in its elections. But although they are part of the social landscape of Mexico City, they share something fundamental and unique to their lives that is hard for others in the city to see: they have all recently returned from long periods of residence in the United States. Olivia ran a successful housecleaning business in Denver, Colorado. Osmundo built computer chips in Silicon Valley, California. With the money from his restaurants, Evaristo bought a lake house and jet skis in Ohio. Five of these former U.S. immigrants are the parents of children who were born in the United States. Most of their children still live there. Evaristo, Mario, Rocío, and Yazmín have more than a dozen U.S.-born grandchildren between them! Although they once made their lives in the United States, and many of their family members continue to do so, their current and future lives are unfolding in Mexico.

Olivia, Osmundo, Evaristo, Yazmín, Mario, Paolo, and Rocío are not alone. They are seven of the more than two million Mexican migrants who returned to Mexico from the United States in the first two decades of the twenty-first century.[1] The number of people who returned to

Mexico in this period was so large that, for the first time in at least fifty years, more people entered Mexico from the United States than entered the United States from Mexico between 2010 and 2020.[2] In other words, after decades of large-scale Mexican immigration into the United States the flow reversed direction in 2010.[3]

In this book, we offer insight into this recent transformation in Mexico-U.S. migration with a study of the lives of thirty-four people who returned to Mexico from the United States. We found them in Mexico's capital city. Mexico City has a long history of migration, dating from long before the arrival of Hernan Cortés in the 1500s. Mexico City sits on the capital of the Aztec empire, Tenochtitlan, which was founded in the fourteenth century. After massive domestic migration in the twentieth century, Mexico City is now one of the largest metropolitan areas of the world, and the second largest outside Asia. Mexico City's role as a destination for domestic migrants shifted in the 1980s and 1990s as domestic migrants began to head north, drawn by manufacturing work in Mexico's northern border states. As the destinations of domestic migrants changed, so did the origins of international migrants. By the 1990s, the majority of first-time emigrants to the United States were urban emigrants, originating from places like Mexico City.[4] Between 1995 and 2000, nearly one out of every ten emigrants departing Mexico for the United States originated in Mexico City.[5] This flow of emigrants out of Mexico City in the late 1990s included Rocío, Paolo, Yazmín, Evaristo, Olivia, and Mario.

Before 1990, most Mexican migrants to the United States did not originate in large Mexican cities but in rural places in Mexico: ranchos, hamlets, and small towns.[6] This demographic history of Mexican emigration contributes to a widespread assumption today that the Mexican migrant to the United States is a rural-origin person. The migrants we spoke to were aware of this assumption. For instance, the barber Paolo told us about an interaction he had with other migrants at the border. As Paolo and these migrants talked about where they came from, the other migrants expressed disbelief that Paolo would emigrate from Mexico City. In our interview with Paolo, he recounted their dialogue:

> "Ay, where do you come from?" they [the other migrants] ask.
> One says, "I come from Guadalajara." And another came from . . .
> I don't remember what other state. . . .

I said, "No, well, I am from the city."

"*Oye, un chilanguillo!*" he says. "Why do you cross [the border] if . . . you don't seem so fucked?"

"No, well, I want to cross, no?"

"But there in the [Federal] District, there are more opportunities. I don't know why you are crossing!" they would comment.

The other migrants Paolo encountered on the border teased him for being from Mexico City—"*Oye, un chilanguillo,*" they said to him, using a diminutive version of the word *chilango,* slang for a Mexico City resident. They could not believe that Paolo would cross the border if he came from the capital city, also known as the Federal District, where "there are more opportunities." In their view, Mexico City residents are surrounded by opportunities, and someone like Paolo, they assumed, would have the resources to take advantage of those opportunities. By contrast, the cultural image of the Mexican migrant to the United States is someone of rural origin, from places where there are few opportunities and only enough resources to finance leaving.

The cultural contradiction of a Mexico City emigrant is surprising to other migrants on the border. Back in Mexico City, the return migrant is invisible in the vast urban social environment. Even as large numbers of people from Mexico City emigrated from the city and returned there after 1990, Mexico City is too large and complex a place for return emigrants to stand out. Emigrants departing households in Mexico City for the United States between 1995 and 2000 numbered more than 140,000, but in 2000 they made up a tiny share of Mexico City's enormous population, less than 1 percent.[7] By contrast, emigrants departing from the ten states located in the center-west region of Mexico—a region commonly labeled the Traditional (emigrant-sending) Region of Mexico—comprised 3.4 percent of the entire regional population over the same period.[8] In some rural municipalities in the Traditional Region, more than one-fourth of the adult population emigrated between 1995 and 2000.[9]

As in small, tight-knit rural communities everywhere, emigrants are visible in rural places in the Traditional Region of Mexico: others in the community note their absences and returns, and their neighbors know they are an emigrant or a returnee. Moreover, when migrants make up a sizable share of a community's population, their migration often has an economic, social, and political impact on their community.[10] The prominent social science story that has been written about return migration from the United States to Mexico is about the demographic, economic, and political transformation that rural-origin, U.S.-bound migration and return have brought about.

What about return to the city? In this book, we study the experiences of return migrants in Mexico City at the beginning of the twenty-first century, when millions of Mexican immigrants in the United States returned to Mexico, many destined for urban areas like Mexico City. In studying return migration from the United States to Mexico City in particular, we consider what it means to be culturally and demographically invisible as a return migrant, encountering a social environment and physical space that did not notice that the migrant was missing, is not profoundly affected by their absence or return, and fails to recognize their experience as an immigrant.

This book is about the particularities of return migration to Mexico's capital city. It is also about the particularities of emigration and return in the 1990s and 2000s, a period in which U.S. immigration policy became increasingly focused on restriction and enforcement. We call this U.S. immigration regime the Policy Trap, a term that refers to the set of laws, policies, and practices that have characterized U.S. immigration policy since 1986, when the U.S. Congress passed the last major comprehensive immigration reform. Since then, U.S. laws and policies have militarized the border, restricted noncitizen immigrant rights within the country, and made it easier for the U.S. government to deport noncitizen immigrants. The Policy Trap enabled more than three million deportations during the Obama administration (from 2009 to 2016), a significant increase over the number of deportations during the tenures of George W. Bush (two million from 2001 to 2008) and Bill Clinton (one million from 1995 to 2000), as well as in comparison to the first presidential term of Donald J. Trump (six hundred thousand from 2017 to 2020).[11] Some deported people as well as many others who were not deported brought their U.S.-born children with them to Mexico, a flow of first-time immigrants to Mexico that contributed to negative net migration from Mexico to the United States.[12]

The return migrants we interviewed all lived in the United States with legally precarious status; most were undocumented upon entry, but some entered legally and later fell out of legal status. A few obtained lawful permanent residency or discretionary status after a period of undocumented status in the United States but were later deported. Regardless of differences in their immigration statuses, the return migrants we interviewed were all exposed to the hardship of life as noncitizen immigrants in the United States during the Policy Trap.

To understand migrant experiences returning to Mexico City during the Policy Trap, we studied the circumstances surrounding their departure and return and their experiences in both the United States and Mexico City—that is, the historical and geographic specificity that informs migration, interlaced with individual life courses and family dynamics. We did this by collecting and analyzing life and family histories through in-depth interviews with thirty-four return migrants in Mexico City in 2019.

Through our research, we found that the experience of return migration to Mexico City after a relatively long period living with noncitizen (mostly undocumented) status as an immigrant in the United States subject to the Policy Trap leaves the return migrant *norteado*, a Spanish word meaning "disoriented" or "lost."[13] The general usage refers to the direction north, without reference to the United States. The etymology of "norteado" is not that different from the word "disoriented" (in Spanish, *desorientado*), which also means "confused" or "lost in space." "Desorientado" refers to the east (the Orient), while "norteado" refers to the north. This meaning of the word "norteado"—directional confusion—captures the experience of the return migrants we spoke to, who upon arrival in Mexico City had to find their way in a massive and dynamic urban environment that had changed while they were gone and forgotten about them in the meantime. The city as a site of return causes returnees to be norteado.

But the word "norteado" refers to more than a feeling of disorientation. In Mexico, the term *el norte* (the north) is not just a direction in space but is also a specific reference to Mexico's northern neighbor, the United States. With "el norte" referring to the United States, the word "norteado" has come to refer to the experience of having lost one's way after migrating to the United States. Confusion for those who are desorientado and norteado emerges from separation from a place of power and meaning—whether the rising sun (in the east) or the United States (in el norte). The experience of being norteado reflects the particularities of return migration to Mexico after a long period of residence in the United States. The United States as the destination of immigration also causes returnees to be norteado.

One more dimension of the word "norteado" is important: the loss it conveys. In some translations, the word "norteado" is interpreted as "north-less," a translation that captures the experience of forced separation from el norte upon return to Mexico.[14] The word "norteado" describes the experience of returning to Mexico from the United States during the Policy Trap. Through border control and other mechanisms, the Policy Trap has made it more difficult and costlier to enter the United States legally and safely. The Policy Trap prevents immigrants in the United States from returning to Mexico when they lack the legal means to subsequently reenter the United States; in other words, migrants without travel visas are trapped in the United States by their fear of being trapped in Mexico if they return there. Among the return migrants we spoke to in Mexico City, the fear of being trapped in Mexico had become their reality: they were unable to reenter the United States legally or safely. As a result, they were separated forcefully from their lives in the United States—including children, partners, and other family, as well as jobs, homes, and communities—when they returned to Mexico. The Policy Trap limits cross-border mobility and separates families. The Policy Trap causes returnees to be norteado.

In this book, we explore what it means to be norteado after resettling in Mexico City in terms of family life and work. Returning there after living in the United States as a noncitizen immigrant subject to the Policy Trap is a difficult, disorienting process of reintegration with uncertain outcomes. It is hard to find the health care and social services one needs, family life is upended, and economic mobility is limited. Being norteado emerges from the experience of returning to the city from the United States and becoming culturally, demographically, economically, and politically invisible. Being norteado made it difficult for the returnees we studied to feel comfortable or settled in Mexico City, even as they made their daily lives there.

The particularities of returning to Mexico City from the United States during the Policy Trap reflect general processes of human migration in the twenty-first century. The experience of return migration is shaped by the context of emigration, immigration, and return, which must be defined in geographic and historical terms.[15] Being norteado is not unique to former noncitizen migrants who returned from the United States to Mexico City during the Policy Trap era. It could describe the experience of returnees to other cities in Mexico or Central America, or any other destination of return where locating oneself in the spatial and social context is challenging. It could describe returnees to rural places or the (northern) Border Region of Mexico, where one's identity as a migrant is known by others, and even valued, but remigration is unfathomable, owing to the costs and risks imposed by the Policy Trap. It could describe returnees who, for a wide variety of personal, environmental, or political reasons, not just the Policy Trap, are deprived of the safe and legal possibility of remigration.

In this book, we uncover the experience of being norteado through a study of return to Mexico City from the United States during the Policy Trap. These particularities of space and time fit into the recent history of Mexican emigration and return, which has been called the "Great Mexican Migration."[16]

The Great Migration from Mexico to the United States

The Great Mexican Migration began in the middle of the twentieth century and lasted through the first decade of the twenty-first.[17] As a result of this migration, the Mexican immigrant population in the United States grew to 1.0 million by the 1970s and to 12.8 million by 2007.[18] The migration flow peaked in the 1990s and early 2000s. From 1991 to 2005, more than 370,000 Mexicans migrated to the United States each year; the annual flow of Mexican migrants to the United States reached its highest level in 2000, at 770,000.[19]

The Great Mexican Migration was part of Mexico's twentieth-century economic and demographic transition.[20] As Mexico's economy grew and transformed from an agrarian to an industrial basis, people moved away from rural places. These migrants were members of very large youth cohorts, owing to a historically brief demographic moment in the middle of the twentieth century when high fertility rates coexisted with low mortality rates.[21] In response to economic change and demographic pressure, most Mexican migrants moved to Mexican cities, supplying labor for urban manufacturing and service industries, but some moved abroad, to the United States, following labor recruiters to U.S. fields or family members to U.S. cities. Many emigrants originated in rural places in the Traditional Region of central-western Mexico, which was connected to the U.S. Southwest by train. Many were recruited directly to work for U.S. growers through the U.S.-Mexico labor migration treaty, the Bracero Accord, which lasted from 1942 through 1964. These historical origins impacted the geographic shape of Mexico-U.S. migration for decades. From 1970 to 1992, more than 75 percent of all migrants to the United States from Mexico originated in rural places or small towns, and half originated in the Traditional Region.[22]

The duration and structural determinants of Mexico's Great Migration are similar to those of other countries. Emigration from Europe to the Western Hemisphere in the nineteenth and early twentieth centuries responded to industrialization, which disrupted rural livelihoods; demographic transition, which generated large youth cohorts; and rising wages, which provided individuals with the means to pay for travel.[23] Migrant networks developed over time, contributing to increasing emigration. In European countries, the declining fertility and economic development led to the decline and end of mass emigration. The process of mass migration lasts about nine decades.

As economic and demographic pressures subsided in Europe, emigration slowed. The same has recently occurred in Mexico. Mexico's economy is eight and a half times larger in absolute terms, and two and a half times larger per capita, today than it was in 1960.[24] Mexico's population is now 80 percent urban.[25] In 2024, its fertility rate was projected to be 1.9 births per woman, well below replacement level.[26] Mexico's emigration rates began to decline after 2000.[27] Shortly thereafter, return migration from the United States to Mexico began to increase. Between 2009 and 2014, one million people left the United States for Mexico, a larger number than left Mexico for the United States in the same period.[28] Included among migrants from the United States to Mexico in this period were hundreds of thousands of U.S.-born children who immigrated to Mexico with their parents.[29]

After 1990, Mexican emigrant origins diversified to include increasing numbers of emigrants from states outside the Traditional Region, as well as from urban areas.[30] Geographic diversification in new emigrant origins is a predictable outcome of the migration process, as information and networks spread beyond migrant origin communities. At the same time, migration flows within Mexico shifted away from cities in

Mexico's interior toward the northern border, and internal and international migration became linked.[31] The data we collected for this book reflect the experiences of people emigrating and returning at the end of the era of the Great Mexican Migration, some originating from and all returning to a place, Mexico City, that represents the new (post-1990) origins of emigrants and a destination for many people returning to Mexico after 2007.[32]

The Social Process of Mexican Migration

An important difference between the Mexican and (many) European emigration experiences is the role of circularity, or back-and-forth migration. The communities and cultures spanning the borderlands between Mexico and the United States render one-way, permanent emigration unrealistic for their inhabitants. But even for Mexican emigrants departing from communities hundreds of miles south of Mexico's northern border, one-way, permanent emigration was not often the goal, at least not at the outset.[33] The proximity of the United States to Mexico makes circular migration and short-term emigration plausible. Mexican migrants could envision the dream of a new life while maintaining strong connections to the old life. Often, the migrant's vision of a new life was a new life in Mexico, one achieved through dollars earned as a U.S. immigrant.

Circular migration and return migration to Mexico from the United States were such common features of the Mexico-U.S. migration experience from the 1950s to the 1980s that many classic research studies found migrants not in the fields of California or the construction sites of Houston but in the small towns and farms of the Mexican states of Jalisco, Guanajuato, and Michoacán, places where migrants would return to celebrate the winter holidays with their families. Such was the case for the Mexican Migration Project (MMP), the forty-year-old (and ongoing) research study developed by the social scientists Jorge Durand and Douglas Massey.[34] In combining anthropological with sociological and demographic methods, Durand and Massey created a large set of valid, systematic data on emigration from Mexico. The project has generated substantial knowledge regarding the social process of Mexican migration.

Along with the social scientists Rafael Alarcón and Humberto Gonzalez, Durand and Massey first described the social process of

Mexican migration to the United States in the 1987 book *Return to Aztlan*, which reported on an analysis of MMP data from four communities in the Traditional Region.[35] Emigration and its impacts on the communities of origin were a key focus of the book, as reflected in the title of the Spanish version of the book, published in 1991: *Los ausentes* (The absent ones). *Return to Aztlan* laid out a model of Mexican migration as a predictable, spatially bounded, and socially limited process in which Mexican households adapted to social and economic change in Mexico with emigration, using income earned in the United States to solve economic problems at home, such as the need for capital and insurance. This argument has been subsequently developed in a large corpus of research using MMP data and other sources of data.[36] A key insight from this research is that emigration occurs predictably at the community level. At the beginning of a community's emigration experience, a select group of emigrants makes the trip, and their emigration reflects an interaction between their characteristics, household arrangements, and macro-structural factors, such as wages, employment, and gender norms. As a community gains emigration experience—as more and more people emigrate from a particular place—the social, economic, and demographic context of the community is changed by migration. Migrants contribute to the transformation of their origin communities through their departures and returns, remittances and capital investments, and new ideas and priorities. These changes at first lead to greater emigration, especially through the development and sharing of migration-specific capital, but eventually they lead to the stabilization and decline of emigration.

An important part of the social process of migration is the return of migrants, the remitting of migrant earnings, and the impact of return and remittances on migrant-sending communities.[37] In the tight-knit communities of small towns and ranchos in the Traditional Region, migrants are known by those left behind. In these communities, return migrants are visible through the houses they build, the trucks they drive, and the clothes and shoes they wear. Migrants from small towns and rural communities transform their communities of origin, sending money to support their families, constructing homes, building businesses, expanding local consumption and commerce, and investing in new community projects. Migrants bring fresh ideas and modes of being, interact in new ways with their family and community members, and energize politics. Studies documenting these sorts of changes in rural Mexico have argued that international migration to the United States is an engine of development and modernization in Mexican places otherwise removed from those same processes unfolding in Mexican cities.[38]

This idea is not without controversy. For some observers, migration is a form of dependency of Mexico on its northern neighbor; for others, migration is a form of U.S. hegemony and the extraction of value from its southern neighbor.[39] Theories and evidence regarding migration's impact on sending communities suggest that the relationship between emigration and development is heterogeneous, dependent on the contexts of departure, reception, and return, especially on conditions that enable or discourage international migration, migrant economic outcomes in the destination, and reasons for return.[40]

One important contextual factor affecting the degree to which migration contributes to economic growth and change in communities of origin is state policy controlling migration. The restrictive and enforcement-based U.S. immigration regime that we call the Policy Trap, which began after 1986, increased the cost of migrating without documents and made circular migration less feasible for undocumented migrants.[41] The Policy Trap also undermined immigrant economic well-being in the United States by increasing the cost of employing undocumented immigrants, a cost that employers passed on to undocumented workers.[42] Because the transformative potential of migration in the origin community depends on immigrant economic success in the destination and on migrant circularity (or, at least, on sustained remitting to the origin), scholars warned that the U.S. Policy Trap was disrupting and unintentionally extending Mexico's migration process, delaying the point at which Mexican emigration rates would begin to decline.[43]

While the Policy Trap disrupted circular migration and the remitting of money back to migrant origin communities in the Traditional Region, it also helped to create a new locus of migrants along the Mexico-U.S. border. Communities in the "borderlands" had existed long before the border was imposed upon them after the United States invaded Mexico in 1846 and Mexico lost half of its territory in the ensuing war. Since then, the Mexico-U.S. border has been a site of transit and the movement of settled people back and forth across it for work, school, and commerce.[44] In the 1980s and 1990s, the Border Region emerged as an important migrant destination, as Mexico's investment in the *maquiladora* (manufacturing for export) industry attracted large numbers of migrants from the country's interior, including from Mexico City. More recently, the border has also become a site of protracted displacement, or forced immobility. Border control buildup during the Policy Trap has turned rural places and small towns along the border into sites of migrant transit, border industry, and control by criminal organizations that engage in human and drug smuggling.[45] As a result of the large-scale deportation of long-term migrants in the United States during the Policy Trap, many deported people settle along the border to be physically close to their prior homes and families in the United States. Others stay on the border because they have nowhere else to go.[46]

Return to the City

In some ways, we view our research monograph as a thirty-year echo of the book *Return to Aztlan*, which examined emigration from and return to the Traditional Region in the 1970s and 1980s using MMP data, complemented by in-depth contextual and historical analysis. Instead of returning to Aztlan, the mythical ancestral homeland of the Aztecs (later named Mexicas) located somewhere in the northwest of Mexico, from which the Aztecs fled around 1064, we study the return to Mexico City, which sits on the Aztec capital Tenochtitlan, formed in 1325 CE, years after the Aztecs fled Aztlan.[47] Instead of emigrating to address problems at home and leaving family behind, most of our respondents moved to accompany or follow family. Instead of returning as part of the social process of international migration, in such a way that would transform origin communities and generate additional emigration, many returnees in our study were forced to return, and most seemed to have returned for good.

The question we ask in this book is how migrants fare upon returning to Mexico City after spending time in the United States with noncitizen immigration status during the Policy Trap. Scholars have termed the process of how migrants fare upon return as "reintegration." Return migrants are not integrating into a different society, but reentry into the origin society is not automatic or seamless after the experiences of exit, absence, and return.[48] In the early 2000s, the migration scholar Jean-Pierre Cassarino provided a theoretical accounting of the forces affecting reintegration after return migration.[49] He proposed that reintegration reflects the interaction between the conditions of return (or reasons for return) and preparedness for return.

In describing conditions of return for voluntary migrants, Cassarino revisits economic theories of international migration. "Neoclassical economic" theory suggests that in the absence of strong economic pulls back to the origin, returnees are people who were economically unsuccessful in the destination. In the Mexican case, therefore, "neoclassical economic" theory views return migrants as failed economic immigrants. Cassarino suggests that neoclassical returnees, having limited resources to mobilize, would need to depend on family for support through the reintegration process. By contrast, the "new economics of labor migration" theory argues that migration is a household strategy by which a household member emigrates to reduce risk through the diversification of household income sources and to earn income to use for consumption or investment at home. In this case, return signals the successful execution of household economic goals: return migrants, with substantial resources to mobilize, experience reintegration as a process of rediscovery and distinction.

Cassarino also emphasizes the importance of preparation, while acknowledging the non-economic aspect of some returns and the variation in the degree to which returns are planned. According to Cassarino's model, highly prepared returnees can better adapt upon return. To some extent, preparedness overlaps with successful or failed economic migrations, insofar as successful migrants are more prepared, but in some cases, such as deportation, a returnee's preparedness upon return has little to do with their motivations for migration, economic or otherwise, nor with the outcomes of migration.

Cassarino's typology of returnees can be mapped onto the geographic history of Mexican emigration and return. The sociologist Filiz Garip, after discovering geographic and temporal (as well as sociodemographic) regularities in the patterns of first-time migrants to the United States from Mexico in MMP data, linked these patterns to both "neoclassical economic" theory and the "new economics of labor migration" theory.[50] In the 1960s and 1970s, "neoclassical economic" migrants left the Traditional Region and migrated circularly; reintegration was not relevant to them insofar as they continued to remigrate, but their exits and returns never-theless had profound impacts on their origin communities. In the 1980s, "new economics of labor migration" migrants left rural places in the Tra-ditional Region in response to the economic crisis in Mexico and emi-grated for longer periods. Although a greater share settled permanently in the United States, the majority returned to Mexico, bringing resources and skills with them to invest in their homes and communities.[51]

In the 1990s and 2000s, two new types of migrants became promi-nent among first-time emigrants: urban migrants and family migrants. Urban migrants originated in urban areas largely outside of the Tra-ditional Region, and one out of five originated in Mexico's Border Region. Family migrants, mostly women, emigrated permanently with the intent to accompany or reunite with family members. Conditions of return are less defined for urban or family migrants than they are for economic migrants; the urban or family migrant's return is not antici-pated by the causes of their emigration. Moreover, these migrants have no opportunity to prepare when they are deported, as happened to many returnees during the Policy Trap decades. These circumstances hint at the experience of being norteado upon return to Mexico.

One result of family-based migration in the 1990s and 2000s has been family return. Studies of return have uncovered the remarkable experience of the immigration of more than 500,000 U.S.-born chil-dren to Mexico since 2000.[52] The migration scholars Víctor Zúñiga and Silvia Giorguli-Saucedo call these children the 0.5 generation.[53] Chil-dren in the 0.5 generation were born in the United States during the Policy Trap to Mexican immigrants who have since returned to Mexico, bringing their families with them. Some immigrant parents were deported, resulting in the de facto deportation of children who accom-pany their parents returning to Mexico.[54] Research has emphasized the difficult transitions these children have, especially in schooling, as well as in accessing needed services like health insurance.[55]

Other studies of return to Mexico during the Policy Trap have drawn a less positive and more varied picture than the story told of emigra-tion from and return to rural places in the Traditional Region during the periods of circular and economic migrations. One body of research has focused on deported people, who are forced to return to Mexico with little to no preparation through an often violent experience of state removal from the United States. Much of the research on deported people has studied the Border Region and found that deported people in cities along the border face a difficult process of reintegration, including a high risk of unemployment, living on the street, mental health problems, and drug use.[56] The border may be the unplanned destination for the most vulnerable of deported people, who have no other place to go or who lack the resources to travel someplace else following their removal from the United States.[57]

What about reintegration in Mexico City during the Policy Trap period? Two key elements of return to Mexico City are different from return to the border, and each of these relates to how returnees to Mexico City are uniquely norteado. In border cities, the United States is physically present in everyday life. The physical proximity of the United States can promote cross-border family life by enabling the possibility of connection with family who remain in the United States and have the legal right to cross, such as U.S.-born children. In these ways, returnees to the border are less north-less than returnees to Mexico City.

A second element of difference involves the visibility of the return migrant in their destination of return. Migrants in the Border Region are a known element of society precisely because of the unique historical and geographic experience of border cities as a locus of migration. This visibility translates into material resources. In border cities, migrants find support from a strong civil society infrastructure providing food and shelter, health access, legal aid, and other kinds of assistance.[58] Civil society organizations in the Border Region are often linked to and receive support from wealthy academic institutions that have funded studies focused on border life, migration, and/or deportation.

Even cities located miles south of the border but still in the Border Region are affected by border dynamics. Monterrey, Nuevo León, is the second largest metropolitan area in Mexico, with 5.3 million people (one-fourth the population of Mexico City). Monterrey, a key industrial and economic center in Mexico, is located 140 miles away from the Nuevo Laredo–Laredo and Reynosa-McAllen border cities (in the Tamaulipas-Texas section of the border). The almost three-hour drive from Monterrey to the Mexico-U.S. border implies different kinds of connections to the United States for those who live there, and in the large urban context of Monterrey, returnees are not as visible as they are in Mexican cities directly on the border. Still, the relative physical, economic, and social closeness of Monterrey to the United States has generated a strong migration industry there that coordinates and enables migration from Monterrey and serves migrants upon return—as one of the first people to study urban emigration from Mexico, Rubén Hernández-León, found in his study of the Monterrey-Houston migration corridor.[59]

In Mexico City, return migrants are invisible, at least compared to returnees in the Border and Traditional Regions. Return migrants in Mexico City are not a predominant topic of concern in local politics; the city has far greater problems, political battles, and economic opportunities. Return migrants in Mexico City are not subjects of social and economic change, as they are in rural places, where they often maintain a strong sense of place-based connection.[60] What defines the return migrant in Mexico City is a sense of mobility rather than a connection to place, as the sociologist Liliana Rivera found in her study of migrants in the Mexico City neighborhood of Nezahualcóyotl.[61] The possibility of social invisibility in the city may be why some return migrants go there, as the sociologist Abigail Andrews found in her study of deported men in Tijuana (on the border), Oaxaca (in southern Mexico), and Mexico City.[62]

The conditions of invisibility, which emerges from the large, complex urban environment of Mexico City, and of being north-less, which emerges from the city's geographical distance from the United States, characterize the experience of being norteado upon return to Mexico City. We find that separation from the United States is not just physical but also metaphysical: the returnees we interviewed did not envision returning to the United States, at least not anytime soon, mostly because of the costs and risks imposed by the Policy Trap. This metaphysical separation—the impossibility of return—results in a sense of loss of one's past life, of disconnection from that life, even as some aspects of that life continue in the United States in their absence. We find that both people who were deported and those who were not deported experience this sense of being norteado as loss.

Our Study of Return Migrants in Mexico City

To study return migration from the United States to Mexico City during the Policy Trap, we interviewed thirty-four return migrants in the Mexico City metropolitan area in the spring of 2019. The map in figure 1.1 shows where Mexico City is located within Mexico and orients

Figure 1.1 *The Mexico City Metropolitan Area and the Thirty-Two States of Mexico*

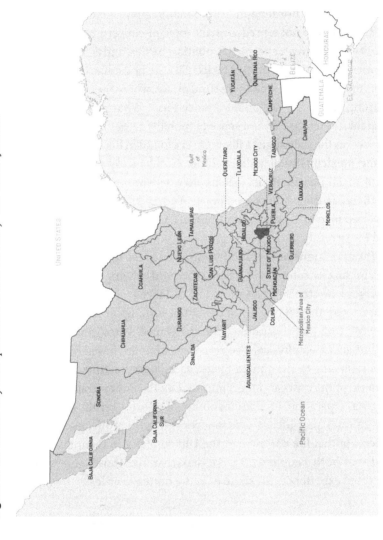

Source: Authors' map.

the reader to the location of other states in Mexico. We recruited participants broadly within the metropolitan area, advertising on social media, approaching people near workplaces and universities that are common gathering places for returnees, partnering with receptive migrant-serving organizations, and finding connections through our networks and those of study participants.

The people we interviewed lived all over the metropolitan area of Mexico City. The map in figure 1.2 shows their residential locations. Although we did not exclusively sample in neighborhoods with high levels of international migration, the geographic distribution of the residences of the people we spoke to reflects where return migrants are concentrated in the city.[63]

In the interviews, we delved into respondents' life experiences, focusing on key themes of family, work, education, health, and political and civic involvement. We asked about each of these themes in specific life-history moments related to migration: before the first migration to the United States, during their time in the United States, and after the final return to Mexico. These interviews form the backbone of our analysis. The methodological appendix discusses in greater detail the study design and ethical considerations that informed our work.

In addition to the thirty-four interviews with returnees, we spoke to and spent time with activists, lawyers, government officials, and members of organizations serving migrants and deportees in Mexico City over a much longer period. We attended events related to the topic, including academic book releases; academic, government, and activist conferences and seminars; and citywide gatherings. We conducted formal and informal interviews with officials at the U.S. embassy and consulate in Mexico City. This background research was invaluable to our understanding of the experiences of migrants and returnees in Mexico City.

The People We Talked To

This book focuses on the experiences of people living in Mexico City in 2019 who spent significant time with noncitizen status in the United States. Their migrations back to Mexico meet the geographer Russell King's straightforward definition of return migration, which is "when people return to their country of origin after a significant period abroad," with "significant periods" defined as one year or longer.[64] Figure 1.3

Figure 1.2 *Municipalities Where Return Migrants Resided*

Source: Authors' map.
Note: Light gray boundary lines designate municipalities. Dark gray boundary lines designate states. Darker and thicker line designates the Mexico City metropolitan area. Dark shading and pins designate the municipalities where the respondents in our study resided.

Figure 1.3 *The Migration Life Course of the Thirty-Four Return Migrants in Mexico City in 2019, from Birth to 2019*

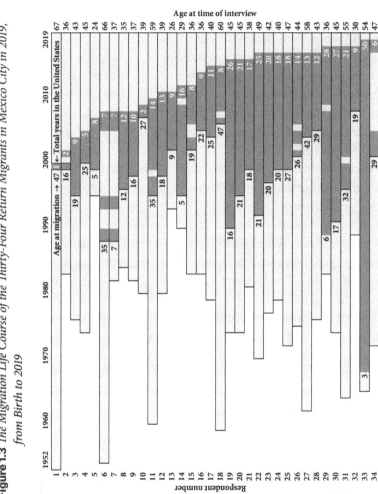

Source: Authors' diagram.
Light gray: Years of life spent in Mexico.
Dark gray: Years of life spent in the United States.

reveals that each of the people we spoke to met King's definition. The figure displays the life course–migration trajectories of the thirty-four people we interviewed, with each row representing a person's life, starting at birth and ending in 2019, when we interviewed them. Each year of life is colored in either light gray, which indicates primary residence in Mexico in that year, or dark gray, which indicates primary residence in the United States in that year. The rows are sorted by the year of last return to Mexico, from earliest to latest.

Figure 1.3 reveals the age-period variation in the migration histories of the people we spoke to. By glancing at the shape of the dark gray–shaded area across rows, it is clear that the people we spoke to migrated to the United States most commonly between 1990 and 2010. Everyone we spoke to returned to Mexico (for the last time as of 2019) after 1999, with most returning after 2010. The amount of time spent in Mexico after the last return ranged from one year (in row 34) to twenty years (in row 1); the average time spent in Mexico after return was seven years.

Each person's age at the time of their first emigration is superimposed in black font at the end of the first light gray–shaded period of each row. Most people we interviewed were young when they first emigrated, with an average age of twenty-one years. Six people we interviewed were children under the age of twelve when they first emigrated; another five were between the ages of twelve and seventeen when they first emigrated.

The total time spent in the United States in years is superimposed in white font at the end of the last dark gray–shaded period. Most of the people we interviewed had spent a significant amount of time in the United States. The average amount of time spent in the United States was fourteen years, and half of the people we spoke to had spent eleven or more years in the United States. It is also apparent in the figure that most of the people we spoke with took only one unique migration trip to the United States. Ten out of the thirty-four had returned to Mexico for a year or longer and then remigrated to the United States.

At the end of each row is the age of the person at the time of the interview (in 2019). When we interviewed them, study participants were between the ages of twenty-four and sixty-seven. We talked to people just leaving school, people in the prime of their working years, and people in retirement. Not shown is their gender or family status. We interviewed twenty-five men and nine women. Most of them (three out of four) were parents, and about half of them had children who were born in the United States. Our interviewees had lived throughout the United States (see map in figure 1.4), but clustered in California, Chicago, and New York City. Appendix table 1.1 provides additional information about the people we interviewed for this book.

While King's definition of return migration fits the experiences of the migrants we talked to, it is important to explain a few ways in which our sample is more narrowly defined and focused. King's definition of "return" includes anyone who emigrated and returned for any reason. Our focus is on labor and family migrants to the United States who migrated without legal documents for entry or who found themselves without legal documents to reside or work after being in the United States for some time. Half of the people we interviewed returned to Mexico for economic or family reasons, while the other half were deported by the U.S. government. This latter group's return migration was forced, but many who returned for reasons other than deportation also did so with little aspiration, planning, or readiness. We did not talk to professional migrants or people who emigrated to work in well-paid or legally sponsored positions. None of the people we spoke with migrated to the United States on a work visa. We did not talk to lifestyle or retirement migrants who had the resources and legal privilege to choose where to live. None of the people we spoke with had a U.S. visa or U.S. citizenship at the time we interviewed them in 2019.

Because of our interest in migrants who had lived in the United States with noncitizen immigrant status, as well as in people who were deported to Mexico, the people we interviewed are not representative of all return migrants to Mexico City. In comparing our sample to the characteristics of all return migrants in Mexico City in a similar period, we see that our sample was less educated than the general population of recent return migrants in Mexico City, which included people who traveled to the United States on short-term work and student visas as well as people who were U.S. lawful permanent residents and who returned to Mexico with the right to reenter the United States.[65]

Back to Mexico City

Our interviewees were different from each other in many ways: their age and stage in life, how long they went to school, their family's origins and history in Mexico City, where they lived in the United States, what

Figure 1.4 *Locations of Primary Residence in the United States of the Thirty-Four Return Migrants*

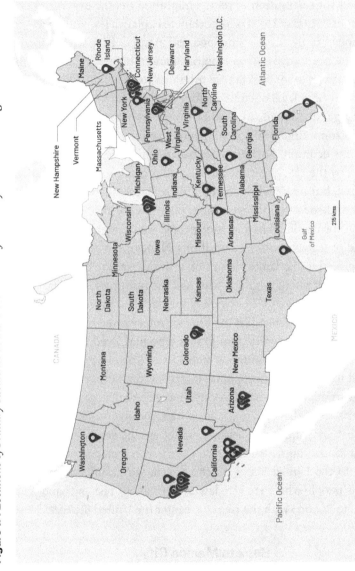

Source: Authors' map.

Note: There are multiple pins on the map for immigrants who lived in more than one place. We define a "primary residence" as residence for a year or longer.

they did there, why they returned, their family structure and relationships, whom they lived with and where in the city, and how they made a living. However, these unique aspects of their lives were similarly shaped by their experience of emigrating to the United States, living there with noncitizen status during the Policy Trap, and returning to live in Mexico City by 2019.

Our study participants were part of the historical moment in Mexico-U.S. migration history in which Mexican cities became the key site of U.S.-bound migration and return migration. In the next chapter, we describe Mexico City as a site of migration: a migrant metropolis, it grew dramatically over the twentieth century as the result of domestic migration to the city, and then, at the end of the century, it became a place of emigration and return. As we will show, domestic and international migration flows are intricately linked, as the Mexico City residents we interviewed who emigrated to the United States were themselves either domestic migrants or the descendants of domestic migrants to the city.

The migrants we spoke to were subject to the Policy Trap, the U.S. immigration regime in effect after 1986. The rules regarding immigrant visas and laws governing the border shaped how they entered the United States. Laws restricting the employment of foreign workers affected how they found work and how much they were paid. Worksite raids, laws designed to identify and detain undocumented people, and rules that restricted immigrant access to U.S. social services shaped how they interacted with schools, police officers, and health care providers. And though the immigrants we interviewed devised creative strategies to live and even thrive in the United States during the Policy Trap, their strategies were unable to protect them from Policy Trap restrictions at the time of their return to Mexico. In chapter 3, we explain how the Policy Trap traps returnees in Mexico, even as they feel free of its grip.

The experience of being norteado begins upon return to Mexico and is heightened upon return to Mexico City. In chapter 4, we focus on the immediate disorientation upon return that makes it difficult to meet basic needs, such as for housing and social support, particularly for people who arrive in insecure and violent neighborhoods and those who are older, disabled, or alone. We also describe migrant organizations, a unique source of support that some return migrants turn to or create in the absence of family and state support.

Over the longer term, two main aspects of life in Mexico City, family and work, continue to be norteado, even as return migrants adapt to city life. Chapter 5 delves into the difficulty of family life for returnees during the Policy Trap. Most of the people we spoke to had children in the United States; some brought their U.S.-born children with them upon returning to Mexico. We also spoke to people who were children when they migrated. As family life continued to unfold on both sides of the border, the Policy Trap kept families apart. These family migration experiences made for a difficult long-term adjustment to life in Mexico.

Finding work in Mexico City after a long period of residence and work in the United States also turned out to be difficult for most of the people we spoke to, as we discuss in chapter 6. Mexico City employers failed to value work histories and skills gained in the United States, especially among older migrants. We find that return migrants largely engaged in survival work. Some migrants mobilized their premigration skills and networks, but they still paid a price for time spent outside the Mexican labor market. Facing these disadvantages, some returnees mobilized their migrant experiences and identities for work purposes.

What can be done about the hardships of return migration to Mexico City? Is it possible to alleviate the experience of being norteado? In chapter 7, we draw from the reflections of the people we spoke to about expanding existing policies and creating new policies or programs to better serve the needs of return migrants in Mexico City and beyond. We also describe the need articulated by some of our respondents for new narratives around return, an issue we also return to in the methodological appendix. In reflecting on these issues, we discuss the conundrum of making visible the invisible.

Across these chapters, the stories of Paolo, Rocío, Yazmín, Evaristo, Olivia, Mario, and Osmundo unfold alongside the stories of the other twenty-seven interviewees to help us understand the lives and experiences of return migrants. Their stories give us a sense of the richness and complexity of the lives of migrants returning from the United States to Mexico City in the twenty-first century. We end the book by discussing what these stories teach us about the recent history of Mexico-U.S. migration, the contributions of our analysis, and what we might expect in the future.

CHAPTER TWO

MEXICO CITY: A MIGRANT METROPOLIS

Osmundo's family did not come from Mexico City but from a small town in the southern state of Guerrero known for its handicrafts. Osmundo's father spearheaded a family business that had been selling colorful painted art for more than fifty years. Their art, filled with colorful images of mythical animals, landscapes, and fantastic characters, represented what many visitors would call "Mexican art." It is hard to tell from their art that many members of Osmundo's family had migrated to the United States and returned to live in Mexico City. But hearing Osmundo's older son speaking English to clients at one of Mexico City's famous handicraft markets, an observer would guess that he learned English as a child. And in fact he did, at public schools in the San Francisco Bay Area. Today Osmundo's family's art is commissioned and sold worldwide thanks to the entrepreneurial skills and English proficiency of Osmundo's son.

Osmundo migrated as a young adult to California, where several of his family members already lived. He was working in the construction industry when it was hit hard by the 2008 financial crisis. When his work dried up, he returned to Mexico to explore the possibility of helping his father with the family business. He and his wife and children first went to Guerrero, but after a few months they moved in with a brother-in-law who had a home in Valle de Chalco, a neighborhood in the southeastern part of the Mexico City metropolitan area. From Chalco, they could commute easily between Guerrero, where the family's art was mostly produced, and the Mexico City markets where it was sold. Living in Chalco has been a successful arrangement for

https://doi.org/10.7758/kokl2957.8057

Osmundo's family in the more than ten years since they migrated back to Mexico from the United States.

When Osmundo and his son drove the forty kilometers (twenty-five miles) from their home in Chalco to a handicraft market in central Mexico City, they followed a well-traveled commuting path. Osmundo and his son were two of millions of people who commute across one or more of the fifty-nine municipalities in the Mexico City metropolitan area. Although long, Osmundo's trip covered only about one-third of the city's expanse. If he continued north, he could drive another forty kilometers without exiting the city limits. Officially, the metropolitan area covers nearly 8,000 square kilometers (3,100 square miles), roughly the size of Delaware and Rhode Island combined, or slightly smaller than Puerto Rico (9,100 square kilometers). The 2020 Mexican census counted 22 million inhabitants in Mexico City, equivalent to the entire population of Florida. By population size, Mexico City is the fifth largest city in the world, after Tokyo, New Delhi, Shanghai, and São Paolo, and the second largest city outside Asia. One out of five people in Mexico lives in the Mexico City metropolitan area.

In this chapter, we describe the city, setting the geographical and historical context in Mexico to which our interviewees returned. When we refer to "Mexico City," we mean its metropolitan area, which includes municipalities from Estado de México (State of Mexico) and Hidalgo, in addition to the sixteen *alcaldías*, or districts, in Mexico City. We give a brief history of the city's development—largely driven by domestic migration from places like Guerrero—into the huge metropolis it is today. As in Osmundo's family, domestic migration from rural places in Mexico to the capital and international migration to the United States are closely linked in the stories of the migrants we interviewed. Some migrants to the city drew from rural-based networks in the United States to make their trips abroad, and some who originated from rural places later returned to the city, no longer connected to their origins.

The international migrants returning to Mexico City experienced something very different from what the migrants who returned to rural settings experienced: an urban context in which their identities and experiences as former migrants to the United States were invisible in their surrounding social environment.

Growth and Transformation in the Capital City

Mexico City owes its origins to the migration and settlement of pre-Hispanic peoples. The Aztec (or Mexica) people founded Tenochtitlan around 1325 CE. According to historical myth, the Aztecs left Aztlan, which was located somewhere north of central Mexico, and followed the god of the sun, Huitzilopochtli, who told them to settle where they saw an eagle on a cactus, eating a snake.[1] When they saw this exact scene on an islet in Lake Texcoco, they interpreted it as a sign from their god and founded the capital of their empire there, naming it Mexico-Tenochtitlan. In 1521, Mexico-Tenochtitlan was invaded and captured by the Spaniards and became Ciudad de México, the capital of Nueva España (New Spain) during colonial times. When Mexico gained independence in the early nineteenth century, the capital city was renamed the Distrito Federal (DF, or Federal District), according to the 1824 constitution. In the 1970s, the Distrito Federal was divided into sixteen *delegaciones* (government districts) that were later renamed alcaldías. In 2016, the city formally became Ciudad de México (CDMX, Mexico City).

From the end of the Mexican Revolution in 1917 through the 1970s, state-sponsored industrialization led to booming economic growth as Mexico transitioned from a rural, agrarian society to an urban, industrial one. The Mexican government's policy of import-substitution industrialization subsidized domestic industries and protected them through restrictions on foreign investment, import tariffs, and trade quotas, a project financed through oil revenue and foreign debt. From 1940 through 1970, the Mexican economy grew at an annual rate of 6 percent. As the national economy grew, so too did Mexico City, the center of Mexico's industrial economy.[2] Mexico City's population grew between 4 and 5 percent each year from 1950 to 1980. Whereas the country doubled its population from 22.3 to 52.4 million between 1950 and 1980, the population of the Mexico City metropolitan area more than quadrupled, from 3.5 to 14.5 million, over the same period.[3]

Two demographic forces were responsible for population growth in the Mexico City metropolitan area in the twentieth century: natural increase, or the difference between births and deaths; and net migration, the difference between in-migration and out-migration.

The demographic transition brought rapid population growth through natural increase to Mexico, especially in the middle of the twentieth century, when mortality rates were quite low but fertility rates had yet to start declining. In the second half of the twentieth century, fertility rates fell rapidly. Declining fertility was notable in the lives of our respondents. Paolo's mother Rocío, for instance, was the oldest of three siblings and had three children herself. She was sixty-seven when we interviewed her. She told us, "My grandmother had twelve children, but her sons all had few children. My father had three, his brother four, another of my uncles three, and yet another of my uncles three also. The men did control themselves."

Mexico's total fertility rate declined from a high of about seven births per woman in the 1950s and 1960s to three births per woman in 2000.[4] In 2024, Mexico's total fertility rate was projected to be 1.9 births per woman, but the rate was heterogeneous across Mexican states, ranging from 1.4 births per woman in Mexico City to 2.8 births per woman in the state of Chiapas.[5]

As fertility in Mexico City declined, the city's population growth was driven by the arrival of migrants from other parts of Mexico.[6] Internal migrants moved in response to the substantial demand for their labor in the manufacturing plants of the city, but the governments of the Federal District could not keep up with their need for housing. Rent controls, housing shortages, and bans on land subdivision within the Federal District forced internal migrants to purchase land or construct housing in undesirable areas in the outer parts of the city.[7] Migrant settlement on the outskirts of the city was largely irregular, established as it was through land invasions or illegal purchases, such as from *ejidos* (communal land)—whose community members were generally prohibited from selling the land (prior to 1992)—or from developers who lacked full title to the land. Local governments, unable to provide housing, tolerated, accommodated, and eventually serviced and formalized the irregular settlements.[8] Scholars have described this physical expansion of the city as the formation of a series of peripheral areas, or *contornos*, between the 1960s and 1980s.[9] As the peripheral areas were settled, each saw rapid population growth. Eventually, wealth became concentrated in the city's center and poverty was decentralized.[10]

By the 1970s, the failures of the import-substitution industrialization program had become apparent. Budget deficits, debt burden, unstable currency, and capital flight were managed with oil revenue in the late 1970s, but the international oil crisis of the early 1980s drove Mexico's economy to near-collapse in 1982, marking the beginning of a severe economic recession that lasted well into the mid-1990s. The peso was devalued twice, in 1982 and again in 1994. From attracting huge numbers of internal migrants in the middle part of the century, the Federal District became a place of out-migration by the 1980s, when migrants headed mostly to the State of Mexico—where the population continued to grow in peripheral settlements—but also to states in northern Mexico.

Amid the economic recession, Mexico City was struck by a massive earthquake, measuring 8.1 on the Richter scale, on September 19, 1985. While the earthquake's death toll is uncertain, it is estimated that as many as ten thousand people died.[11] Mario, whose quip about dogs in Mexico City introduced our book, worked in a textile manufacturing plant where many seamstresses were killed when the building collapsed in the earthquake.[12] He told us, "I went to work here in Pino Suárez in a T-shirt company where there were seamstresses. I don't know if you read the news that in '85 the last to be rescued were the seamstresses. Those were my coworkers, those who were left crushed in '85."

The 1985 earthquake left a physical and emotional scar on Mexico City residents and transformed architectural styles and regulations. As some Mexico City residents decided to leave the city, internal in-migration slowed down and out-migration increased.[13] Some migrants lost their housing after the 1985 earthquake or were impacted by the economic crisis; others decided to move to less crowded cities. The 1985 earthquake is recalled every year on September 19 as Mexicans all over the country practice how to respond to a potential disaster with the National Simulacrum. On September 19, 2017, the city was hit again by another massive earthquake, measuring 7.1 on the Richter scale. Five years later, on the same day, it was hit again by an earthquake measuring 7.7 on the Richter scale.

In the wake of the 1985 earthquake, and in response to Mexico's economic crisis of the 1980s, the import-substitution industrialization model of economic growth was abandoned in favor of a model embracing neoliberal principles, including loosened trade restrictions, an increase in foreign investment, and the privatization of key industries. Globalization started to become visible in the city. For example, the first McDonald's restaurant in Mexico opened in 1985 in southern Mexico

City, very close to El Colegio de México. In 1986, Mexico joined the General Agreement on Trade and Tariffs (GATT, later the World Trade Organization [WTO]), and in 1994, Mexico, Canada, and the United States signed the North American Free Trade Agreement (NAFTA). These changes led to shifts in regional economies and growth in the maquiladora industry in Mexico's Border Region.[14] Internal migration flows within Mexico responded accordingly: fewer Mexicans migrated to Mexico's interior cities and greater numbers headed north.[15]

Neoliberalism was also brought to governance in Mexico City. In 1992, two important legal changes transformed housing development. One was a constitutional amendment that allowed the sale of ejido land, increasing land values and leading to the densification and regularization of some irregular settlements.[16] In the same year, reforms to government lending programs made loans to public and private employees much more available and increased growth in private housing developments. In response to new housing developments and new mortgage programs for state and private employees, massive numbers of internal migrants moved to eastern sections of the city.[17]

One city neighborhood that grew rapidly in the wake of neoliberal reform was Valle de Chalco, where Osmundo and his family lived. The municipality of Valle de Chalco Solidaridad was formally created as a new municipality in the State of Mexico in 1994. In the mid-1990s, nine out of every ten residents in Chalco had migrated there from another municipality in the city.[18] The word *Solidaridad* (Solidarity) was added to the municipality's name because the neighborhood participated in the pilot effort of the national antipoverty cash transfer program, Programa Nacional de Solidaridad (National Solidarity Program), which was later renamed Progresa and then Oportunidades. Chalco was targeted for participation in the pilot program because of the high levels of poverty and the low level of service provision in the newly settled part of the city.

Responding to urban change, officials built the major concentric avenues in the Federal District, such as the Anillo Periférico (Peripheral Ring) and the Circuito Interior (Interior Circuit), which were built between 1950 and 1970, and later, in the 1980s, the major avenues connecting the State of Mexico and the Federal District. In the 2000s, large infrastructure projects were completed, including the construction of the Segundo Piso, the second level of the Periférico highway, and other bridges and tunnels. Massive demand for public transportation called for the creation of the Sistema de Transporte Colectivo (System of Collective Transport) in 1967; construction had already begun on the first metro line, which opened in September 1969 at 12.6 kilometers long. By 1988, the metro system had seven lines and covered 124 kilometers. By 2012, with twelve lines, the metro system's total length was 226.4 kilometers (140 miles). Today that system is complemented by other types of road transportation, including fixed routes serviced by cable cars, trolleys, and the Metrobus (which also has dedicated lanes), smaller buses that cross all parts of the city, an extensive fleet of city-controlled taxis (currently colored pink), private taxis, and, since 2013 or so, a large number of Uber and other app-based ride-share drivers. According to 2017 estimates, a person who lives in one of the sixteen alcaldías of Mexico City spends at least 82 minutes commuting, whereas someone living in Mexico City but working in its metropolitan area (in the State of Mexico or Hidalgo), or vice versa, invests at least 175 minutes (nearly three hours) to commuting each day![19] But commuting times decrease with new transportation innovations. Beginning in 2021, the Cablebus, an aerial cable car system, transports people from the mountainous areas on the edges of the city to inner-city metro stations in gondolas that hang 100 feet above the ground.

Osmundo was one of these commuters, but he was lucky because he traveled early on weekend mornings, when the roads were empty, and he owned a van, which he filled with his family's art to take to market. His commute took about an hour each way. By contrast, consider the commute of a member of our research team who lived in a neighborhood nestled in the foothills of the Sierra de Ajusco-Chichinauhtzin, the chain of lava domes that form the southern border of Mexico City. To get to work in the mornings, the team member traveled by bus for up to an hour to reach El Colegio de México, which is also in the southern part of the city. Getting from El Colegio de México to an interview in Cuautepec, in the north-central part of the city, could easily take another two hours, if not longer. In other words, to travel from home to work and back again in a single day, the team member might spend as much as six hours en route.

Mexico City is defined not just by its expansiveness, population, and history but also by its cultural vibrancy. The city is alive, a playground of riches and possibilities, especially for those with some cash

to spend. Mexico City is a place where in a single day you can explore
Aztec ruins, visit Frida Kahlo's Blue House, watch the national Ballet
Foklórico in the Palacio de Bellas Artes, and later go to see the alterna-
tive rock band Tropikal Forever perform their cumbia-salsa-norteño
(*tropikalizado*) covers of "The Final Countdown" and "All That She
Wants" at a club in Condesa.

Tourists are a constant feature of the central parts of Mexico City,
attracted to the city's precolonial and colonial monuments and world-
class art, architecture, and history museums. In 2019, nearly five million foreigners arrived at Mexico City's international airport.[20] (Five
of these travelers were members of our team or their relatives.) Visitors to the city could get a sense of Mexico City's vibrancy by perusing
a tourist guide. Beyond descriptions of famous sites, they would see
beautiful images of its food, flowers, and handicraft markets, including
perhaps the market where Osmundo and his family sold their art. The
guide would describe restaurants featuring food from all regions of
Mexico at every price point, from bicycle cart vendors selling *tacos de
canasta* (basket tacos) to the world-famous Michelin-starred restaurant
Pujol, where the diner can eat baby corn served smoking in a gourd and
coated in braised ants. The guide would also describe the city's many
international restaurants, like the sushi restaurant that Mateo helped
to build. Visitors would read about Turibus, the double-decker tourist
bus with six routes through the city that once employed Reynaldo as
a guide. They would read about the women selling toys and painting
faces in the park, as Lucía did, and the Uber drivers, like Evaristo, who
make navigating the city as a tourist more convenient.

Although the return migrants we spoke to helped to build and service Mexico City, they were invisible within it as returnees. Return
migrants disappear into the large complex urban environment of the
city. Their migrant savings—the dollars they accumulated working in
the United States—are tiny within the massive Mexico City economy.
With their relatively small numbers and monetary assets, they have
little influence over development projects in the city, and the businesses
and houses they build do not stand out as representative of a successful trip north. Any wealth the migrant remits to Mexico City disap-
pears into the city's vast landscape of riches and poverty. Moreover,
return migrants themselves do not stand out as visibly distinct within
the crowded and diverse population of the city. As Raúl explained,

people in Mexico City do not realize that returnees have been abroad because they

> do not know where you come from or who you are, and they treat you just as they treat everyone in their neighborhood, as a random person you run into in the metro. They see you and they look, so they do a profiling of you as a Latino, and they say, "Oh, someone else who is around." You will not start screaming, "Hey, I am a migrant!"

Their invisibility as return migrants within Mexico City's vastness and complexity is compounded by the contrast they present to Mexico City residents' cultural image of a Mexican emigrant as someone from rural origins. Emigrants from other parts of the country made this association clear, as Paolo related to us. We described this scene in the introduction, but it is worth repeating here. Paolo told us that other Mexicans he met crossing the border into the United States teased him for being from Mexico City—"*Oye, un chilanguillo,*" they said to him, using a diminutive version of the word *chilango* (a Mexico City resident). Their confusion came from the dissonance of his being both an emigrant and a resident of Mexico City. They said to him, "But there in the [Federal] District, there are more opportunities. I don't know why you are crossing!"

Paolo and others crossed for a multiplicity of reasons that reflect the findings of earlier scholars of urban-origin emigration. As we will explain next, the combination of large-scale internal migration to the city, an advanced rural-origin migration flow to the United States, and the national economic crisis set the stage for large numbers of Mexico City residents to make their way northward in the 1980s and 1990s.

Mexico City's Role in Mexican Migration to the United States

As Mexico City grew through the arrival of domestic migrants from rural places in the middle of the twentieth century, the same social, economic, and demographic processes that mobilized domestic out-migrants set the stage for emigration abroad. As we discussed in chapter 1, the Great Mexican Migration unfolded over the course of the twentieth century. Large-scale U.S.-bound migration began during World War II when Mexico and the United States signed the Bracero

Accord, which gave permits to millions of Mexicans to work as *brace-ros* (strong arms), or field-workers, in U.S. agriculture. The program ended in 1964, but migration from Mexico to the United States contin-ued, funneled by U.S. labor demand and social networks that reached across the two countries. The annual flow reached its highest levels in the 1990s and early 2000s; as a result of this migration, the population of Mexican immigrants peaked at 12.8 million in 2007.[21] But by the end of the first decade of the twenty-first century, the number of people entering the United States from Mexico equaled the number leaving the United States for Mexico, and in the 2010s, more people migrated from the United States to Mexico than migrated to the United States from Mexico.[22]

At the height of the Great Mexican Migration, the typical emigrant originated from a rural place in the central-western states of Mexico in the Traditional Region.[23] Rural towns in the Traditional Region were connected to the United States by the railroad and the work of labor recruiters during the Bracero period. However, as the migration pro-cess evolved over time, emigrant origins diversified to include increas-ing numbers of emigrants from outside this region—from rural places in the south of Mexico, in states like Oaxaca, as well as from urban areas like Mexico City.[24] By the mid-1990s, the origins of Mexican emigration had shifted from rural places to small urban places and large metropol-itan areas.[25] Among migrants departing for the first time to the United States in the 1990s, there were more urban migrants than other types of migrants; by the mid-2000s, urban migrants made up the majority of first-time migrants to the United States.[26]

Indeed, Mexico City became a major place of origin for Mexican emi-grants after 1990. Since 1995, the first year in which a Mexican census or population count included questions on international migration, there have been more migrants departing from Mexico City for the United States in the previous five-year period than from any other major Mexican city.[27] Between 1990 and 1995, the 137,000 people who migrated to the United States from the Mexico City metropolitan area comprised more than one in four (27 percent) of emigrants from met-ropolitan areas and almost one in twelve of all emigrants to the United States.[28] Between 1995 and 2000, Mexico City sent more emigrants to the United States than the cities of León, Guadalajara, Tijuana, Monterrey, Puebla, Oaxaca, and Veracruz combined.[29] In that period, nearly one out of every ten emigrants departing Mexico for the United States originated in Mexico City.[30]

Mexico City Step Migration

Does emigration from urban origins in the 1990s follow the pattern established in research on rural origins in the 1970s and 1980s? In some ways, yes, but in other ways, no. In both rural and urban places, social and economic change disrupted life in ways that made emigration abroad a possible and desirable option. Mexico's transition from an agrarian and rural economy to an industrial and urban economy through the middle of the twentieth century disrupted rural life, created new economic problems and wants, and mobilized large cohorts of people born during the height of the demographic transition. Most migrated to Mexico's cities, but some emigrated abroad. After 1980, Mexico's shift from a domestic, industrial economy to a globalized, service-based economy increased unemployment among domestic migrants and their descendants who settled in cities, people whose skills were better suited to work under the old economic model.[31] Although rural- and urban-origin emigration occurred in different moments of historical transformation, in both rural- and urban-origin migration to the United States, emigrants used migration abroad to adapt to economic and social transitions at home.

Although both rural- and urban-origin people emigrated in response to macroeconomic change, the predictable social process of migration that unfolded in rural communities was not replicated in most urban neighborhoods. In urban places, emigration never became self-perpetuating in the way that rural emigration did because urban networks are generally too dispersed and weak to develop and spread migration capital.[32] Scholars have argued that the city environment is too large and complex, too individually oriented and fast-paced, to generate the kinds of ties that concentrate and distribute information, resources, and ideas about migration, as occurs in rural places.[33] Only under certain unique circumstances, as Hernández-León found in Monterrey, has there been evidence of the development of migrant social capital native to the city.[34] The Monterrey neighborhood that Hernández-León studied was characterized by a long history of economic stability and occupational specialization; in this context, residents responded to the

economic crises of the 1980s through emigration, migration was funneled by migration-related entrepreneurs and services, and a strong
binational network formed between Monterrey and Houston, Texas.

In Mexico City, studies have focused on specific neighborhoods where
migration is common, such as the neighborhood of Nezahualcóyotl
in the eastern part of the metropolitan area. In 2010, six out of every
ten inhabitants in Nezahualcóyotl was born in another part of Mexico,
and six out of every ten international migrants were also internal
migrants.[35] Rivera's study of return migration from the United States
to Nezahualcóyotl reveals the disconnection, in the urban context,
between emigration and return that undermines the possibility for
place-based ties.[36] The return migrants she studied originated in other
parts of Mexico or other parts of the city. They may have migrated first
to Nezahualcóyotl before departing for the United States, or they may
have departed from another place and returned there. As a result, they
did not share identities, networks, or migration trajectories anchored
in sites of origin or destination. What they held in common was not a
sense of place or peoplehood but a sense of mobility. The sociologist
Cristóbal Mendoza's survey of residents in Osmundo's neighborhood
of Valle de Chalco also found that residents there felt a strong sense of
placelessness; those who did feel strong attachments to Chalco were
less likely to emigrate.[37]

The return migrants we interviewed did not originate from a single
neighborhood, and none drew from nonfamily networks located in
their urban neighborhood to emigrate. Many people we spoke to emigrated to accompany or follow family members. When we tracked
the information, resources, and ideas of migration to their source, we
found that nearly every migrant we spoke to drew from rural-based
networks to emigrate. Osmundo, for example, emigrated directly from
a small town in Guerrero to California, drawing on connections to
friends and family who had emigrated from the same rural origins.
Osmundo initially returned to his origin in Guerrero, but he relocated
to the Mexico City neighborhood of Valle del Chalco when he realized
that he could enhance his family's business by being close to the Mexico
City handicraft markets. In other words, Osmundo was not an urban
emigrant. He was an urban returnee.

The migration trajectory Osmundo took—from a rural place to the
United States and then returning to the city—was uncommon among

our respondents. Six people we spoke to originated outside of Mexico City.[38] One of those six, Antonio, originated from a rancho in San Luis Potosí. He told us about the first time he emigrated in 1990 with his uncle, who had been in the United States for decades:

> I went for the adventure, not for necessity. . . . I decided just like that. Like, all of my family, the majority of my uncles . . . is in the United States. I had an uncle who would come [to Mexico] two times a year with all of his family. I was about to turn seventeen, and he was here, and he said, "Hey, this time Jesse didn't come," because I have a cousin [Jesse] who is the same age as me. So he said, "If you want to go to the United States, well, let's go." That was a Friday, like at four in the afternoon, when he said that to me. So I got to my house, I took a shower, and I was bathing, and I said to myself, "Ay, I'm going to go." So I just said to my mom, I said, "Mom, I'm going to the United States." And she said, "What? You're crazy." "No, I'm going now." I grabbed three pants, three shirts, and let's go. My uncle came by at like eight PM, and that was it. The next day, it was Saturday, like at two in the afternoon, and we were already crossing through Matamoros.

Antonio emigrated suddenly, without foresight, planning, or, as he put it, necessity. The decision was so sudden that Antonio remembered the time of day it happened, the shower he took, and the brief exchange about it with his mother. Antonio's social ties to his emigrant family made his emigration possible from one day to the next, and his unplanned departure reveals that strong network ties can lead to emigration even in the absence of economic reasons to emigrate. Antonio did not emigrate to solve an economic problem at home, but simply because he could. Later he ended up in Mexico City, rather than back in San Luis Potosí, because he was deported there.

More common in our sample were people who migrated to Mexico City from a rural origin before emigrating to the United States. Respondents in our sample moved to Mexico City from rural places or small towns in Michoacán, the State of Mexico, Veracruz, Hidalgo, Guerrero, Jalisco, San Luis Potosí, and Guanajuato. People who migrate up the urban hierarchy—from a rural place or small town to a big city, and then abroad—are known in the scholarship on migration as "step migrants." In theory, people become step migrants because exposure to new experiences and environments primes them for additional migrations as they develop new aspirations and abilities.[39] In a recent elaboration of this theory, the international migration scholar Anju Paul argues that the process can be planned from the outset: a person migrates along a sequence of domestic and/or international destinations to accumulate sufficient capital to reach their preferred (final) destination.[40]

The experiences of the step migrants we spoke to did not reflect the logic of either of these theoretical accounts of step migration. As they migrated, these return migrants neither developed new aspirations and capabilities (which, according to classic theory on step migration, would have inspired them to migrate internationally) nor strategized domestic migration to the city as a means to accumulate sufficient capital to reach their final destination (the United States). The step migrants we spoke to were domestic migrants who became international migrants by drawing on networks and norms in their rural communities of origin.

Mateo is an example. Mateo's family had moved from a small town in Hidalgo to the south of Mexico City, where he was born. Mateo's aunt and uncle had emigrated to the United States from Hidalgo, and his uncle told him what work was like there: hard but worth the effort. When Mateo was a teenager, he got in trouble with some friends, and his mother sent him to live in the *pueblo* (small town) in Hidalgo where she was from. As he explained, "My punishment, they sent me with some uncles from the town of my mom, so that I would see that life is hard, no?" He was eager to go to the United States, where his aunt and uncle lived, and one day the opportunity arose. He told us, "I was in the town [in Hidalgo] for a year, year and a half, working with a guy. And he said to me, 'Well, now come, there are some people coming from Pachuca,' from Pachuca, Hidalgo. Well, the crazy idea is now in my mind to go [to the United States]." Mateo took the opportunity and left with the group from Pachuca. His idea of going to the United States had originated in his uncle's example and advice; the opportunity arose through social connections based in the pueblo where his mother originated and had sent him as an adolescent needing discipline. She did not plan for him, however, to depart Hidalgo for the United States. As Mateo told us, he emigrated to escape his mother's control.

We examined our data for evidence of a planned process of stepwise international migration, as Paul found among Filipina domestic workers who migrated across destinations in East and Southeast Asia, but we did not find any.[41] None of the people we spoke to talked about using Mexico City as a jumping-off point, a place to temporarily accumulate the necessary capital to emigrate to the United States. Their social capital—connections to other migrants through which they received information, resources, and ideas—was formed before they migrated to the city and was still located outside of the city when they emigrated to the United States. None of the migrants we spoke to talked about the importance for emigration of other sources of capital, such as human capital (education or work experience) or financial capital obtained in the city.

We considered how city life might prime a person for international migration by exposing them to new aspirations or capabilities, as argued by the classic theory on step migration.[42] But contrary to an image that joins migration with modernity, what emerged was the sense of dissonance between Mexico City residence and U.S. emigration, as expressed by the *paisanos* (fellow nationals) Paolo encountered on the border. The perception that a person did not emigrate if there were local economic opportunities, and that there were local opportunities in Mexico City, was common among our study participants. Reynaldo, who was twenty-four when we interviewed him, spent part of his childhood in the United States. He told us that he had no interest in ever returning there, for reasons that reveal his cultural associations with U.S. migration. He said:

> I, for example, am the head of my household, and earning here [in Mexico City], it's enough. I am very well off. I don't have any need to go to another place. And there is no point because those who go there return tattooed or cholos. . . . Yeah, it's like, why do you go? If you go, that's why people speak badly about us, and all that's going to happen is you turn into a cholo. Think about it a bit, no? At least me, never.

In emigrating, Reynaldo believed, one revealed oneself to be economically needy, not well off. He also believed that one ran the risk of becoming stigmatized by emigrating. *Cholo* is a derogatory slang term used in Mexico and the United States to refer to Mexican-origin people who, because they wear baggy clothes and have tattoos, are presumed to be gang-affiliated.[43] Reynaldo's comments reflect the idea of the Mexican emigrant as an economically needy rural person with no local opportunities, either economic or political. In this view, emigration substitutes for local opportunities, but in emigrating, the rural emigrant runs the risk of returning as a cholo. The cultural image of the Mexico City resident is of a self-sufficient person with no such need—"the head of the household" who earns enough, as Reynaldo said. According to these cultural images, adopting a Mexico City identity moves a person further away from an emigrant identity, which thus becomes less culturally plausible as a way of acting or being. Acculturation to Mexico City norms is therefore unlikely to make emigration more likely.

Others expressed the idea that going to the United States revealed some kind of compliance with the system. The father of the barber Paolo felt this way. When Paolo and his mother Rocío emigrated for the first time (a story we tell in chapter 5), Rocío and Paolo's father were separated, but his father was nevertheless dismayed. Paolo told us that his father believed that "you don't need to go to the United States to improve yourself. What we need is to change the government here in Mexico. Well, why don't I use his literal words? '*What the hell am I going to do in a country that is not mine?*' That is how he sees it."

What emerged in our interviews was not that rural-to-urban migrants were transformed by the city in ways that primed them for emigration, but that a sense of geographic mobility predated their or their family's initial move to the United States. Like the migrants whom Rivera studied in Nezahualcóyotl, we found among Mexico City returnees an ambitious and risk-taking desire to improve their life chances through spatial relocation, which related to moves both within Mexico and abroad.[44] For example, Mario, who was born in Veracruz to parents from Puebla and moved to Mexico City when he was a teenager, described the migrant spirit this way: "The key word 'migrant' is that there is not a place, there is no space for a person, no? . . . And so, the moment that one has their worries, the moment that one wants to reach certain goals, well, one turns into a migrant automatically." According to Mario, his family's migrations—which unfolded as step migration across their lifetimes—reflected their sense that there was no local space for them to achieve their goals, whether in Puebla, Veracruz, or Mexico City.

Eduardo's family, whom he described as having a migrant spirit, migrated from Guerrero to Mexico City when Eduardo was five, and later,

Eduardo's father emigrated to the United States. Eduardo defined the migrant spirit as "always looking to improve oneself, one's quality of life":

> Well, my father was the first who began to come to Mexico [City] for work, he was the first to come, and all of us were, my siblings and my mom and I, in Guerrero, in the town where I was born. He worked and found where to live, and that was when they decided to bring us all to the city. I think it was for more work opportunities and to search for a better life . . . than there was in the little town. And to give us a better education. Well, in general for all of the family, I think that was the reasoning, no? Because also, my father . . . I was thirteen years old when my father also went to the United States, he was also an emigrant. That is, always looking to improve oneself, no? One's quality of life.

Like his father, Eduardo also had a strong desire to work and to emigrate. He told us about fighting with his mom when he left school because she wanted him to continue his education, but he was ready to work. Unlike his father, who emigrated permanently (never returning to Mexico City or Guerrero), Eduardo saw U.S. emigration as the way to purchase his own taxi in order to return and work in Mexico City. Although their specific migration strategies differed, Eduardo and his father shared the sense that migration was a preferred route to obtaining a better life. This sense predated and drove their move first from Guerrero to Mexico City and later from Mexico City to the United States.

Conclusion

Among the returnees we interviewed, migration to Mexico City from rural places had enabled their emigration to the United States. They had drawn on cultural and social capital from rural places, located in social networks that predated their own domestic migration, to migrate to the United States.[45] Thus, some urban-origin Mexican migration to the United States—the emigration we observed—was facilitated by social processes that unfolded in rural Mexico.

Step migration helps us understand why, in the popular perception, the chilango (Mexico City resident) doesn't emigrate, as Paolo discovered at the border. Among the men Paolo shared origin stories with at the border, chilangos were assumed to be immobile, tethered to and economically well off in the capital city. The contemporary cultural dissonance between the chilango and emigration is ironic, given the origin of the term. Because the name "Mexico" refers to a city, a state, and a country, and the Mexico City metropolitan area incorporates three different states, it is hard to create a demonym for the Mexico City resident. *Capitalinos* refers to residence or birth in the capital city, and *defeños* refers to the inner city's previous name, Distrito Federal.[46] These terms do not capture, however, the experience of the millions of Mexico City residents who live in the metropolitan area beyond the inner city, especially since many residents migrated internally or were born to internal migrant parents. "Chilango" became the term to refer to rural-origin migrants who settled on the outer edges of the city in the 1960s and 1970s, outside of the Federal District. Later, in the 1980s, it became a pejorative label for metropolitan residents who migrated from Mexico City to other parts of the country, regardless of their precise origin within Mexico City. Upon arrival in other Mexican cities, internal migrants from Mexico City encountered hostility: coming from the capital city, they were perceived as culturally distinct and criticized for a presumed sense of superiority. A xenophobic phrase spread in response to out-migration from Mexico City: "*Haz patria, mata un chilango*" ("Be patriotic, kill a chilango").[47] Today the word has a more neutral meaning and is sometimes used with humor, and occasionally pride.

The people we spoke to, like Paolo, Mario, Eduardo, and Reynaldo, were concerned about their identities as Mexico City residents as well as their identities as return migrants. One of our respondents, Raúl, resolved some of the conflict between these two identities by adopting a distinct title. He believed, he told us, that the same hostility toward chilangos that permeated Mexico in the 1980s was present in the United States. He explained:

> There is a very important thing, that if you go from a state, you are there in the United States, and if you're from a state, no matter which one, Toluca or whatever it is, they receive you with open arms, they give you more opportunities.[48] If you are from the capital, they say to you, "You're chilango," and they give you problems . . . because of the reputation. The reputation that chilangos have. The chilango comes from outside. If you live here, you know your history. We grew up or were born in the great Tenochtitlan, from the city, and so we are *Tenochcas*, misnamed chilangos.

Raúl told us that while Mexican migrants from the states (meaning from outside Mexico City) were received by fellow immigrants in the United States "with open arms" and given "more opportunities," chilangos met with "problems," owing to the chilango's reputation. He therefore embraced an identity that evoked the pre-Hispanic inhabitants of the land on which Mexico City sits, the Mexica who built Tenochtitlan ("and so we are *Tenochcas*, misnamed chilangos").

It was important for Raúl to lay claim to his city's history—a history that continues to unfold as he and other return migrants resettle there.

CHAPTER THREE

THE POLICY TRAP

Olivia and her partner Rodolfo struggled to make ends meet as young parents in Mexico City. She worked selling *paletas* (popsicles) and *chicharrones* (fried pork skins) in front of her mother's house in Gustavo A. Madero in north-central Mexico City, and Rodolfo worked as a *microbusero*, driving a microbus around the city. They had a two-year-old daughter and often lacked money for diapers and milk.

A friend of Rodolfo's named Edgar, another microbusero, had emigrated to Arizona a year before. Rodolfo would still talk by phone occasionally with Edgar, who told him that he could easily find good-paying work in Arizona. Rodolfo didn't have the money to cross the border, certainly not with Olivia and their daughter. Edgar had left his wife and children in Mexico City for the same reason, but now that Edgar had the money to cover his family's journey into the United States, he worried about them crossing the border without him. Then Edgar had an idea: he would pay for Rodolfo and his family to cross if they would accompany Edgar's wife and children on the journey, taking care of them along the way. Rodolfo and Olivia agreed. Rodolfo, Olivia, and their young daughter walked across the border with Edgar's wife and children, through the desert near Douglas, Arizona. It took them three attempts, but the two families eventually entered the United States.

Edgar was right. Rodolfo found good work in Arizona as a dishwasher at a nursing home. Olivia stayed home with their daughter, occasionally cleaning houses or watching other children for some income. A few

https://doi.org/10.7758/kokl2957.7530

years after they immigrated, Olivia became pregnant again and fell into a severe depression. "I missed my family so much, I missed my country, the language [English] was hard, and my child cried every night." When Olivia's mother became ill in Mexico City, Olivia returned to see her. It was Olivia's only trip home to visit her mother in the seventeen years that she lived in the United States. Olivia stayed in Mexico City for a month and a half—long enough to see her mother's health improve but nearly too long to be separated from her four-year-old daughter, who had remained in Arizona with Rodolfo. Because Olivia was pregnant, she reentered the United States this time as a passenger in a car driven across the border. She was caught by Border Patrol on her first entry and subjected to expedited removal. Then she tried entering by car a second time and made it through.

Olivia and Rodolfo had three more children in Arizona and were economically successful there. But things were getting difficult for immigrants in Arizona, and they decided to leave for Colorado in 2010. That year, the Arizona legislature passed Senate Bill 1070 (SB 1070), the "Show Me Your Papers" law, which required local law enforcement officers to ask for immigration papers when they had reasonable suspicion that a person might be unlawfully in the country. Olivia heard that immigration agents were conducting raids in the area and that people were being caught, detained, and deported. She told us what it was like to live in a state of threat: "You live with fear. People who have documents don't worry that migration [authorities] are going to grab you, or that you will be left without work because someone asks for your documents . . . but [people without documents] are always aware that something can happen." Olivia described the experience as *acoso* (harassment): "You started to see the harassment," she told us. "There is so much harassment that now exists."

Although they fled the heightened threat of apprehension in Arizona, it was in Colorado that Olivia's life as an immigrant in the United States began to unravel. In 2013, she was caught driving without a license and detained for four months, subject to deportation. But Olivia was not deported at that time. She argued in the courts that she should be issued a reprieve because of her good moral conduct, record of tax payments, clean criminal record, and, most importantly, the potential hardship to her disabled, U.S.-born daughter if she were deported. The judge agreed, and although Olivia did not qualify for lawful permanent residency, the judge granted her discretionary status, which deferred her deportation and allowed her to obtain work authorization. Olivia credited this turn of events to a mixture of political, spiritual, and personal forces. As she told us,

> Obama gave us a lot of opportunity . . . I am proof of that. Since I had more than ten years living in the country, having paid taxes and all, well, he told me, "Okay, I am going to give you a chance." . . . In fact, they told me that I would be deported, but God was very great, and it was Him who helped me get out. More than anything, it was the situation with my daughter.

Olivia's work authorization enabled her to start her own business cleaning homes and offices; she was very successful, employing several family members and friends. Her oldest daughter, a teenager with discretionary status through the Deferred Action for Childhood Arrivals (DACA) program, worked with her, and her three U.S. citizen children attended public schools in Denver. Sometimes even her husband would work for her.

Under her discretionary status, Olivia was required to check in annually with immigration agents. Olivia told us that, in 2016, her lawyer gave her the following advice: "If Trump ends up being president, there will be a lot of changes because he comes with a very different ideology [than Obama]. There is a risk that he could deport you. Do you want to risk it? Or do you want to hide? Disappear from the map so that there is no problem?" Olivia's status was discretionary, meaning that it could be revoked. By following her lawyer's advice to "disappear from the map" by failing to show up for her immigration check-ins, she could avoid the risk of deportation, but she would lose her work authorization. Olivia did not want to lose her business, so she decided to risk deportation.

In April 2017, when Olivia showed up for her annual migration check-in, she was arrested and detained. Migration officials flew her from Denver to Utah to Nevada to Texas to New Mexico and then back to Texas, all in a matter of six days. She was not able to use the bathroom on the airplane, and she developed a severe urinary tract infection. She told us:

> When I arrived at the jail in Texas, I was with fever, pain in the kidneys— all through my lower back, and my stomach had swollen as though I was four months pregnant. They gave me an antibiotic, but I was getting worse. And so, when they saw that I was getting worse, well, what did they do? They deported me. When I was the sickest, that was when they kicked me out.

Olivia was taken across the bridge to Ciudad Acuña, Coahuila, and told, "Don't turn around because they will shoot you if you turn around." She walked toward Mexican police officers, who brought her to a reception station. When the Mexican police released her, she bought a bus ticket to Mexico City. She never said goodbye to her husband or children.

In the research for this book, we interviewed immigrants like Olivia who had lived full lives in the United States. They did essential work in childcare, cleaning services, landscaping, agriculture, construction, restaurants, and manufacturing. Some, like Olivia, built successful businesses. Some went to U.S. schools. Some had relationships with U.S. citizens. Others had U.S. citizen children. They paid rent and taxes, bought cars and houses, learned English, joined churches, became activists, and raised children. Yet none of the people we interviewed had full legal rights in the United States.

The people we interviewed had been harmed by U.S. immigration policy but by 2019 were getting on with their lives as return migrants in Mexico City. Of the thirty-four people we interviewed, half had been deported from the United States, including Olivia.[1] The other half returned for other reasons, most often citing a desire to reunite with family. Regardless of the circumstances or reasons for their return, none of the people we interviewed were legally able to reenter the United States. U.S. laws trapped both people who were deported and people who returned for other reasons in Mexico. Ironically, despite their inability to lawfully reenter the United States—despite being trapped in Mexico by the U.S. Policy Trap—their return to Mexico after living undocumented in the United States brought into sharp relief for our interviewees what it meant to be free.

In this chapter, we describe the series of major U.S. federal laws and policies created after 1986 that make up the Policy Trap. We then relate our interviewees' trajectories vis-à-vis these policies. Finally, we draw out a key theme of the Policy Trap that emerged in our interviews with former U.S. migrants living in Mexico City in 2019: the paradoxical experience of being trapped on one side of the border and yet free in Mexico.

The Policy Trap

We use the term "Policy Trap" to refer to the U.S. legal and immigration policy regime in effect from 1986 through at least 2024. The Policy Trap began after the passage of the Immigration Reform and Control

Act (IRCA) in 1986, the last major U.S. immigration reform, and continued through the 2012 creation of DACA. The Obama administration designed DACA in response to immigrant activism spurred by the failures of U.S. immigration policy during the Policy Trap period, but DACA hardly signals a shift in federal immigration policy. The Policy Trap continued after 2012 and worsened in many respects with Trump's first administration, Covid-era border protocols, and the arrival at the U.S. southwestern border of large numbers of migrants from Central America and Venezuela, among other places.

The Policy Trap began in 1986 with IRCA, the last comprehensive federal immigration reform passed in the United States (as of 2024). As considerable research on U.S. immigration law and Mexico-U.S. migration has shown, IRCA was a response to earlier failures and gaps in U.S. immigration law, including the failure of ending the Bracero program in the mid-1960s without a replacement to account for the labor relationships developed while the program was in effect, as well as the introduction of limits to legal immigration from the Western Hemisphere in 1968.[2] These pre-IRCA policies transformed a circular, legal migration flow into a circular, undocumented migration flow.[3] IRCA sought to address the issue of undocumented migration with a three-pronged approach: amnesty for the resident undocumented population, employer regulations to prevent the employment of undocumented people, and border control to prevent undocumented entry. However, none of the three approaches addressed the U.S. demand for undocumented migrant labor.[4] Despite its intent, IRCA failed to prevent undocumented immigration.

IRCA began a three-decade-long (and ongoing) focus on enforcing the U.S. southwestern border. This effort picked up in the 1990s.[5] Under the Policy Trap, the U.S. Congress attempted to control the entry of undocumented immigrants by putting more border patrol agents, physical barriers, and technology on the border. Trump's 2016 "build the wall" presidential platform may have been the most extreme policy position on border control, but the agencies assigned to guard the border have seen their budgets increase under all presidential administrations since IRCA.[6]

Although the policy intent of border control was to prevent undocumented entry, very large numbers of people entered the United States without documents through the 1990s and early 2000s.[7] What border control changed was patterns of return to Mexico. Border control had the unplanned effect of trapping undocumented immigrants within the United States. The rising cost of crossing into the United States compelled undocumented immigrants to stay (and work) longer in the United States to recoup the investment they had made to cross. Border control also made border crossings more difficult and dangerous, leading to an increased risk of death on the border.[8] An immigrant could not return to Mexico for a short trip because reentry into the United States would impose new costs and risks; as a result, circular migration became infeasible. Forced to stay longer without making return trips to Mexico, immigrants became more deeply settled in the United States. Because migrants could not cross back and forth across the border, transnational family life became increasingly difficult to sustain. Many undocumented immigrants reunited with their children in the United States to avoid separation, and many more formed families in the United States.[9] The impact of border control on entry, return, and reentry patterns was apparent in the increased population of undocumented immigrants in the United States, largely because of declining return migration.[10] Two other populations profoundly affected by U.S. immigration law also grew: U.S.-born children of undocumented immigrant parents and undocumented child migrants.

Two U.S. laws passed in 1996 transformed the management of immigrant detention and deportation. Passed shortly after the Oklahoma City bombing, the Antiterrorism and Effective Death Penalty Act (AEDPA) expanded the category of deportable offenses. It also mandated detention and severely limited judicial review in the cases of immigrants ordered deported following conviction for a deportable (criminal) offense. AEDPA recharacterized an undocumented person's situation in the interior of the United States as similar to that of an undocumented person apprehended upon entry to the United States, such that both types of immigrants could be processed for removal without consideration of their ties to the United States.[11]

Even more devastating for immigrant rights than AEDPA was the 1996 Illegal Immigration Reform and Immigrant Responsibility Act (IIRAIRA). IIRAIRA expanded the category of deportable offenses well beyond AEDPA by reclassifying the term "aggravated felony" to include any criminal conviction with a prison sentence of one year or longer. Because prior laws allowed the deportation of persons convicted of an aggravated felony regardless of when the conviction occurred, this redefinition vastly expanded the group of people subject to deportation as a result of convictions after 1996, as well as those that occurred before 1996. IIRAIRA enabled the stripping of lawful permanent resident status from immigrants convicted of aggravated felonies and limited judicial review of deportation orders for immigrants who had been convicted of aggravated felonies or crimes of moral turpitude, beyond the limits already imposed by AEDPA. These actions vastly increased the ability of immigration officers and judges to deport immigrants who were settled in the United States.[12]

IIRAIRA also created reentry "bars"—restrictions on reentering the United States—as a penalty for undocumented entry into and residence in the United States: three-year bars for people who had spent more than 180 days and less than a year with undocumented status in the United States, and ten-year bars for people who had spent more than a year with undocumented status in the United States. People who are deported are typically barred from reentry for ten years, but the bar becomes twenty years if an individual is caught reentering after deportation. Olivia's reentry bar was ten years.

After the terrorist attack on September 11, 2001 (9/11), the U.S. Congress passed the Homeland Security Act, which restructured the agencies overseeing immigration and organized them within the new U.S. Department of Homeland Security (DHS). The restructuring included the creation of a new U.S. agency dedicated to enforcing immigration law, Immigration and Customs Enforcement, or ICE.

While the U.S. Congress was passing laws that sought to restrict immigrant rights in this period, laws to expand immigrant rights routinely failed to pass. In 2001, in response to the growth in the population of undocumented child migrants, U.S. senators introduced the Development, Relief, and Education for Alien Minors (DREAM) Act, which was intended to provide a route to citizenship for young, undocumented immigrants who arrived as minors. The DREAM Act failed to become law in 2001 and in every subsequent congressional session when it was reintroduced. During this period, Congress also made repeated but failed attempts at comprehensive immigration reform.

While the border was the focus of immigration enforcement during the 1990s, after 9/11 efforts to enforce immigration law expanded within the interior as well. Drawing on the legal groundwork laid by IIRAIRA, the DHS created programs to formalize collaboration between federal immigration agencies and local law enforcement to increase the surveillance and capture of undocumented immigrants settled in the United States.[13] Some state legislatures, notably Arizona and Georgia, passed laws to assist in these efforts. Arizona's SB 1070, which led Olivia and her family to migrate from Arizona to Colorado, is the most notorious of these laws. The training and enabling of local law enforcement to act as immigration agents transformed even minor interactions with police—traffic stops, emergencies, crime witness testimony—into terrifying moments of possible apprehension.[14] Or harassment, as Olivia called it.

By 2012, these combined policy efforts had created a large population of undocumented people who lived, worked, and raised families in the United States but lacked basic legal rights. The sociologists Daniel Martínez, Jeremy Slack, and Ricardo Martínez-Schuldt call these immigrants "unauthorized permanent residents."[15] Like Olivia's oldest daughter, many unauthorized permanent resident immigrants arrived as children, were educated in a U.S. public school system, and identified as Americans, yet had no rights under the punitive policy regime through which the federal government managed immigration.[16] Furthermore, the U.S. government also generated fear, distrust, and alienation among immigrants with the legal right to live and work permanently in the United States, undermining their rights as well.[17]

In response to activist demands for some resolution, the Obama administration introduced DACA, an executive action that used prosecutorial discretion to defer enforcement actions (detention and deportation) for young, settled people who lacked legal documents and had arrived as children. Under other laws, DACA also provided work authorization. Working much like the discretionary status that Olivia received, DACA is a large-scale program created for a swath of the undocumented population. Eligibility for DACA includes not just age (fifteen to thirty-one in 2012) but also age at arrival (under sixteen), time of arrival (prior to 2007), consistent residency in the United States from 2007 to 2012, and some qualitative criteria such as having a high school degree, being enrolled in school, serving in the military, and having a clean criminal record. Although DACA provides important protections and rights, the program's fate is uncertain, being dependent on executive discretion and judicial oversight, and it provides no route to lawful permanent resident status or citizenship.

Although nearly one million people obtained DACA status, the program excluded the majority of undocumented immigrants in the United States.[18] An extension to the program, the Deferred Action for Parents of Americans and Lawful Permanent Residents (DAPA), which might have protected Olivia and her husband, was proposed but struck down in the courts. As an executive action, DACA remains subject to presidential discretion. As Olivia's lawyer had warned, Trump's first administration did indeed change the Obama policies. Trump attempted to terminate DACA, but the U.S. Supreme Court upheld the program, determining that the Trump administration lawyers had not given sufficient legal reasoning to terminate the program. In October 2022, the U.S. Court of Appeals for the Fifth Circuit ruled that the program was unlawful but allowed it to continue while a lower court reviewed a new rule proposed by the Biden administration. Pending judicial review and without federal legislative action, DACA recipients remain uncertain about the program's future as well as their own.

DACA did not remedy the failures of U.S. immigration law and policy under the Policy Trap. The U.S. policy regime of heightened immigration enforcement with few routes for regularization and legal migration continued as of 2024 (the time of this writing). However, large-scale, undocumented migration between Mexico and the United States has slowed. For the first time in recent history, net migration between Mexico and the United States reached zero in 2012: the same number of people who entered the United States from Mexico left the United States for Mexico.[19] Since then, net migration has been mostly negative.[20] As a result, the population of undocumented Mexican immigrants in the United States peaked at an estimated 7 million in 2007 and declined by 2.25 million between 2007 and 2019.[21]

Policy Trap Immigrants

The immigrants we interviewed are part of the Policy Trap generation in that they migrated too late to benefit from IRCA and too late, or at too late an age, to benefit from DACA. Figure 3.1 is a reconfiguration of figure 1.2, organized in this version by age, from the oldest to the youngest respondent. As in figure 1.2, each row in figure 3.1 represents a single life course, with shading beginning in the year of birth and ending at the time of the interview in 2019. The light gray-shaded blocks represent years lived in Mexico, and the dark gray-shaded blocks represent years lived in the United States.

Figure 3.1 adds information about qualification for IRCA and DACA. The year 1981 is marked with a double-lined black border to designate a person's qualification for IRCA (based on year of residency) and DACA (based on year of birth). Only one person we interviewed qualified for IRCA's amnesty: the legal status of Rubén—who moved to the United States in 1968, when he was three years old—and his family was adjusted under IRCA. No one else we interviewed had arrived in the United States in time to qualify for IRCA. The IRCA amnesty gave beneficiaries permanent residency with the possibility of naturalization. Although Rubén qualified for naturalization, he did not complete the process. As a result of the provisions laid out in AEDPA and IIRAIRA, Rubén was deported following a conviction for domestic violence with no consideration of his deep ties to the United States—a life lived in California since childhood, three grown children and multiple grandchildren, and a long career in civil service.

No one we interviewed was sponsored for a visa by IRCA beneficiaries either. Several people we interviewed were related to IRCA beneficiaries but did not obtain legal status through family sponsorship. In many cases, the family relation did not qualify them for sponsorship. For instance, Julio's aunt, an IRCA beneficiary, could not sponsor him for legal status because U.S. immigration law does not allow for the sponsorship of nieces or nephews. The Uber driver Evaristo had brothers and parents who adjusted their status under IRCA, but because they were not yet citizens when he entered the United States in 1992, they could not sponsor him. Others who may have been related to IRCA beneficiaries who could sponsor them for status may have found the waits imposed by annual caps and country-specific quotas too burdensome. For instance, if Evaristo's siblings had naturalized by 1992, their petition to sponsor him for a visa would not have been processed until 2004, twelve years after Evaristo immigrated. In the interim, Evaristo's mother passed away; the burden of this wait would have been too great for their family.

Other people we spoke to had close ties to an IRCA beneficiary, but other legal circumstances complicated sponsorship. For example, Lety's husband, Alonso, obtained lawful permanent residency through

Figure 3.1 *The Migration Life Course of the Thirty-Four Return Migrants in Mexico City in 2019, Ordered by Birth Year*

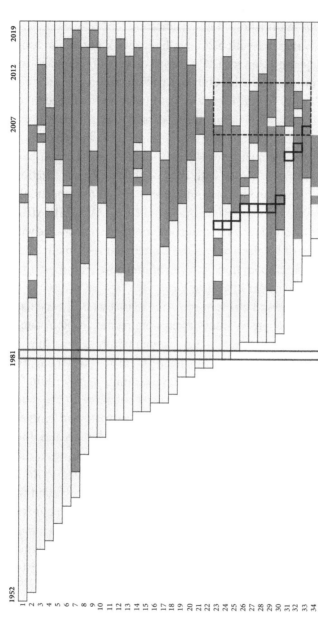

Source: Authors' diagram.

Light gray: Years spent in Mexico.

Dark gray: Years spent in the United States.

Double-lined black border around the year 1981: Eligible for IRCA (based on U.S. residence) and DACA (based on birth year).

Square black border: Age-eligible for DACA (by age at migration) at age sixteen.

Rectangular dashed black border: Eligible for DACA based on constant U.S. residency between 2007 and 2012.

IRCA, but his prior criminal conviction disqualified him from sponsoring Lety. In still other cases, immigration law complicated family matters. Roberto's partner's sponsorship by her mother, an IRCA beneficiary, was in progress when she moved in with Roberto. He adopted her two young children, and they had two children together. Roberto understood that if he married his partner, her pending petition would be revoked, as the law allowed only a parent who was a lawful permanent resident to sponsor unmarried children. Roberto and his partner would have married had it not been for the immigration consequences of formalizing their union.

In addition to defining the beginning of the residency period for IRCA eligibility, 1981 also marks the birth year for upper-age eligibility for DACA. To qualify for DACA, a person had to be between the ages of fifteen and thirty-one in 2012 (born between 1981 and 1997). All interviewees in figure 3.1 rows that begin in 1981 or later (starting with row twenty-three) qualified for DACA based on age. DACA eligibility also required migration before the age of sixteen, which is marked in a black-outlined box within each row from row sixteen to row thirty-four. The final eligibility criterion observed in the figure is constant residency in the United States from 2007 to 2012, a period marked by a dashed black border that takes the shape of a vertical rectangle.

The figure makes clear the narrowness, arbitrariness, and complexity of the DACA eligibility criteria as applied to real lives and migration trajectories. Although many of our respondents migrated as children, none qualified for DACA.[22] But many came close to qualifying. Among the eleven age-eligible respondents, five migrated at a young enough age (rows twenty-nine, thirty, thirty-two, thirty-three, and thirty-four), but none lived in the United States consistently from 2007 through 2012. Two respondents (rows twenty-four and twenty-eight) lived in the United States from 2007 to 2012, but both migrated at too old an age. Row twenty-nine came the closest to eligibility; that person migrated young enough but did not live in the United States consistently from 2007 to 2012. The figure does not include other DACA eligibility criteria, such as school attendance and high school graduation.

The children of several of the people we interviewed qualified for and obtained DACA, including the children of Olivia, Mario, Yazmín, and Evaristo. DACA recipients are protected from deportation and can work legally in the United States so long as the DACA program exists and they continue to renew their status. But when their parents live in their country of origin after a period of residence in undocumented status in the United States, U.S. immigration law makes it very difficult for parents and children to be together. Olivia, Mario, Yazmín, and Evaristo faced IIRAIRA bars on reentry to the United States; even if they had qualified for and obtained a visa, they would have had to wait for the expiration of the reentry bar before they could legally reenter or obtain a waiver to the bar under extraordinary hardship criteria. Because DACA is a temporary protective status given to undocumented immigrants, travel outside of the United States is possible but difficult. DACA recipients can obtain Advance Parole to travel under certain circumstances, but lawyers warn DACA recipients that, even with Advance Parole, there is a risk of getting stuck outside the United States.[23]

The Policy Trap and Return to Mexico

Olivia and the other people we interviewed were a few of the millions of Mexicans who reside in the United States, or who used to reside in the United States and now reside in Mexico, who are trapped by the Policy Trap. A large and growing body of research documents their experiences.[24] The experiences of the migrants we interviewed echoed much of what is known about the harms of U.S. immigration policy to individual, family, and community well-being.

Olivia's experience was not unique. Mario also experienced a sudden arrest and eventual deportation after years of living well in the United States. His story shares many similarities with Olivia's, as well as with those of many other return migrants we interviewed.

Like Olivia, Mario emigrated from Mexico City to the United States in 1998, searching for economic opportunities but with no way to qualify for a visa. He crossed the border in the California desert, walking for two days with a paid guide. Our interviewees described a wide range of border crossing points and strategies, including entry through the turnstiles with fake documents, hiding—or even sitting in plain sight— in a vehicle, walking across the desert, and swimming across the river. Like Olivia, some were apprehended and returned multiple times before they succeeded in entering the country. Only a few of them entered with temporary visas granted to them as tourists or students. They became undocumented after they violated the visa's terms, such as by working or overstaying the expiration. Visa overstayers have become more common among undocumented Mexican immigrants in the United States in recent years.[25]

Both Olivia and Mario crossed the Mexico-U.S. border in harrowing ways, risking illness, injury, violence, and even death. Owing to the cost and risk of crossing, Olivia and Mario could not return easily to Mexico if they wanted to subsequently reenter the United States. Like many other Mexican immigrants in the United States, they reunited with and formed families in the United States rather than remain separated from them. After four years in the United States, Mario paid a guide to bring his wife and three children across. They joined him in unlawful status in the United States.

The Policy Trap made circular migration infeasible and short trips home extremely costly. Nearly everyone we spoke to said they would have liked to return home frequently to visit family or to celebrate the holidays, but they could neither afford nor risk the journey. When we asked the artist Osmundo about going back and forth, he was very clear in explaining to us that he crossed only once, intending to stay, work, and save as much money as he could. He would be in the United States for ten years. We asked him if he ever left the United States and reentered during that time. "No. Never," he told us. Entering the United States, he added, "is too much stress, too much threat from the migration [authorities]." People returned only under dire circumstances, such as an illness or death in the family. Olivia, for instance, returned to Mexico to be with her ill mother. Like Osmundo, Mario never returned to Mexico during his time in the United States. As a result, he lost contact with his family in Mexico over time.

For twenty years, Mario, much like Olivia, did well in the United States. He was a sought-after farmworker who worked hard and saved enough money to buy his own mobile home. Like Olivia's oldest daughter, Mario's children obtained work authorization and protection from deportation through DACA. They earned college degrees and started careers. They married. Mario now has eleven U.S.-born grandchildren.

Although the Policy Trap makes life for undocumented immigrants in the United States difficult and stressful, the immigrants we interviewed were creative and strategic in managing the daily complications presented by immigration law. They devised strategies for safely navigating social spaces, finding work and dealing with employers, resolving conflicts, and obtaining needed services. Much like the sociologist Asad Asad has argued, these immigrants both engaged and evaded: they sought out the services they needed, interacting with institutions and bureaucrats to establish a record of good conduct and take care of themselves and their families, and they evaded apprehension as best they could.[26] Immigrants found ways to get licenses and license plates (driving across state lines), Social Security cards (purchased on the black market or "borrowed" from deceased family members), affordable rent (apartment sharing, renting rooms), and health care (emergency Medicaid, free clinics, loans from friends). These strategies made life in the United States doable despite the hardships of limited rights and the threat of apprehension.

Yet the threat of apprehension was ever present, and sometimes strategies to cope with it backfired. Such was the case for Mario. His troubles began when he sold his car to a brother-in-law. Because it is complicated, costly, and risky to conduct legal transactions in the United States without legal status, he did not change the name on the title. Then Mario's brother-in-law was in a traffic accident and fled the scene, fearing that any entanglement with law enforcement could lead to his deportation. Instead of tracking down the brother-in-law, law enforcement tracked down Mario, whose name was on the title, and charged him with various crimes committed by his brother-in-law.

Mario wanted to fight the charges because he was innocent, but the public defender assigned to his case convinced him to plead guilty to reduce the sentence. The lawyer assumed that Mario would be deported regardless of the outcome of the case because he had no authorization to live in the United States. The lawyer reasoned that Mario was likely to be convicted, and because a U.S. criminal record would not affect Mario in Mexico (after he was deported), it was in his best interests to shorten the time he spent in prison before deportation. Mario recounted the discussion with his lawyer:

> He [the lawyer] told me, "Listen, your problem, it's solved. Your problem, you have it on a silver platter. Why? Because you don't have anything to fight [for] in this country. You are illegal. You don't have papers. What does it [a criminal record] affect you if they deport you? So I am going to fight [for you], why?" Because the judge wanted to give me thirty-two to thirty-six months in prison. So the lawyer told me, "Look, I am going to try for them to cut [the time] in half [if you plead]."

Mario pleaded guilty, and his lawyer negotiated the sentence down from thirty-six to thirteen months. When the thirteen months were up, ICE authorities transferred Mario to an immigrant detention center, where he spent a month and a half before he was deported.

Although Mario's lawyer was right that he would be deported, he was wrong about the cause. Mario was not deported because of an immigration violation but because of the criminal record that he pleaded to in court. It is not a given that Mario would have been deported as a result of his unlawful status. As Olivia's case revealed, there is discretion in when and how immigrants are deported for unlawful status, and an undocumented person interacting with the criminal courts is not automatically charged with immigration violations. Moreover, Mario's outcome—criminal deportation—is a worse outcome than deportation for unlawful status. Criminal deportation implies more severe immigration consequences, including, in Mario's case, a long-term bar on reentry and criminal charges if he was caught unlawfully reentering the United States. From what we could tell, neither Mario nor his court-appointed criminal defense attorney understood the immigration consequences of his plea at the time when he made it.

When we interviewed him in 2019, Mario lived in Mexico City, separated from his family after a deportation caused by Policy Trap conditions. Owing to the same set of U.S. laws and policies, Mario had been trapped in the United States while he lived and worked there; he could not afford to return to Mexico during that time, because reentry to the United States was too costly. But then, in 2019, following his deportation, he was trapped in Mexico. He could not lawfully reenter the United States. Moreover, Mario's children, who were protected by DACA status while in the United States, could not travel to Mexico to visit him without substantial risk to their status. They, too, were trapped in the United States.

Free in Mexico

Everyone we spoke to for this book had returned to Mexico, some having made plans to return, some having been forced to return, and some having neither planned nor been forced to leave the United States. Regardless of the process of return, a recurring theme among return migrants in Mexico was the sense of relief that came from escaping the surveillance and threat in the United States. Before we elaborate on formerly undocumented or deported immigrants' sense of being trapped in Mexico after returning there, thanks to the Policy Trap's restrictions on reentry, we focus on the simultaneous relief they felt upon leaving the United States during the Policy Trap. Some return migrants described this relief as freedom.

Olivia told us how good it felt to walk safely in the streets. "I am here, and I love my country," she said. "I love to walk on the streets without the fear that migration [agents] will grab me, because here I know that if I don't get into trouble, then I don't have any reason to think I will be persecuted by the law."

Sergio migrated to the United States as a child and was apprehended in a home raid at age eighteen. He was detained for two years before he was deported. He put it plainly: "When I was in the Mexican territory, I felt happiness because I was free again. I felt at ease." Later he told us, "I like to feel free. I like to walk in the streets without thinking that they are going to deport me, they are going to do this [other bad thing] to me."

Olivia's and Sergio's descriptions of the safety and freedom of being in Mexico point to the lack of safety and freedom they felt in the United States—the sense that they might be detained at any minute or persecuted for no good reason. Return migrants' sense of freedom in Mexico reveals how unfree they were in the United States.

Rocío and her son Paolo returned to Mexico for the last time in 2007. She told us that she felt some mixed emotions upon return, but that the most important point for her about being in Mexico was the sense of freedom she gained. "Look," she said, "at first it made me sad because you arrive in Mexico and you see your country is filthy . . . full of smog. But it also made me happy because, well, I will repeat it: I'm free. My spirit is free, no?"

Carla, who migrated back to Mexico to accompany her son who was deported, expressed similar feelings:

> Well, it's beautiful to be Mexican, because you are free here in your country. You don't have to go around hiding from anyone. It's just that you bring another perspective of life, that here you now see that there is a lot of trash, dogs in the street, that the city is dirty. But it's your country, your place, where you are not drowned, where you can go where you want and nobody says anything. You're free.

Both Carla and Rocío drew a contrast between orderliness and personal freedom. The United States provides orderliness and cleanliness, but also creates an environment of fundamental personal insecurity, or unfreedom.

The U.S. government deported Matías in 2016. He described his sense of freedom in Mexico slightly differently—not as freedom from surveillance, persecution, and capture, but as empowerment. In the United States, his status as an undocumented immigrant had prevented him from standing up for himself in the face of abuse. By contrast, when he went to obtain his elector's document—colloquially called the INE (for the Instituto Nacional Electoral, National Electoral Institute)—from a government official in Mexico City, he refused to be treated badly. He told us:

> I don't like being treated poorly, I hate it. There [in the United States], I permitted it because it was a whole different situation. I didn't want to lose my papers nor my kids, but here I didn't have anything to lose. So when they treated me poorly [at the government office in Mexico City], I said, "Hey, why do you treat me like that? They are paying you to help me, not to come and yell at me. If you don't want to help me, then let me speak to your supervisor."

In the United States, the threat of immigration enforcement actions against him meant that Matías had to tolerate poor treatment by others, but in Mexico he was able to stand up for himself.

Others found freedom in Mexico from the U.S. culture of money and work—dominant concerns for undocumented immigrants, who often justify the costs, risks, and hardships of their experience in economic terms. The artist Osmundo told us that in the United States, "it's just the question of money, work, and money. Here you are more free, or you feel more free, more relaxed. Returning here, you feel better than you did there. . . . Having gone there and returned, one feels much better here." While Osmundo found the focus on work and money stressful, another respondent, Eduardo, found it simply boring: "It was never my idea to stay in the United States to live . . . because I don't like it [there]. I prefer life in Mexico; life there is boring. It was work to house, house to work, from Monday to Saturday."

In a context where money is prime, lack of ownership is yet another reminder of being unfree. Renting symbolizes the economic dependence on and control by others that many undocumented immigrants experience in the United States. Paolo's mother Rocío explained that in the United States

> we rented . . . in a trailer, imagine, one of those mobile houses, because I did not have enough money for an apartment. Here, I have my apartment, I had a house that I rented, in Zihuatanejo, I had another property. I mean, there [in the United States] when do you get to buy property? I tell you, my daughter [who had been in the United States for thirty years] still rents. No, how ugly. As my grandmother says, you have to have your own corral! That's why I'm better here. It was very pretty, the little trailer, but it wasn't mine. They make you sign papers when you rent it that you are going to leave it as it was when you moved in, but how are you going to leave the stove and the oven the same if you use them? Even if you wash them, you know? They don't stay the same. No. Here you get it together and buy a piece of land.

Returning to Mexico brought into relief the lack of freedom for undocumented persons in the United States: the personal insecurity in public, the threat of unlawful persecution by the state, the inability to stand up to mistreatment and abuse by others, the incessant focus on work and money, and their own economic dependence. In Mexico, returnees were free of these constraints on life—or, as Rocío put it, one's "spirit is free."

Yet existing alongside this sense of relief and freedom was the feeling of being trapped by U.S. laws and policies that prevented safe and lawful reentry to the United States. Even interviewees who had no wish to reenter the United States experienced the legal impediment to migration as a threat to their well-being.

Trapped in Mexico

Our data give us unique insight into the experience of returning to Mexico during the Policy Trap. The long arm of the Policy Trap was felt by returnees in seemingly contradictory ways: on the one hand, they described a profound sense of freedom from immigration surveillance and threat, but on the other hand, they felt trapped in Mexico because they could not lawfully or safely reenter the United States.

Most of the people we spoke with would have liked to return to the United States legally, if only to visit; Lucía, for example, told us that she wanted to see the "princess castles" at Disneyland. Others would have liked to earn U.S. dollars again, or to return to good jobs they had in the United States. Many maintained contact with their former U.S. employers. Those who were separated from their families were desperate to return. Seeing his family again, Evaristo said, would be a dream come true. As Matías put it, "Yes, I want to return. I want to be there. There I have my job, there I am somebody. Here I am not anybody. There I have my kids, there I am a dad. I don't even have that here."

Although Olivia felt free back in Mexico, she also felt trapped between two worlds: the world of her prior life and family in the United States, and the world she inhabited in Mexico City. She said:

All the people I know who have been deported or who have decided to return, we are all locked in those two worlds. We are here, we like our country, we can breathe freedom, but at the same time, we are with our souls in the United States, wanting to return to our family, for what we lived there, for the opportunities there. And so, it is very complicated. And for me, sometimes it does cost me a lot of work, like . . . how to see my life towards the future. . . . To me they have said: "It's that you are here, but your mind is there." And that is the truth. I am here in body, but my mind and spirit are in another place.

For Olivia, returning to the United States would reunite her body with her mind and spirit, which resided with her former life and her children.

Yet, despite the desire to return, the people we spoke with expressed significant uncertainty about returning to the United States because of the legal barriers to lawful reentry and the costs, risks, and potential legal consequences of unlawful reentry.[27] Return migrants who experienced the threat, surveillance, and violence of immigration enforcement while in the United States felt a sense of freedom once they were back in Mexico, yet the U.S. immigration policy created during the Policy Trap period continued to affect them, nearly eliminating the possibility for lawful reentry. This was true even for migrants with family in the United States, including U.S. citizen children, and migrants whose U.S. employer would gladly have sponsored them for a visa. The returnees were free in Mexico, but they could not freely leave—at least not to head north of the border lawfully.

Olivia described the experience of being trapped in Mexico as being caught between a pack of wolves and a cliff edge. Upon being deported, Olivia was barred from reentering the United States for ten years. "Imagine ten years without seeing my children," she said.

> For me, it is a lot. And so, yes, it is difficult, because you know you cannot wait ten years, but you also know that if you go, you risk that they detain you and you spend two years in prison. And so, you are in . . . like in a limbo about what to do. . . . I feel like I am at the top of a mountain, of Everest, and behind me, there is a pack of wolves, and in front of me is the precipice. What do you do? Do you jump? Surely, you'll die. But if you turn around, the wolves get you.

Olivia felt the IIRAIRA bar on reentry as a direct threat to her existence; others experienced it as a sentence, like a prison term that had to be waited out. Juan was deported, leaving behind a small U.S. citizen child, who remained with the child's mother and her family. He said he wanted to return, but "not now. I am aware that I have to wait the time that they gave me. They gave me ten years, and then I will see what I can do."

Unlawful reentry was a possibility for return, but nearly everyone we spoke with perceived the border as having become more difficult and costlier to cross since they had done it previously. "Not the same as it used to be" and "things are different now" were common ways of describing how the border (as well as the risk of apprehension in the interior) had changed during the Policy Trap, especially during the Trump administration. Some also felt too old to cross; most were at least fifteen years older when we interviewed them than they had been the first time they crossed.

We do not mean to imply that everyone we spoke to wanted to return to the United States. Many respondents were happy in Mexico, such as Paolo's mother Rocío, who was content to be in Mexico. As she put it: "Imagine that, you think I am going to return? Even if they gave me papers, no. Because there everything is so expensive, and here I have my pension that I earned through work. Another reason? I never liked that country. Never! . . . [Mexico is] my land, it's my country, and I love it."

Conclusion

The migrants we interviewed moved between Mexico and the United States in a particular historical moment in which U.S. policy aggressively tried to control undocumented immigration. As more and more people sought entry to the United States in order to fill jobs that demanded their skills and labor and to follow and reunite with family who had gone before them, U.S. immigration policy not only failed to support them but deprived them of fundamental rights to travel, to work, to be safe, to receive welfare services, and to be accorded due process. In doing so, Policy Trap policies created a tractable workforce that has served the essential needs of the U.S. economy at a low cost. By trapping immigrants and their families across borders, the Policy Trap increased the population of undocumented immigrants and their children who settled in the United States without basic rights. Since 2012, this population has decreased as many have returned to Mexico, but the Policy Trap continues to affect them by preventing their safe and legal reentry, thereby separating them from their lives in the United States.

Although large-scale undocumented migration from Mexico to the United States has waned since 2012, Policy Trap policies remain in effect. The U.S. Congress has still failed to pass comprehensive immigration reform. The border remains a playground of political opportunism. DACA, although designed to rectify some of the failures of U.S. immigration policy toward some of the most vulnerable members of the immigrant community, has been a partial solution at best: it provides only temporary (renewable) status, it is politically contingent (and continuously threatened), and it protects only a small share of the undocumented population.

Our research reveals what the Policy Trap has meant for people who entered the United States during this period, lived there with (mostly) undocumented status, and returned to Mexico City. Formerly undocumented migrants, both those who were deported and other returnees, noted a sense of relief upon return and felt the freedom that came with being fully endowed with citizenship rights again. But this relative freedom was curtailed by the inability to legally reenter the United States: return migrants were trapped in Mexico by the U.S. Policy Trap. This is one way in which the Policy Trap extends beyond the borders of the United States to affect the lives of former migrants.[28]

Being trapped in the United States has been said to have a caging effect. The idea is that policy has caged immigrants as long-term residents, interrupting circularity and impacting everyday life.[29] For example, the sociologist Kristina Fullerton Rico studied how unauthorized immigrants in the United States grieve and mourn the death of beloved ones in Mexico.[30] This notion is also present in popular culture, such as in the 1984 song by the Grammy-winning band Los Tigres del Norte, "La Jaula de Oro" (The Golden Cage), in which a Mexican migrant reflects on how imprisoned he feels by the perennial hard work, fear of deportation, lack of interest of his U.S.-born children in moving to Mexico, and longing for the homeland. As we show, however, even after returning to Mexico, to their birth country, returnees remain trapped. The "golden cage" keeps them trapped from both sides of the border, preventing their return to Mexico as well as their return to the United States.

CHAPTER FOUR

SETTLING BACK IN THE CITY

Evaristo was born in Michoacán but moved to Mexico City with his family when he was a baby. In his midtwenties, he and his wife and children traveled to the United States on tourist visas to visit his siblings and mother, who lived in the Midwest. But his plans unexpectedly changed after they arrived. "I got there and they told me that my mother has terminal cancer. . . . The doctor told us, 'She has three to six months to live, no more.' 'Well,' I said, 'I can't just stay on vacation.'" Evaristo's extended stay eventually turned into settlement. He found work, and his kids enrolled in school. He lived in the United States for nearly twenty years. He told us about Thanksgiving dinners and Halloween parties, trips to Miami, Florida, and Disneyland, and time spent on the lake close to their home during the summers.

In 2017, he arrived alone in Mexico City, fleeing the threat of incarceration and deportation. Evaristo's arrival in Mexico City was sudden and unplanned, but he was able to bring some money with him. He purchased a car and started his own business in Mexico City as an Uber driver. He managed the construction of his family home in a Mexico City suburb, financed by remittances sent by his brothers. Although Evaristo was fortunate to arrive with some financial stability, the experience was extraordinarily difficult. He sympathized with the experiences of other, less fortunate return migrants: "How do they go? Walking? Towards where? North or south? Where is north and where is south? They arrive norteados . . . and no one helps them."

As we explained in the introduction, the notion of "norteado" has two meanings. It is a Spanish word that means being disoriented or lost

https://doi.org/10.7758/kokl2957.3779

in space, and it also connotes the North, as if returnees, still somehow in the United States, are northless in Mexico. "Norteado" captures the simultaneous experience of disorientation and loss upon return to the city from the United States.

U.S. migrants are disoriented in many different ways upon return to Mexico City. Most basically, they are overwhelmed and lost in the massive, complex, and ever-changing landscape of the Mexico City metropolis. But they are also disoriented socially; after their long absence from the city, they are disconnected from family and old friends. The disorientation is worsened by having few social advantages from their status as return migrants. At best, their emigration to and return from the United States is an invisible status in the city; at worst, they are stigmatized for exhibiting a U.S. style or presumed to be criminals. Nevertheless, over time, they settle into life in Mexico City.

How does this process of settlement unfold? In this chapter, we explain what we learned from our interviews with return migrants in Mexico City in 2019. We first explore how returnees navigated the city, explaining how their experiences differed by age, health, and level of disability. We then describe how, in securing housing and getting around, returnees had to (re)learn how to navigate corrupt bureaucracies and violent and insecure neighborhoods. While many navigated these processes alone or with limited support networks, others organized to pool resources and support each other in the metropolis. Through these efforts, they had to navigate a tension between making the returnee experience visible and avoiding the creation or enactment of stigma. In the subsequent chapters, we focus on the two aspects of social life that were most profoundly transformed by emigration and return over the long run: family and work.

Navigating the City after Arriving Norteado

As mentioned in the introduction, most of the returnees we interviewed left Mexico in the 1990s and early 2000s and returned to Mexico for the last time after 2008 (see figure 1.3). Most made only one trip to the United States. The average length of time they spent in the United States was fourteen years; half of our respondents spent more than twelve and a half years there. When we interviewed them in 2019, returnees' time back in Mexico averaged six years, and half had been back more than four years. In other words, when we interviewed them, they had been in Mexico City for less time after returning than they had spent in the United States. They also arrived in a metropolitan area that had changed dramatically in their absence. Their first and most pressing need was to figure out how to get around the city.

Carla, who was fifty-eight and had lived in the United States for fifteen years, migrated back to Mexico to accompany her deported son. She felt that she had to move with him because he did not know Mexico. Their family had migrated to California when he was just a toddler. She described what it was like to return: "It was very difficult. We didn't know how to cross the streets, oh, no! We walked holding hands, and it was very difficult for me because I had already been driving for ten years. I didn't even know how to ride a bus. The money had changed. It was very difficult for us."

Roberto, who was forty-four years old when we interviewed him, emigrated to the United States in 1999 and was deported seventeen years later. He too was disoriented upon return, even though he had lived in Mexico City for twenty-five years before emigrating to the United States. "There were already new streets, bridges, and new subway lines and all that," he discovered upon his return. Similarly, Alberto, who was forty-seven years old and spent sixteen years in the United States, also found that the city had changed while he was gone. He said the city "changed in many things. When I left, there was no metrobus, it wasn't there. When I left, there weren't some subway lines. . . . We did not have the suburban train, and there is also more movement now and all that."

The complexity of Mexico City's environment affected returnees' ability to adjust socially and reestablish connections with friends and family. María Luz, for example, told us that both her experience of being away and her experience of returning to the city shaped her close relationships:

> To begin with, I was back to the other side of the city—this city is huge. I used to live in the north, in Naucalpan, and now I'm back living near the National University [in the south], at the apartment where my daughter lives because I don't have a house. I don't have anything, right? I left everything. But after all this, I know that I am another person, right? It is important to realize who is going to understand it, and who is going to support you. For many people, it's like,

"She's exaggerating, well, she's lived here all her life." And you say, "Well, right, I don't need this now." I mean, yes, they love me a lot, but they don't understand what's happening to me, and so we better end it there, right? This city is chaotic, and it's also that I'm very far away, that I'm very busy.

María Luz was cut off from people who "love [her] a lot" because she lived with her daughter on the opposite side of the city from where she had resided before. She was separated from those networks by her dependence on her daughter, as well as by distance and chaos. But she also felt socially alienated. She had the impression that old friends could not understand her migrant experience, that they believed she was exaggerating the difficulty of her experience. As revealed in María Luz's experience of disconnection, it can be difficult for returnees to disentangle the chaos of the city from the chaos of being norteado. For María Luz, the chaos of the city was interwoven with her sense of social alienation in part because her close friends had no understanding of her migration experience and didn't realize that, "after all this," she had changed into "another person."

Others also commented on how the size, traffic, and economic life of the city shaped their free time and the possibilities for connecting with others. Rigoberto, who was away for twenty-three years, felt that he now lived in a city that was not enjoyable, even if it had a perfect climate. The people of Mexico City, he said,

> have one of the most beautiful cities in the world, and they don't know how to take advantage of it because they work too much. Only those who have money enjoy it, because regular people lose four hours of their lives in transportation. . . . In four hours, you can do so many things, take your son to a certain place, visit a museum. [Traveling in the city] takes away the desire, it takes away the desire to do something because you arrive annoyed with everything, and the only thing you want is to get to rest, really.

Some confusion or disorientation arises because the city itself has changed. Most people arriving in a city after being away for a decade or longer expect some degree of change, and coping with it is consistent with the culture shock that migrants experience upon arriving in a new place where they must learn strategies to cope and adapt to unfamiliar or unexpected circumstances.[1] However, returnees are often shocked by this first experience of disconnection, which affects their experiences not just of navigating the city but also of reconnecting with old ties and creating new ones. However, not all people experience return to the city the same way. As we discovered in our data, how people navigate the city is contingent on health, disability, and age.

Health, Disability, and Age

Rubén was fifty-four at the time of our interview and had been in Mexico City for two years when he shared his story with us. He was born in Guadalajara, Jalisco, and emigrated to the United States when he was three. After living in Los Angeles for fifty years, he no longer had family in Mexico; his three sons and grandsons all lived in the United States. Mexico City was strange and unfamiliar to him.

Rubén and his parents had benefited from the IRCA amnesty, managing to "fix their papers" in 1986. But like thousands of Mexicans who can naturalize but have not, Rubén never became a U.S. citizen.[2] He passed the citizenship exam in 1996 but missed the appointments for the naturalization ceremony, first because he was traveling and then because he had moved and the notification arrived at the wrong address. Rubén was deported from the United States in 2017. As we explained in chapter 3, in 1996 (the same year Rubén almost became a citizen), new U.S. laws, AEDPA and IIRAIRA, expanded the offenses for which a noncitizen could be deported (by redefining the term "aggravated felony" to include any convictions with sentences of one year or longer in person) and eliminated deportation relief (cancellation of removal orders) for noncitizens convicted of aggravated felonies.[3]

Being a U.S. permanent resident was not enough to ensure Rubén's well-being in the United States, even though other legal statuses are more precarious.[4] As a young adult in the United States, Rubén suffered a devastating illness that left him paralyzed from the waist down. But Rubén had a long and successful career. He studied administration and worked in a series of jobs in management, including in public service. Like many others who could be considered well integrated into U.S. society, however, having a "green card" (the identity document for lawful permanent residents) did not prevent Rubén from being deported to a country he hardly knew, a place where he had no support networks and his disability created substantial needs.[5] Although much of the current discussion about immigration policy highlights the vulnerabilities of those with uncertain and precarious legal status, current U.S. immigration law does not consider strong family ties and arrival in the United States under age five strong enough factors to allow individuals, not even lawful permanent residents, to remain there, in many cases of removal.

Rubén's health condition dramatically limited his ability to move around in a city that did not accommodate disabilities. "I am unemployed, I have not been able to find a job here, it is very difficult, especially being in a wheelchair, mobility is very difficult here in Mexico, since many places do not have access," he said. Although there is volunteer work that Rubén is interested in that relates to work that he had done in the United States, he cannot get there. "I have to take the subway . . . I don't remember how far, and then after the subway, I have to take a taxi from the subway station to where they are, and all of that would be out of pocket because they are not going to pay me," he explained.

Disability status interacts with social class not only by constraining social and spatial mobility but also by translating into a presumption of indigence. As Rubén said: "If you are in a wheelchair, many people act as if you don't exist. Yes, some people are considerate, but most are not. When I first arrived, I went here to the market to eat or whatever, and they looked at me as if I was going to ask for money, they didn't serve me." In addition to arriving in a completely unknown city, he was shocked to realize the differences between the two countries in the treatment of disabled people. He told us that "in the U.S., they don't look at you differently. There they treat you the same, almost everywhere, and by law, all public spaces need to be wheelchair-accessible. It's by law there! If they don't have it, you can sue them, and that doesn't exist here."

Evaristo, who suffered from disabling pain resulting from an old injury, echoed Rubén's words in describing the lack of accessible infrastructure and the lack of consideration for people with disabilities: "Here our rights are violated . . . and being disabled is a crime. I just went to the secretariat of foreign affairs, and I told them, 'I can't climb many stairs.' They don't have ramps, and the elevator is just for the employees." Evaristo saw the lack of accessibility as a structural measure of exclusion, of both the migrant population and more generally the population of those with disabilities. He said, "Here you are separated from your family, and they don't care about you. You go to the secretariat of foreign affairs, but their rule is, 'These people do not enter, bye-bye.' They close the door on you."

Rubén and Evaristo were not the only return migrants we interviewed with mobility-related disabilities. In fact, a good number of Mexican returnees were disabled, in part because the migration journey and return, at times involving detention and deportation, present substantial health risks.[6] Eduardo was in a car accident in the United States when he was twenty-eight, after living there for ten years, and was left with limited mobility. He returned with the support of the Mexican consulate in 2004. He was forty-three in 2019 when we talked to him. When he first returned to Mexico City, Eduardo had been very active. He lived in Coyoacán, where he sold used clothes from the United States, fake designer suits from China, and electronics, with support from his mother and sister. This arrangement ended when his mother's health declined. He and his younger brother, Marco Antonio, then moved to Tláhuac, an alcaldía located in southeastern Mexico City, where they lived in a house they built on land inherited from their mother. He explained that life in a wheelchair was harder now, given the hilly area where he and Marco Antonio lived:

> There [in Coyoacán] I could get out and move more, but here [in Tláhuac] it's more difficult to move. Yes, it's more difficult . . . and since my hands don't work well, it's hard for me. . . . I mean, downhill it's hard for me to hold the chair, the weight gains me. . . . I have no strength in my fists. I don't close my hands well; they were damaged from the accident. If it is flat, well, yes, I can move more, and since the streets were better over there [in Coyoacán], I would get out of the apartment complex and I would grab my chair . . . alone, I would leave.

Eduardo's experiences show the clear interconnections between family, health, housing, and work, which are key to a returnee's ability to reintegrate in Mexico in a context where experience in the United States and the reason for return are intertwined. Because access to social benefits and health services in Mexico is strongly related to formal work, returnees with health conditions and precarious job conditions depend on family support.

Some may think that Rubén and Eduardo could have capitalized on their U.S. experience upon return. Rubén had grown up in the United States and spoke English fluently, but like Eduardo, he was prevented by his disability from working in Mexico City. To the explicit question of whether he believed that there was an advantage to his U.S. migratory experience, he answered:

> I don't know, but until now it seems there is no advantage. I would think that it should be an advantage, wouldn't it? Because you come from there, you speak two languages, you know U.S. culture. Mexico and the enterprises here should take advantage of that, use it by employing you . . . but here they discriminate against you a lot, because of your age and because of your disability and for anything else that comes to mind. I thought it would be easier to find a job here than there, but it's more difficult here.

Rubén's experience contrasted markedly with the experiences of Julio and Reynaldo, who had migrated to the United States as children and arrived back in Mexico young and in good health. Both managed to capitalize on their English language proficiency at work back in Mexico, as we describe further in chapter 6. Youth and health are often necessary to capitalize upon the advantages associated with time spent in the United States.

Housing

Limited institutional support implies that people must depend on the support they receive from family and friends. But returnees often lacked family, social networks, and support in Mexico precisely because, after their long stay in the United States, their families and friends were there and their ties to friends and family in Mexico had been severed or lost. Given the lack of institutional support and his own lack of family support, it was the support of other deported people that enabled Rubén to survive and not end up on the streets like other returnees, such as Manuel, who had emigrated to the United States at the age of eleven. When Manuel was deported in 2008 and arrived in the city, he said, "I had no family in Mexico. Neither friends nor capital. That's why I lived six months on the street. That's why I became a clown and [worked] again at the windshields at traffic lights. But that's how I was saving little by little. I was buying more decent clothes because I understood that in Mexico, they treat you as they see you."

Another returnee who suffered from lost and severed ties was Mario, whose story of deportation we told in chapter 3. Mario had lost the phone numbers of his family members when his possessions were stolen while he was living in farmworker housing. This happened at a time before cell phones and the internet, and Mario had written the phone numbers of his father and nephews on a piece of paper. Without these contacts, he lost all communication with family in Mexico and had no way to send them money. As he told us, "The problem is that I never sent anything to my dad, and so now how can I arrive at a place where no one will understand? They will say, 'He was in the U.S. and it's unbelievable he did not send anything to his dad.'" An unfortunate event that transpired while Mario was an immigrant in the United States had compromised his relationships and his ability to rely on his family upon his return to Mexico.

Without family to help him, Mario expressed how difficult it was to find a place to live that he could afford on his low wages:

> Yes, well, it is not enough at all because, look, it would practically help you if you found a room for 1,000 pesos [US$50]. But I am earning, well . . . almost 3,000 . . . like 3,200 per month [US$160]. But here you can only find rooms for 4,000 pesos [US$200] per month. So what do you have left? You have nothing, you just work for nothing . . . just to pay rent, and then they don't just charge you that, they want you to give a deposit or two deposits, they want you to give a guarantor.

Mario cannot afford housing on his salary, much less the deposits and other monies demanded of renters.

Reconnection was difficult for others as a result of interactions with immigration enforcement. ICE officials took Juan's cell phone and never returned it prior to deportation. When he arrived at the Mexico City airport, he couldn't reach his family:

> I do not memorize my phone numbers, so after seventeen years without seeing them, I did not know how to reach them because I brought nothing with me. Another deportee that I met in the process invited me to his home. He let me use his internet, and I logged into my Facebook so I was able to contact my nieces living in Texcoco. They would not believe me when I told them, "Come pick me up, I was deported."

Juan first spent a couple of weeks with one sister, then stayed with another sister before finally moving to downtown Mexico City, where he received support from other deportees. Due to limited resources, deportees and returnees try to support each other and often live together because renting a place is expensive. Many of the people we interviewed who had been deported relied on other deported people for housing.

Others rent space to fellow returnees. We interviewed Lety, who, after returning to Mexico, began renting rooms in the family home to which she returned in the Gustavo A. Madero municipality in the north of Mexico City. She rented rooms to other internal and return migrants, including a single man who was deported and left his family in New York, a man who migrated from Puebla, and a woman who lived with her children. Lety had a technical degree in computing and was an executive secretary before emigrating, but now, besides renting rooms, she cared for her sick mother and cleaned houses sporadically.

Renting rooms from one's home is an economic strategy that links family arrangements and home ownership. The strategy allowed Lety to address the health problems faced by her family and provide care work while generating income for the household. If she and her son had been in the United States, they might have been able to take care of his learning disability, which made it difficult for him to study. Now, given the lack of institutional support, she supported him from home.

Other returnees saw being a landlord as an "ideal job." Forty-year-old Mateo, who was deported in 2010 after living fourteen years in Washington, D.C., explained that he wanted to build rooms at his mother's house, on top of where he lived. He saw this project as an improvement over the work he did in construction, which he disliked because it involved traveling a long distance—across the city, from La Joya in Tlalpan to Santa Fé on the western edge of the metropolitan area in the alcaldía of Cuajimalpa. After such a long commute, he told us, "You arrive very stressed out."

Insecurity, Violence, and Corruption

Not only did returnees feel stressed out from spending a long time on public transportation, but they also often felt unsafe moving around the city. Such insecurity made the commute even more stressful. For example, Raúl told us that he saw someone stealing a cell phone in the metro. He reported the incident to the police, but since the police did nothing about it, he was deterred from interacting with the police in the future. In fact, he now suspected that the police would harass him:

> I told him [the police officer], "He stole his cell phone. . . ." and the police did nothing. Then you even get into trouble with the police,

because that's what it is. I have learned of cases in which the police pick up people in the subway because they are supposed to help them and they leave them afterwards without money, without cell phone, without anything. So, those types of situations make me more tense, right?

Adjusting to insecurity, violence, and corruption in Mexico City requires adapting away from the different norms and experiences of crime in the United States. Humberto, who spent nine years in North Carolina and returned in 2014, explained that in the United States there is terrorism and shootings in schools, but "there are very few, so few that they make the news, it is not common. Here in Mexico, it is common, and because it is common it is no longer news. It is common for someone to be killed."

Julio, who spent much of his childhood in New York City, said he worried about how normalized violence had changed Mexican culture. He told us: "Since I arrived, I have noted the narcoculture. Violence here in Mexico is so bad that we already sell it, it is already part of the culture. We consume it even in the Mexican films that have been made because they only sell violence, and that greatly affects children's development."

Having been in the United States affected returnees' experience of insecurity in Mexico City in different ways. For instance, Alejandra told us that she was "a little more afraid of being here in this city. I don't like being around alone, like, I still don't have the courage to walk in places I don't know, because it does cause me a little fear and insecurity. And in the United States I didn't feel that way."

Olivia, on the other hand, said that she was not used to the crime, but her experience of being fearful in the United States and avoiding problems there as an undocumented migrant had prepared her for Mexico City. Olivia lived in Ecatepec, located in the State of Mexico and one of the municipalities within the metropolitan area of Mexico City with the highest crime and homicide rates (along with Cuauhtémoc, Miguel Hidalgo, and Cuautitlán).[7] She told us:

> I'm not used to it, no. It is an area where there is a lot of crime. . . . Well, Ecatepec is also very . . . they say that right now it is one of the ugliest neighborhoods, but . . . thank God until now nothing has happened to me. In the neighborhood where my mother's house is, every now and then there are shootings wherever you want. Oh well, you come from the United States, and you come with more fear, and also you already come thinking, "Why do I get into trouble?" I avoid problems.

Other returnees highlighted the relative safety they felt in Mexico after being targeted for other kinds of violence and crime in the United States. For example, Sergio, who had lived in Chicago for seventeen years, told us that he saw a man get robbed of his earnings next to the Monumento a la Revolución (Monument to the Revolution) about a month before we interviewed him. For him, this seemed like a small crime compared to what he experienced growing up without gang affiliation in Chicago. He said:

> Yes, of course there is insecurity [in Mexico City], but given what I have gone through, I don't feel insecure or fearful. I have always been alert. I grew up in the south of Chicago, where gangs would take over all the city, where you walked two blocks and you were already walking in the territory of another gang. Then the gang members asked you where you were from, why you were wearing these colors, why you were wearing a hat in a certain way, or the pants in a certain way, so you couldn't even wear gang colors, or put on your clothes in any way, because everyone would question, and sometimes they even shot you, because they thought you were from another gang. So, for this reason, I feel more freedom [in Mexico]. Here I can dress as I want, I can walk as I want, without the fear that some gang member will approach me and tell me why I am dressed like that, that he wants to fight me, or wants to shoot me, or something like that.

Some of the people we interviewed had experienced gang violence directly. Julio told us that his family had moved from a very dangerous Brooklyn neighborhood with frequent conflict between Mexicans, African Americans, and Puerto Ricans to Queens, where they felt safer. Julio's family moved after one of his cousins witnessed a shooting of an African American man by a Mexican man. The killer ran away, leaving Julio's cousin open to blame for the death from gangs.

Insecurity shapes not only neighborhood choice but also internal migration within Mexico. Reynaldo returned in 2004 to Chilpancingo, the capital city of the southern state of Guerrero, after living five years in Arizona. There he worked as a bartender to put himself through college. To earn more money, he got involved with drug cartels and sold drugs at the bar. He said, "I didn't want to do those things, but I needed money. I had to pay rent and university." He quit university after a year, however, because he could not keep up with his schoolwork. One day he decided to quit that lifestyle and implored his mom and sister to leave Chilpancingo with him. Once in Mexico City, he told his mother about his involvement with the cartels, confessing that was the reason why they suddenly left Chilpancingo. As Reynaldo explained to us, "There, they kill you and all your family. . . . Everyone I know there was already killed. They are all dead. . . . I felt good when I arrived [in Mexico City]. I knew they would not find me here."

Violence and insecurity also deter crossing back to the United States and affect the decision to leave or stay in Mexico City—as illustrated by the testimonies from Rocío and her son Paolo, as well as from Reynaldo and Marco Antonio.[8] As described at greater length in chapter 5, Rocío and her son Paolo emigrated three times to the United States to reunify with Rocío's daughter. However, insecurity was behind their decision to emigrate for the third and last time. Rocío's oldest son, Ramón, owned a successful hair salon in the Tláhuac alcaldía in southeastern Mexico City, next to Chalco (where Osmundo lived). Rocío told us that Ramón's hair salon was famous for having so many clients. Paolo also worked there at the time. He told us, "People believe that you earn a lot, and the truth is that, no, you don't earn that much, but well. . . . They got in, they assaulted us, they grabbed my brother." Ramón died from the injuries he sustained in the attack. His mother Rocío fell into a deep depression and sadness after losing Ramón. She felt that she could no longer live, and her daughter convinced her to remigrate to the United States. She told us, "I started to think, 'Well, I am creating decent, hardworking children, and for someone to come and take away the tower that you are building, it is not worth it.' Then it's the end, because you feel bad, they take your life, you no longer want to live. And my daughter told me, 'Come here.'" She and Paolo remigrated to the United States to help them cope with the tragedy of Ramón's death.

While violence in the city inspired some to leave, violence in border areas and along the route to the border motivated others to stay. Marco Antonio explained that the increase in violence in northern Mexico had made the trip to the United States riskier, costlier, and more difficult. Marco Antonio returned to Mexico City in 2012 after living for almost ten years in New York. He returned, planning to stay for only a few months while visiting his mother and family, whom he missed. "I was thinking of returning to the United States. My idea was not to stay here in Mexico, because I had already made my life in the United

States." But when he tried to return to the United States, he realized that things had changed. He told us:

> The cost of the passage [across the border into the United States] increased, and it got more complicated. I already had a way to go again, but it didn't work. On the first trip, I didn't go because I couldn't get a plane ticket from here to Sonora; they were sold out. I said to myself, "Well, I'm leaving in eight days," but then on the first trip they [the drug cartels] kidnapped all the people.

Marco Antonio felt that he was given a second chance at life: he would have been kidnapped too if he had been able to buy a plane ticket to Sonora and gone with the group. He decided that the second chance meant he should stay in Mexico City.

In addition to learning how to navigate new forms of violence and insecurity in Mexico, returnees learned how to deal with another problem that is normalized in Mexico: corruption.[9] Corruption in Mexican schools, where U.S.-born and Mexican returnees are asked to pay bribes to facilitate enrollment, has been documented in other studies.[10] Returnees felt particularly vulnerable to exploitation because of their unfamiliarity with bureaucratic norms and procedures. For example, Julio described his mother's experience trying to register his sister Abril at school:

> The moment they see my mother confused and not knowing what was happening, they tell her, "It's very difficult," and this and that, and they made excuses to get money from her. The same thing with me. When we arrived at the SEP [Secretaría de Educación Pública, or Secretariat of Public Education] offices to validate our U.S. school certificates, the same thing. In other words, for the simple fact that we didn't know how everything was going, they took those 5,000 pesos [US$250] from us.

Evaristo was also frustrated by corruption. While directing the construction of a home in Mexico City for his family, who remained in Ohio, he was in charge of paying the bills and obtaining permits. He explained to us that he was also in charge of paying bribes:

> Here in Mexico, unfortunately, it is like that. It scares me when I get the permit and suddenly the delegate of the area arrives, those who

supervise, everyone comes. You need to give money to everyone even if you don't want to and try not to. It happened to me, I have my permit, everything is fine. But they closed the construction site, and I had to give money under the table, and then the director told me, "Anyway, when my boys come, you have to give them something," and that's how I'm working. Otherwise, the building would be closed. Even if you have all the permits required by law, there has to be something under the table.

Others, like Osmundo, believed that corruption would not end if people didn't stop paying bribes. He told us that he had seen police get payoffs, referred to in Spanish as *mordida* (bite) or *mochada* (cut), but then added, "We want them to change, but if I give it to them, how will they change?"[11] Although violence, insecurity, and corruption were disorienting for returnees—and discussed by many of them in relation to what they had lived through and observed in the United States—they shared this context and the impacts of relatively normalized violence, insecurity, and corruption with those who had no migration experience at all.

Organizations: Orientation to Find One's Way

Migration to and from the United States is not considered a local political problem in Mexico City, at least not on the same scale as in other places or in comparison to other local problems. In Mexico's northern border cities, where deportation and transit migration (of migrants from other countries seeking entry to the United States) are local problems, the deported migrant and the migrant seeking to cross the border are subjects of political concern, the target of civil society organizations, and actors in border politics.[12] By contrast, the issue of migrant return to Mexico City is overshadowed by other issues that affect the capital city's residents—health and housing, access to jobs and fair wages, anti-corruption and safety efforts, education and transportation—as well as by national political concerns, including migration, which is assumed to be a problem affecting places outside the capital city.

Yet the paradox of the migrant's political invisibility in the city is that Mexico City offers substantial political opportunities to the return migrant, given that it is the capital city and the location of the federal government. This is important for returnees' ability to act on their basic citizenship rights, especially in obtaining documentation, as the sociologist Gabriela Pinillos has shown in her work on returnees to Mexico City and Tijuana.[13] Unlike the returnee in rural Mexico, the Mexico City returnee does not face long travel distances to the closest government office issuing birth certificates or electoral registrations. Moreover, with proximity to the national political stage and the headquarters of the country's organizations of civil society, the Mexico City returnee can access political capital that is unavailable in a rural area or border city.

Indeed, a number of migrant organizations based or active in Mexico City have emerged in the past two decades—including Otros Dreams en Acción (ODA, Other Dreams in Action), Instituto para las Mujeres en la Migración (IMUMI, Institute for Women in Migration), New Comienzos (New Beginnings), Hola Code (Hello Code), F*ck La Migra (F*ck the Immigration Authorities), Estado 33 Aztlán (33rd State Aztlan), Deportados Unidos en la Lucha (DUL, Deportees United in Struggle), and Comunidad en Retorno (Community in Return)—to address concerns specific to return migrants, including family separation and issues of work and housing for deported people. Most are organic activist organizations—that is, members of the community formed them to serve members of the community. Some organizations were formed in response to returnees' experiences of social isolation. DUL and Estado 33 Aztlán, for instance, were organized by deported people who banded together out of mutual need and solidarity and became an essential source of support for other deported people who arrived in the city without local family or friends. Organizations like DUL and Estado 33 Aztlán meet newly arriving deported people at the airport and help them find shelter, work, and legal advice. With a unique focus on migrant youth, ODA is the leading organization dedicated to the experience of people whose childhoods, identities, and families are based in both the United States and Mexico. This group provides sanctuary, support, and community to its members at its headquarters, called Pocha House.

In their efforts to bring attention to and address issues affecting return migrants in Mexico City, these organizations have created a presence in civil society, government, and media as well as online. We attended events at the Mexico City offices of the National Commission of Human Rights where members of migrant organizations shared their stories and argued for their rights. We watched and read news stories documenting the experiences of organization leaders. We were told about the courting of various migration organizations in the city by presidential candidates in the runup to the 2018 presidential election. We followed the social media activities of Mexico City migrant organizations that, through their online presence, network with other activists, politicians, researchers, artists, religious leaders, and the media on issues of migrant rights around the world.

Their impact has been felt on the national stage. In 2016, the Mexican federal government launched the strategy Somos Mexicanos (We Are Mexicanos) to facilitate the reintegration of returnees, deportees, and their children and to provide immediate food and transportation assistance after their arrival. Later, in 2020, these federal efforts were later renamed the Estrategia Interinstitucional de Atención Integral a Familias Mexicanas Repatriadas y en Retorno (Interinstitutional Strategy for Integral Assistance to Mexican Repatriated and Return Migrant Families) by President Andrés Manuel López Obrador. In April 2017, then-mayor Miguel Ángel Mancera declared Mexico City a sanctuary city for migrants to ensure that returnees and foreign-born populations had access to social programs.

In February 2017, deported migrants arriving in Mexico City became temporarily visible when President Enrique Peña Nieto (2012–2018) visited the airport to meet with a group of deported people. Peña Nieto's visit was a response to the threatening rhetoric of Donald Trump during his first presidential campaign and first month in office about the Mexican migrant community. Peña Nieto took pictures with deported migrants, and media outlets covered the news. Later, months prior to the 2018 presidential election, return migrant organizations were approached by candidates José Antonio Meade (Partido Revolucionario Institucional, PRI, the Institutional Revolutionary Party), Ricardo Anaya (Partido Acción Nacional, PAN, the National Action Party), and Armando Ríos Pitter (Partido de la Revolución Democrática, PRD, the Democratic Revolution Party), a senator who intended to run as an independent candidate. The May 2018 presidential debate featured a story of a deported person, along with the *costal* (bag) where that person's belongings were held. During that time, appearances in the media put returnees and the issue of deportation at the center of the city's political debates. After the election, migrants continued to arrive at the Mexico City airport, but none were again welcomed by the Mexican president. Instead, they were met by fellow return migrants who had organized to greet them. Media and political attention had dissipated.

Conclusion

The emergence of a local civil society dedicated to migrant rights in Mexico City over the past two decades reflects the development over the same period of emigration from the city and return to it. This can be seen in the changing agenda of the Asamblea Popular de Familias Migrantes (Popular Assembly of Migrant Families, or APOFAM), which shifted from focusing primarily on the experiences of families left behind by emigrants to addressing the concerns of migrants who returned or were deported. APOFAM's approach has been unique. Focusing historically on women—the wives and mothers of emigrants—the program trains women in handicraft arts and then helps them obtain visas to attend handicraft fairs in the United States, enabling them to visit their migrant family members while there. This strategy has been harder to implement since APOFAM's recent shift to incorporating returnees, like Carla, who accompanied her deported son back to Mexico. Obtaining visas for formerly undocumented migrants in the United States is more difficult than obtaining a visa for a person who has never emigrated.

Evaristo described returnees as norteados, as disoriented or lost in space after returning to a city that was transformed while they were away, but being norteado was harder for some than for others. Some returnees had to learn how to navigate the city after suffering disabling accidents or health crises in the United States that predated or even precipitated their return. Learning to navigate the city required not only learning how to drive the Segundo Piso or how to take a new metro line, but also learning how to move through new political environments and institutions, as well as in violent and insecure neighborhoods. As with any global city, Mexico City's size and dynamism, violence and insecurity, economic vitality and inequality, political barriers and opportunities, make it hard to navigate and reorient to life.

Evaristo's remark "Where is north and where is south? They arrive norteados . . . and no one helps them" puts us in mind of a compass oriented toward a specific geographic direction. This metaphor is key for understanding return to Mexico City. Compasses use a pivot that points to magnetic north, which is used for navigation. We now use GPS and other methods to orient ourselves and navigate through space. But compasses and GPS are not useful to returnees, who are disoriented socially by the experience of U.S. migration. In the absence of easy tools, as well as in the absence of both family support and significant state support, returnees created or joined organizations as a way to find and provide support to one another. In the next chapter, we discuss the role of family in emigration and return and its transformation in the process.

CHAPTER FIVE

FAMILY

Yazmín spent her days between the market stall where her sister and brother-in-law sold vegetables and her home in the hills of Cuautepec in the northern alcaldía of Gustavo A. Madero in Mexico City. She lived on the money she received from her second husband, who lived and worked in New Jersey, and talked to him every day. She also talked regularly to her adult children, who also lived in New Jersey, in fact, within walking distance from one another. As she explained to us, her family was "accustomed to being very dependent on one another. And so, my children have that custom, and they live very close to one another. They see each other very often. They get together often. Imagine. And the mom? Here." In Mexico City.

Yazmín's life in Mexico City in 2019, separated from her husband, children, and grandchildren in the United States, cannot be understood without knowing what came before: the multiple migrations she and each of her family members made between Mexico and the United States. In Yazmín's life, and in the lives of so many other return migrants in Mexico City, family separation is a fact of life, the result of all sorts of migrations. Even people who migrate to accompany or reunite with family experience family separation in the process. This is an outcome of migration between Mexico and the United States during the Policy Trap era, when U.S. laws and policies have denied the legal right to travel to hundreds of thousands of people who migrate from Mexico to the United States.

We can trace Yazmín's experience of family separation back in time. In 2014, five years before our interview, Yazmín lived with her husband

https://doi.org/10.7758/kokl2957.8685

in New Jersey, near her children and grandchildren. When her elderly mother became very ill, Yazmín returned to Mexico City, acting on a strong obligation to her mother to be with her. As Yazmín explained to us:

> My mother begged me, "I want to see you. Come, child. I am going to die, and I won't see you. Come, Daughter." And there are two loves, right, very strong, very strong loves. I returned against the will of my children, who were left crying, "Don't go, Mom." But I said, "Well, my mom is going to die and she wants to see me."

In the context of Mexico-U.S. migration, Yazmín's two loves—her love as a mother for her children, which manifested in the United States, and her love as a daughter for her mother, which manifested in Mexico— were incompatible. In reuniting with her mother in Mexico City, she separated from her children (and husband) in New Jersey.

Yazmín's migration story involves many more moments of separation and reunion, loss and change, that came before 2014. Ten years earlier, in 2004, Yazmín lived in Mexico City with her four younger children, all girls. One day her youngest daughter came home from school complaining of a stomachache. The child's health deteriorated rapidly, and she tragically died from a severe case of pancreatitis. Yazmín's grief over the loss of her daughter felt insurmountable. Her surviving children—two older children, both boys, who were in the United States, and three daughters, who were with her in Mexico— decided together that migration to the United States, by bringing the family together, was the best way to help Yazmín overcome the depression. As she told us:

> My daughters didn't want that [to go to the United States], but for the despair I felt for my baby who died. . . . I became very emotionally unwell. One of my older sons who was there [in the United States] told me, "Mom, you need to come," because I was entering a nervous breakdown. I told my children, "Children, don't hold it against me if one day I try to take my own life." I was here alone with the younger children, and my older children in the United States told me, "You need to come." And we went, thanks to God. The change helped me immensely to overcome that crisis from the death of my daughter.

When Yazmín migrated to the United States in 2004 with her three surviving daughters, she reunited with her two older sons in New Jersey. Her first emigration, four years earlier, had been different. In 2000, Yazmín emigrated alone, leaving her four daughters in Mexico with her mother. For two years she worked in Florida, sending money home to support them, but that was as long as she could stand being apart from her young children. Although she earned good money in the United States, Yazmín returned to Mexico City in 2002 to reunite with her daughters.

Yazmín emigrated for the first time in 2000, but her migration story began decades earlier, when her first husband, the father of her children, first emigrated to the United States to work. She told us, "He would come [to Mexico City], and I would get pregnant, and I would be happy. He would leave again, but I would be content because I was expecting a baby." Over nearly two decades of her husband coming and going, Yazmín had six children. Her two oldest children, both boys, followed their father to the United States once they became adults.

While Yazmín's family grew in Mexico through her husband's circular migration, her marriage unraveled. Her first husband found a new partner in the United States, and their divorce left Yazmín responsible for their four young daughters after he stopped sending money. So, in 2000, Yazmín emigrated, as she put it, "for the necessity of the children." Yazmín did not follow her first husband or her older sons to the United States, but a new love interest, a U.S. permanent resident who knew of good work in Miami. She eventually married him.

In Yazmín's story, we see how migrations are related to one another across a life course embedded within a network of family ties. Earlier migrations create the conditions for subsequent migrations. Yazmín first emigrated because of conditions created by her first husband's emigration: his separation from her led to her need to emigrate. Yazmín's first emigration involved separation from her younger children; she returned to Mexico to reunite with them. Yazmín's second emigration, which brought her five surviving children together in the United States, separated her from her mother; then she again returned to Mexico to reunite with her mother. Many of Yazmín's migrations reveal the basic motivation underlying "family migrants," who move to enact family roles and obligations when geographical separation threatens them.[1]

The dilemma of family migration for unity is that new separations are created in the process and, in the context of the Policy Trap, become long-term. Substantial research has studied the well-being of families left behind in Mexico by emigrants to the United States, while our research has uncovered the experience of return migrants in Mexico, like Yazmín, who are separated from family who remain in the United States.[2] Yazmín could not reenter the United States to reunite with her husband, children, and grandchildren. She lacked legal authorization for travel into the United States and felt too old to attempt unlawful entry.

In addition to separating return migrants from family in the United States, the Policy Trap creates two other unique family forms in Mexico: de facto deported families, or families with people who migrate to Mexico to accompany a deported family member; and binational, mixed-status families, or families with U.S. citizen children in Mexico. Sometimes a single family takes both forms, as when U.S. citizen children migrate to Mexico because a family member was deported.

In this chapter, we describe the process of family migration, showing how family migrations are linked across the individual life course and between family members. In addition to describing migration to unite families, we also describe migration to separate family members, a distinct form of family migration. We then focus on three family types among return migrants in Mexico that emerge: separated families, de facto deported families, and binational families.

Migration for Family

The most common form of family migration is migration to unite families—that is, family migrants moving to accompany or reunite with a family member. As seen in Yazmín's story, Rocío and Paolo's migrations reveal the dilemma of family migration: migration for unity also causes separation.

Rocío's first emigration involved reunion. She first emigrated to find her daughter Ana, who had met and fallen in love with a man who would come and go from Mexico City to California. Then, on one of his trips, Ana left with him for California. Rocío "went crazy" when Ana ran away. For all she knew, the man Ana had followed "was in the business of selling girls—at least, that was my imagination," she said.

In emigrating to the United States, Rocío defied her family's expectation that emigration was not something they did. As Rocío put it:

> My grandmother and all of her ancestors going back always told us that we don't have any need to go as wetback or braceros, that there is always enough to eat here. Here we never have seen in the newspaper that "someone died of hunger." Here the person who doesn't eat, it's because of laziness. "Your Mexico is rich and is plentiful," they taught us since we were little, saying, "If you sow tomatoes, they will grow." Ever since we were children, they raised us to believe that . . . we never had the necessity, it's true, to go to work on the other side [in the United States]. They made us love our Mexico and they taught us to work.

Rocío told us that when her grandmother found out that she emigrated, the grandmother "nearly died"—of anguish, presumably. Yet Rocío emigrated, selling everything she owned to finance the trip and taking her five-year-old son Paolo with her. Rocío migrated in spite of the tremendous financial cost and the potentially even greater social cost, including her grandmother's admonition, the direct disapproval of her ex-husband, and the reluctant support of her older son, Ramón, who stayed in Mexico. Rocío told us, "As my older son would say, 'In the end, you are a mother, no? You have to go look for her.'" Fulfilling her obligations as a mother by ensuring her daughter's safety and well-being was more important to Rocío than the cost-saving, and face-saving, of staying in Mexico.

While Rocío followed Ana to reunite with her, Paolo migrated to accompany his mother and avoid separating from her. In migrating to unify, the family migrant responds to another person's migration, with the primary purpose of being physically present in a family relationship. Family migrants seek to avoid the social costs of migrations that separate or threaten separation, leaving them physically apart and unable to provide in-person care and companionship. Family migration solves the dilemma of family life lived at a distance, but it often creates new dilemmas in the process, as it did for Rocío and Paolo.

We interviewed both Rocío and Paolo, a mother-son pair who emigrated together three times to the United States and returned three times together to Mexico. Each time Rocío migrated, she was responding to a dilemma of family separation created by an earlier migration. Paolo migrated with his mother three times between the ages of five and seventeen, each time to accompany her and avoid separation from her. Like other young child migrants, Paolo had no choice in his early migrations, since he was dependent on his mother, but as he aged he migrated with greater autonomy, that is, he chose to migrate with his mother to fulfill a strong sense of obligation to her.

On their first trip to follow and reunite with Ana, Paolo was five years old. They found Ana and determined that her husband was a good person, but they decided to stay in the United States for a while because Ana was pregnant and Rocío wanted to help Ana with the baby. After Rocío enrolled Paolo in the local kindergarten, he quickly learned English. He remembered his time in the United States fondly. Paolo described his elementary school in the United States to us:

PAOLO: The school had playgrounds, no? Just playgrounds totally different from those here. Here at most, they put a soccer field.

INTERVIEWER (*laughing*):   Some swings.

PAOLO: I never had swings in the elementary schools here! (*laughing*) Well, in the U.S., there were swings, games, railings, and really big open spaces. The schools did not have walls [around them]. For me, that was the coolest, no? I had arrived to another world. We had lockers, the cafeteria area was totally covered, carpeted, and you ate things that I had not eaten here. For me, I liked it a lot.

Although Paolo was happy in elementary school in California, Rocío decided to return to Mexico City after a year and a half because she could not adjust to life in the United States, so far from the rest of her family, especially her older son, Ramón. Rocío had assuaged her concerns about Ana's marriage, so she decided to return to Mexico. Paolo recalled his mother's position:

My mother didn't adapt to being there. . . . The Mexican family is like *muégano* . . . *muégano* is a sticky candy. Even though we are not always together, we like to know how everyone is doing. . . . She wasn't comfortable [in the United States]. I imagine also because of like, "Okay, I saw the daughter who is there, I saw that she is okay, that the husband, even though he is older, he treated her very well," or to say that my brother-in-law, the dad of the little ones, is a good person, we don't have complaints about him. And so, I think she saw that Ana was okay and began to worry about my other brother [Ramón], who was alone, who worked. Later on a phone call, he [Ramón] tells my mother that he is thinking of starting a business [a hair salon]. And so, I don't know, my mom, like, started to worry about that. She had seen my sister was okay, and so she decided to go back.

Rocío was a mother torn across borders, with one child and a grand-child in California, another child in Mexico City, and the third, Paolo, too young to do anything but accompany her. After their first trip to find Ana, they returned to Mexico to be with Ramón. They then reemigrated to California to be with Ana a second time, with Paolo enrolled in U.S. schools for a second time, and then after a while they again returned to Ramón in Mexico City. After that second return trip, the family suffered a tragedy, which we mentioned in chapter 4. One day Paolo, Ramón, and Rocío were assaulted by armed men at Ramón's hair salon, and Ramón died from the injuries he sustained in the assault. Paolo described the impact on him and his mother:

> My mother fell into a profound sadness, no? And that's when she decided to go [to the United States] again [for the third time]. And this time she did ask me, she said: "Do you want to go?" But she didn't ask me frankly because she tells me: "You want to go because now here in Mexico we don't have any reason to stay, no?" She says, "And I would like you to go because I do not want my children separated." No?

In the wake of the tragedy, Paolo and Rocío emigrated again to the United States. This time, Paolo was old enough to work in the United States, and he was very successful in a series of jobs in the food indus-try. Rocío and Paolo lived together in California, but she felt she never saw him; he was always at work. She was too far away to easily visit Ana and her grandchildren. Although she was in the same city as her two living children, Rocío felt a strong sense of social disconnection in Cal-ifornia. When her father became ill, Rocío decided to leave California for good. This time she told Paolo that perhaps he should stay in the United States, and she meant it earnestly. He had a good job there, and he would never earn that kind of money in Mexico City. But for Paolo, it was being with his mother that meant family to him, so he returned to Mexico City to be with her. As he told us, he returned "for my mother, how do I explain? I have a commitment to her, no? More than anything with myself. It is a moral obligation. It would be easy to leave her and do my own thing, but for the basic gratitude, I don't do it. I am attached to her."

Rocío and Paolo's migration experiences reveal how family considerations can take precedence over economic ones for family migrants. When Rocío emigrated for the first time, she sold everything she had to enact her role as a mother to Ana. In addition to selling property to fund the trip to the United States, a loss she would not recuperate in the United States, Rocío suffered her family's admonition. When Rocío decided to return to Mexico the last time, Paolo returned with her, even though he earned more money in California than he would in Mexico City. He did so to enact his role as a son, out of a feeling of a strong "moral obligation" to his mother. Rocío and Paolo paid high economic and social costs to be family migrants.

Like Rocío and Paolo, other migrants we interviewed moved for family reasons even when the costs were high. When Evaristo, for example, traveled to Ohio with his wife and children on tourist visas to visit his mother and brothers who lived and worked there, he had a good job in Mexico City as a government official. Evaristo decided to stay in Ohio only because his mother received a terminal diagnosis. He stayed to care for her through her death, but in doing so lost his job in Mexico City and overstayed his visa, becoming undocumented.

The obligations that family members enact through migration are obscured in theoretical models of migration that consider cost only in pecuniary terms.[3] Paolo's, Evaristo's, and Rocío's migrations cannot be understood in those terms. The stories we heard subvert the economic primacy of migration theory in other ways as well. In Yazmín's case, for instance, family dynamics—the divorce from her husband— created the economic conditions that led to her first migration to work in Florida to support her dependent children, who stayed in Mexico with their mother.

In other cases, economic rationale was used as a front for family-motivated migrations, as was most obvious when people migrated to escape from unhappy or violent family situations. We heard stories of children who emigrated to escape their parents and partners who emigrated—or convinced their partner to migrate—to bring separation to a conflicted union. Migration can provide a physical solution to a problem of family togetherness when togetherness is not wanted. In these cases, separation was a hidden goal, one not shared among all family members. When the goal of family dissolution or separation is hidden, migrants or their family members may use the logic of economic rationale to achieve the goal.

We heard several stories of youths emigrating to escape the control of a parent. Lety's husband, for example, migrated when he was fourteen years old to escape abuse in his family home. She told us that "he went all alone . . . because he didn't live well here. His father hit him a lot, so for that he went." We asked her if her husband knew a lot about migration or the United States before he went or if he had friends or family there. "No!" she said. "He told me that because they mistreated him here, he simply tried to get as far away from here as possible."

Mateo, whose emigration we described in chapter 2, left as an adolescent to escape the control of his parents after his mother sent him to work and live in her rural village of origin. As he told us, his mother was disappointed in his choices regarding school and work, and they frequently fought. After one argument, his mother told him he could not stay with her in Mexico City any longer, and she sent him to live and work in her hometown in the state of Hidalgo. Mateo experienced this punishment as his mother's way of extending her control over him when he was not under her roof. When a friend suggested that he emigrate to the United States, he saw an opportunity: he could emigrate to find his freedom from his mother. He told us that he emigrated to escape *la chancla*, a reference to the sandal used to swat children who misbehave.

While Lety's husband and Mateo emigrated to escape a controlling or abusive parent, Sara convinced her first husband to emigrate to bring an end to their unhappy and violent union. Sara used an economic rationale to achieve a family outcome when she convinced her husband that he could make more money if he emigrated and that through emigration they could reach their economic goals in Mexico. Although outwardly her husband's emigration was economically motivated, Sara's true intent in encouraging him to leave for the United States was to resolve the crisis of their marriage. She described it this way:

> My marriage, I tell you, was getting worse over time until, at some point, to get out of the relationship, I said, "I have to do something," and convinced my ex-husband to go to the United States, and that was the way that I freed myself from him. I said, "Go, go, so that things will be better for us, we can do various things. . . . (*laughing*) He was

an administrator for a local organization, but we started to have many, many problems, and as an administrator, he did not make very much money, so I told him: "Better you go to the United States, so we can build a home, so we can do this and that." But what I wanted was to get out of that toxic relationship, because in reality, it was a lot of punches and many problems. So he went to California.

Sara found a solution to the problems in her marriage in an economically motivated emigration that separated her from her husband.

We also interviewed someone who believed that he was in Mexico because his partner had accused him of a crime in order to have him deported. Matías and Rachel had a volatile relationship marked by passion, arguments, breakups, and emotional reunions. Their last argument ended with a threat. Rachel warned Matías that he would "see everything she could do." Shortly after she issued this warning, police arrived and arrested Matías on charges of domestic violence. He was advised to plead guilty to reduce his sentence. Like Mario, whose story we told in chapter 3, Matías was unaware of the immigration consequences of the plea and was deported as a result.

According to Matías, his ex-partner Rachel used migration achieved through state power—that is, deportation—to resolve a domestic crisis. Matías had no desire to return to Mexico but ended up there, he believed, because of Rachel's actions against him. Having Matías deported achieved the separation she allegedly sought from him, and it also punished him by separating him from his children.

Family Separation

Family separation is far more often an unwanted cost of migration than the (hidden) goal of migration. It is well known that migration to the United States from Mexico often involves family separation. For decades, Mexican migrants who moved to the United States left behind spouses, children, parents, and siblings in a family migration strategy that involved risk diversification, access to capital in the United States, remittances sent home, a presumption of eventual (permanent) return to Mexico, and the ability to make trips home for short reunions.[4] By focusing on those who returned to Mexico, we might therefore have expected to hear stories of family reunification. But in fact we heard about return migration involving separation just as often as it involved reunion. In the context of the Policy Trap, when migrants do not have visas to migrate freely across the border and the consequences of unlawful migration are severe, people who return to Mexico are commonly separated from family left behind in the United States.

Many of these return migrants living in Mexico, like Yazmín and Matías, were irreparably separated from their closest family members in the United States owing to U.S. policy restrictions on legal migration, as we described in chapter 3. U.S. laws and policies made it impossible for Yazmín to legally or safely reenter the United States. Her older children, who were undocumented but had U.S. citizen children, could not leave the United States and later lawfully reenter. Yazmín's younger children had DACA status, but that allowed them to travel internationally only under limited circumstances. The Policy Trap traps undocumented immigrants and immigrants with tenuous legal status (like DACA) in the United States, and it traps in Mexico formerly undocumented immigrants who have returned to Mexico, separating families across the border.

Forced separation is often the situation that people find themselves in when they are deported, as deportation typically invokes legal bars on reentry, and a previously deported person risks criminal charges and (additional) immigration penalties if caught unlawfully trying to reenter. When a family faces the deportation of one of its members, there are no good options to help them stay together. Either the deported family member attempts to (unlawfully) reenter the United States or the family accompanies them to the country of origin.

In Matias's and Juan's cases, family separation was the outcome. Indeed, nearly every person we interviewed who was deported was separated from family. Evaristo, whose migration to visit family in Ohio on a visa turned into a long-term undocumented stay when his mother became ill, was forced to leave the United States by the threat of deportation. By the time he left the United States, he had a successful work life and a lake home, and his children had obtained DACA status. When he left, he was irreparably separated from his family and his life in the United States and found himself in a place—Mexico City—where he no longer had family ties. Evaristo was like other deported people who find themselves alone and without support in their country of origin. He turned to a community of deported people who had formed an organization to provide housing and work opportunities to others in their situation, as described in chapter 4 (and again in the context of work in chapter 6).

Being deported and leaving children behind is heartbreaking, even for those who have relatives in Mexico. This was the case for Matías, whose dispute with his partner Rachel ended with his deportation. Matías had family to return to—he now lived with his mother and brother in Mexico City—but he nevertheless experienced deportation as the end of his family life. He told us that when he first arrived, "I hugged my mom, and the first thing I said to her was, 'They took my children from me.' It was the most, most painful," Matías said. We later asked him what it meant to him to be a dad, but he replied by saying that he no longer believed he was a father:

> Well, I believe I am not a father because I don't have them. . . . (*long silence*) If I had my children, I would be able to tell you what it means, but it is a process. I know that they exist, but in this case, they were taken from me. I would just be a dad by name, right? I am a dad, but being one means taking care of them, bringing them to school, providing for food and clothes, making sure they become good people. But they [the U.S. government] did not allow me to be a dad.

In depriving him of contact with his children, Matías believed, deportation had deprived him of fatherhood.

Juan was also deported, leaving behind a son in the care of his grandmother. For Juan, deprivation of contact with his son left him incredulous at times. He explained: "Sometimes it's hard for me to believe [I am a father], and I say, 'OMG, I have kids?' I have been alone for a while, and I feel alone, like I have no one, I have nothing, but I really do have a family. I have a son." Juan and Matías had children, but they were irreparably separated from them by restrictions and penalties imposed by U.S. immigration policy.

De Facto Deportation

Less common than family separation after deportation is "de facto deportation" when family members migrate to accompany a deported family member.[5] De facto deportation is government-forced family migration. Although de facto deportees are not directly forced by the government to migrate, they are forced to migrate to avoid family separation. A recent study of de facto deportation estimated that approximately eighty thousand U.S.-born children lived in Mexico in 2018 owing to a parent's deportation.[6] Mexican-born children and U.S.- and Mexican-born family members who are not children—especially spouses, partners, and parents—can be de facto deported as well.[7]

Lety, who was de facto deported along with her two U.S.-born children, met her husband, Alonso, in her sister's *tienda de abarrotes* (small grocery store) in northern Mexico City. Alonso first migrated to the United States as a teenager in 1981 in order to escape a violent father, as described earlier. Alonso became a lawful permanent resident through the 1986 IRCA amnesty and traveled back and forth to Mexico City. On one of those trips, he met Lety.

Lety made two attempts to enter the United States. On the first attempt, she entered with false documents, was apprehended, had her fingerprints taken, and was detained for a short while before being returned to Mexico. When she attempted to enter again by walking across the border, she was successful. Lety and Alonso had two children in the five years they lived together in Oakland, California. Their family was a "mixed-status" family: Alonso was a lawful permanent resident of the United States, the children were U.S. citizens, and Lety lacked legal status. In an earlier era, Alonso could have rectified this situation by sponsoring Lety for legal status, but that option was now complicated by changes to immigration law under the 1996 IIRAIRA, which we described in chapter 3. Alonso had served time in a California prison before he partnered with Lety. His offense was not deportable at the time he committed it, but it became deportable after IIRAIRA was enacted in 1996. Because IIRAIRA reclassified Alonso's offense as an aggravated felony, he became both deportable and ineligible for "cancellation of removal." In other words, IIRAIRA made it impossible for a judge to consider the well-being of Alonso's children or any other extenuating circumstances or context in issuing a deportation order against him.

At the advice of a lawyer, Alonso, Lety, and their young U.S. citizen children returned to Mexico rather than fight a deportation order against Alonso and were thus de facto deported themselves. Their choice to return to Mexico had little to do with where the schools were best, the quality of the housing, the security of the neighborhood, or economic opportunities. They migrated to Mexico to remain with Alonso and to prevent Alonso from having to serve a potentially long period of immigration detention. If not for these circumstances, they might have made different choices. Lety told us that schooling in the United States was more accessible and that she admired the lack of tolerance there for absences and gaps in schooling. She was also impressed by the bilingual preschool program her son was enrolled in. In returning to Mexico, Lety's children experienced a long delay in school enrollment. Although they were also Mexican citizens (by their birth to Mexican citizen parents), Lety's children did not have the necessary paperwork to enroll in Mexican public schools right away. Lety had been frustrated by the inconsistency in scholarship and student support programs in Mexico City. She told us that her son, who had a learning disability, did not have the kind of support he needed in his neighborhood school.

Binational, Mixed-Status Families

Lety's children were U.S. citizens, but their parents had no legal way to travel or reside with them in the United States. Lety and her family were a mixed-status family in the United States, and now they were a mixed-status family in Mexico, as defined by the different citizenships of their family members. We refer to families like Lety's as "binational" mixed-status families: members of these families have dual citizenship and/or live across countries.

Lety's children were two of the more than half a million U.S.-born minors who lived in Mexico in 2015.[8] One study estimated that about one in six U.S.-born children in Mexico in 2014 were there owing to a family member's deportation, suggesting that the majority had migrated for other reasons.[9] In 2015, most U.S.-born minors in Mexico lived with a Mexican-born parent, and their arrival in Mexico was strongly linked to the return migration of family members.[10]

We interviewed multiple members of binational mixed-status families, whose presence in Mexico was the outcome of the massive return migration and deportation of parents with their children to Mexico during the Policy Trap. Binational mixed-status families in Mexico are similar to mixed-status families in the United States in that their mobility is severely constrained by U.S. immigration law: even though they reside in Mexico, some members—typically the parents—cannot reenter the United States lawfully to be with their U.S. citizen children there.

They also experience disadvantages in Mexico that emerge from their children's birth in the United States, resulting in paperwork dilemmas and delays in accessing social services and schooling.

The inability to lawfully reenter the United States prevented Lety from considering a trip there with her children. She would have liked to return to the United States someday, but she would do so only with a visa. Lety's children had U.S. citizenship and could return to the United States on their U.S. passports. When they turned twenty-one, they would be able to apply to sponsor their parents for immigrant visas, although their father's prior conviction and their mother's prior apprehension at the border made it unlikely that they would be successful. Lety's children were curious about the place of their birth. They believed that there were more opportunities for them in the United States than in Mexico, and they understood that their citizenship would protect them from their parents' experiences of hardship as undocumented and deported people. But they had few memories of California. They did not speak English. Although they would have had full legal rights in the United States if they migrated there, their experience would be more like that of a first-generation (foreign-born) immigrant arriving as an adult without language or cultural knowledge, without the affinity or connections that one develops growing up in a place. This is the outcome of Policy Trap conditions: the de facto deportation of U.S. citizen children forces them into exile from their country of citizenship in order to remain with their parents, and the Policy Trap prevents parents from moving freely and safely back to the United States with their U.S. citizen children.[11]

We also interviewed Julio, who was a member of a binational mixed-status family. Julio's experiences reveal some of the hardships in Mexico for a family of different citizenship statuses. Julio emigrated from Mexico in 2002, when he was in second grade. He was therefore a 1.5-generation migrant in the United States; as a child migrant who grew up in the United States, went to schools there and learned English as a child, but lacked citizenship or legal status. Julio was a Dreamer.

Julio's sister Abril was born three years later, in 2005, in New York City. Abril was a U.S. citizen by birth. When we interviewed Julio in 2019, Abril was a binational citizen living in Mexico, and Julio and his mother were return migrants without the legal right to reenter the United States. Meanwhile, Julio's father remained in New York City with undocumented status. Although Julio was educated in the United States from kindergarten through the end of high school, felt like an American, and spoke fluent English, in legal terms Julio was a return migrant no different from the adult migrants in our study: he had no legal right to reenter the United States. His sister, on the other hand, was a U.S. citizen with less English language ability than Julio and fewer memories of her country of birth. She was much younger than Julio when she, her mother, and her brother migrated to Mexico. The differences in the two siblings' legal rights vis-à-vis the United States owed to the locations of their births, one in Mexico and the other in the United States.

Like many U.S.-born minors who migrate to Mexico, Abril was bullied at school in Mexico. Julio reflected on their different experiences of socialization in Mexico and the United States:

> One of her biggest problems was that she couldn't speak Spanish well, not because she didn't speak it, but she did the translation from English to Spanish and instead of saying, "I want to go home," she said, "I want home." . . . She came home with tears from primary school and did not want to go because her world changed a lot.

When Julio had first arrived in the United States, he said, "the teachers were great, but the children were not." Unable at first to communicate "the nerve and rage" he felt, Julio learned English in a year, and "when I got to high school they said, 'You're American.' I mean, I felt like an American."

Abril now no longer felt the rejection she suffered in elementary school. She had lost her English language ability, partly because of the time that had passed, but also partly because of the rejection of other members of the community of Milpa Alta in southeastern Mexico City, where they lived. Julio explained, "They obviously believed we wanted to show off and they called me the gringo. . . . We used to go out to the patio and play and speak English, right? We would get comments like, 'Oh, they feel superior because they continue speaking in English,' 'They feel they are gringos,' right? And that was the most hostile thing we suffered."

Abril was not the only U.S.-born student attending her school, but what was important, Julio explained, was the age at which these minors arrived in the Mexican community and how they had been socialized in the United States. "They didn't know how to deal with my sister's case. . . . She was the one who arrived with more schooling in English [than] the other girl who had arrived, because she arrived when she was two years old, that is, when she was barely born. I mean, she grew up like a Mexican. But not my sister."

Abril had arrived with dual citizenship because "luckily," Julio said, "my mom thought it through very well and they did the paperwork for her dual citizenship while in the United States. So coming here there were no conflicts at school, she was Mexican." However, the family fell prey to the corruption of Mexican schools faced by many immigrant and returnee minors, discovering that they needed to pay bribes to enroll the children in school or to receive services that should have been free (as described in chapter 4). Julio told us that Abril "enters primary school and, well, she is Mexican but they still do not recognize her. I mean, she had trouble getting recognized too, and that meant a bribery here, and a bribery there." Several studies have analyzed the educational contexts of return migrant and U.S.-born children and highlighted the social integration challenges they face.[12]

While Abril and Lety's children suffered some disadvantages of migration to Mexico in a binational mixed-status family, Osmundo's story reveals that having a U.S. citizen in the family can bring economic advantages in Mexico. Osmundo lived in California for ten years and returned to Mexico in 2008 with his wife and three children. His two younger children, who were ten and sixteen years old at the time of the interview, were born in the United States but did not speak English because they arrived in Mexico when they were very young, ages five and one. The oldest son, however, was like Julio: he was born in Mexico, migrated to the United States at age two, and returned at age twelve. He was a 1.5-generation migrant in the United States. That son was now in his twenties and still spoke almost perfect English. He put this skill to good use in the family's handicrafts business, which we described in chapters 2 and 6.

The U.S. state treats members of binational mixed-status families differently and unequally with respect to the legal rights it accords them. Osmundo and his wife would have liked to obtain U.S. tourist visas, since, without them, they were unable to legally reenter the United States. Their oldest son was able to obtain a visa, and he traveled back and forth with his younger siblings, who were U.S. citizens, while their parents were trapped in Mexico. Osmundo had no plans to return to the United States to live, but he would have liked to be able to go to his family's art shows and visit his younger children when they spent time in the United States. He explained: "I sent my middle son to study . . . so that he can help me. I am not sending him telling him that they [people in the United States] will help him there, no, I tell him, 'Help yourself.'" He added that, "right now, at work, we need English, and if you can try to study, it's fine, it's much better because you're going to learn more, you're from there. I tell him, 'Take advantage of it [U.S. citizenship].'" Several studies have documented the comings and goings of young people who cross the Mexico–United States border to study daily, both in San Diego, California, and in Tijuana, Baja California.[13] Our finding that the U.S.-born in Mexico City engage in similar practices confirms that binational family life also unfolds outside of border cities.

The case of Rosa, Lucía's daughter, is different from the experience of Osmundo's children in many ways. Rosa arrived in Mexico City with her mother when she was only six months old. Lucía had lived for a very short period of time in the United States before returning with a U.S.-born baby under tragic circumstances: Lucía's husband (Rosa's father) had been murdered by a Honduran member of the Mara Salvatrucha gang—commonly known as MS-13—a month before Rosa was born. Lucía lost her daughter's "American papers" and her husband's death certificate in the chaos of their migration to Mexico. Rosa now lived with her mother at her uncle's house and received support from her father's relatives, and Lucía struggled to make ends meet as she reconciled family and work as a single mother with limited resources. Rosa was a dual national but had no sense of a binational identity; her country of birth was foreign to her. She was now growing up in Mexico City facing a great deal of precariousness and vulnerability.

Current literature studying 1.5- and second-generation immigrants in the United States emphasizes that their integration depends on their parents' legal status and the family's corresponding degree of legal inclusion.[14] This is also true in Mexico among the hundreds of thousands of U.S.-born children of immigrants who have emigrated out of the United States, children like Lety's and like Abril and Rosa.[15] An important question is what will happen if and when these children return to the United States. Abril planned to return because "she does not stop being an American," even though she said, in Julio's words,

"'I don't know anything [about the United States]. That is, I'm from there, but I never knew anything, I don't remember anything.'"

Gender and Family Migration

Family separation and the creation of transnational families has largely been studied in the case of the "sole sojourner" who leaves behind his wife and children (or her mother and children) to work in the United States and send money back to support the family left behind. As our stories of return and the experience of transnational family life from Mexico City reveal, this pattern of transnational family life was upended by the Policy Trap.[16] In the interviews we conducted among people who migrated during the Policy Trap era, there were few such sole sojourners. Yazmín migrated this way at first, leaving her young children in Mexico with her mother, but her story reveals the limits of the family migration strategy based on the sole sojourner during the Policy Trap. Yazmín could not easily travel back and forth across the border to visit her children. To make her migration investment (in crossing the border) worthwhile, she had to stay and work for a long period in the United States. As she told us, she "couldn't stand" the separation, and she took her youngest children with her on her second trip to the United States to avoid a long separation from them. Of course, as we learned, Yazmín's story was more complicated than a simple story of family reunification: her second migration trip was made to bring her family together to cope with the tragic loss of her youngest child.

Although the family is the meaning and rationale that migrants frequently give to migration, theories that seek to explain and predict international migration treat the family as secondary to economic motivations. The stories told in this chapter upend the primacy of economic motivations, but there are no theories squarely interested in non-economic, family-based emigration that could be brought to bear on them.[17] Feminist researchers have pointed this out, criticizing the theoretical accounts of international migration for ignoring how gender structures the social process of international migration for non-economic reasons—a process dominated, at least in the Mexican case, by women.[18] As a structuring force, gender refers to the social expectations, norms, and practices that guide and inform the identities, roles, actions, and opportunities of women, men, and people outside the gender binary. Gender is embodied and enacted by individuals but regulated and enforced through social systems and institutions outside the individual, including the family, the community, schools, the labor market, the church, and the state. Because people experience economic and social life differently as a result of gender, gender informs who migrates, at what point in their lives, with what resources, for what reasons, and with what consequences.

Patriarchal norms have meant that women are less likely to emigrate from Mexico to the United States than men are, and when women do emigrate, they often do so for different reasons than men, under different circumstances and using different resources.[19] Women are more likely than men to migrate to follow or accompany family—a reason to migrate that is normatively sanctioned as safe and appropriate for women.[20] In identifying women's emigration as its own phenomenon, the research has defined family migration as a type of migration that is theoretically distinct from economic migration.[21] Although there is no predictive theory of family migration, Garip's analysis of MMP data identified the unique demographic profile of the Mexican family migrant.[22] She found that family migrants are slightly older than other migrants and that the majority are women, though one out of every three are men. She also found that family migration from Mexico to the United States became common after the enactment of IRCA in 1986, during the Policy Trap period.

The social scientists Gabriela Pinillos and Francisco Flores Peña, using these same interview data, have analyzed the particularly difficult experiences of women who returned to Mexico City during the Policy Trap.[23] In this chapter, we drew inspiration from their work as well as from gender scholarship that uncovers the meanings of family migrants, irrespective of their gender. In exploring the meanings and motivations of family migrants, regardless of whether they are women or men, we build on long-standing critiques of theories of migration that have prioritized economic motivations and therefore men's migration (at least in the Mexican context). Here we have prioritized family migrants, who are mostly women but include men—mothers and fathers, sons and daughters. The story told here is one of families struggling to enact their primary roles and obligations as family members in the context of the Policy Trap, which stymies family migration and separates families.

Conclusion

When hundreds of thousands of Mexican migrants in the United States returned or were deported to Mexico in the 2000s and 2010s, families were again separated, but this time they were separated as migrants returned to Mexico, leaving families behind in the United States. If we think of migration to accompany or reunify as acting out a family role or obligation—roles and obligations that can be fulfilled only in person—then separation limits the possibilities for family fulfillment. People forced by deportation to separate from their families experience it as the state depriving them of their family life. Although deported people strive to parent their children from afar, the experience is still one of deprivation—of not being allowed to fulfill their role as a parent in the day-to-day, in-person lives of their children.[24]

Some others, like Lety, Osmundo, and Lucía, brought their children with them to Mexico and formed new kinds of families there, including families with Mexican-born children who were raised in the United States and families with U.S.-born children now being raised in Mexico. Today mixed-status families live on both sides of the Mexico-U.S. border. In the United States, parents who are Mexican citizens without U.S. lawful status raise U.S. citizen children; in Mexico, parents who are Mexican citizens with no possibility of attaining lawful status in the United States raise U.S. citizen children. In the United States, growing up in a family denied full legal rights harms children in many different ways.[25] Our data suggest that this may also be the case for young U.S. citizens growing up in Mexico. With parents who cannot accompany them to their birthplace, these U.S. citizen children are growing up without access to the rights of U.S. citizenship granted by residence in the U.S. territory. It is not known what the future holds for them.

CHAPTER SIX

WORK

With Agnieszka Wieczorek

By the time Mario became entangled in the U.S. legal system, he had mastered the intricacies of multiple harvests: onions, five varieties of apples, cherries, asparagus, broccoli, and carrots. For almost twenty years, he learned which knives were appropriate for which crops, how to protect his hands from vines, roots, tools, and other hazards, and how much he needed to do to make good money on each fruit or vegetable.

"Let me tell you, in the asparagus, you have to be crouching, crouching, crouching, crouching, crouching all the time," he told us. Planting onions wasn't much better: the transplanter's spikes used to create holes were as big as fingers and had to be spaced so closely that one could barely walk across the field. Mario didn't mind cleaning vegetables like carrots and onions too much, because he used a machine to separate the greens from the vegetable, but he did have to watch out for the barbs when cleaning onions. Picking cherries was easier because of the ladders. But apples were the best: he could pick different varieties all season, starting with Golden Delicious, followed by Fujis, Pink Ladies, Granny Smiths, and Red Delicious.

Although Mario became a skilled farmworker in the United States, his pathway into agriculture was not assured. A native of Veracruz, he was raised in Puebla. After finishing some high school, he migrated to Mexico City, where he joined an older sibling, who got him a job in a sheet metal factory. He later left that job to work in a garment factory in downtown Mexico City (a building that would collapse shortly after he left, in the earthquake of September 19, 1985). He next joined a transport unit of the army, work that offered substantially higher pay. Over

https://doi.org/10.7758/kokl2957.6392

the next ten years or so, the military took him to different parts of the country, during which time he married and had children. When he was discharged, he worked as a caretaker and driver at a tiles factory. By age thirty-five, he had considerable experience in both manufacturing and transport and had secured formal work in the military and various private factories.

Yet, at thirty-five, Mario and his wife decided to cross into the United States to join her sister, leaving their children with a grandparent. When Mario arrived in their new home, he could find only one job—harvesting asparagus. He took the job, but after slicing the tip of his finger with asparagus scissors, he discovered that he could make money on cherries without having to crouch. He kept discovering the pros and cons of each crop—their health risks and their payoff potentials—until he had worked with six types of fruits and vegetables. His pay allowed him to buy a mobile home and a car, to support his children—who arrived a few years after him—and to weather a divorce from his wife. When he was deported at age fifty-five, one of his daughters, by then an adult, tried to salvage his belongings. But in the end, he arrived in Mexico City with almost nothing.

After twenty years in the United States—and forty years after he first migrated to Mexico City at fifteen—he had to start anew. Unlike in the United States, where the only job he could find was in agriculture, he could survive in Mexico City by stringing together a series of service jobs. None of the transportation jobs he applied for were interested in him. He was too old, and his experience in transportation was too long ago. His agricultural experience in the United States did not transfer to the city.

Mario's experience mirrors the disconnect that many migrants faced between their work lives in the United States and the possibilities for work upon returning to Mexico City. Mexico City is a diverse and vibrant economy, a major center of commerce, government, manufacturing, and professional services, and a hub of informal work in markets, restaurants, and small businesses. Yet return migrants faced many barriers to stable and secure work in the city. They often encountered discrimination based on age, gender, family status, appearance, language skills, and presumed criminality. These status-based exclusions were associated with unique channeling of job applicants into or out of certain types of work. For instance, older returnees like Mario found that they were either excluded altogether or perceived as capable of doing only low-paid or difficult service work. Returnees also faced profound difficulty in having their foreign credentials and work experience abroad recognized by Mexican schools and employers. Even validating U.S. primary and secondary school records proved challenging. The process took so long (and sometimes was impossible) that returnees gave up on schooling or employment goals and took up survival work. Some returnees also noted that they were unable to access records of their experience in Mexico before migration. Such barriers were a source of frustration and discouragement and led them to settle for less-than-ideal employment.

Other barriers reflected the process of return. Deportation disallows preparation for return. Deportation is a swift network interruption that disconnects people, deprives them of resources, and places their health and safety at risk.[1] Even as many people in our study indicated that they had good job opportunities in the United States or could send money to family in Mexico, forced or unplanned returns divested them of resources and prevented them from preparing for reentering the Mexican labor market. Some were deported after spending decades in the United States without plans to return at any point. Many had lost or not kept track of schooling or employment records in Mexico because they had not planned for a future there. In this context, people pieced together employment to survive.

The return migrants we talked to encountered a complex and unequal labor market in a city where return migrants have not been perceived as a critical part of its development story. As demonstrated in table 6.1, they experienced little mobility in the jobs they held upon return relative to their previous U.S. or Mexican work experience. Most people we interviewed worked in low-wage, informal, and insecure work in services, small-scale manufacturing, or construction. Many were working in the same industries and occupations they had worked in before they left for the United States. The self-employed largely pursued informal survival work rather than starting up stable or profitable small businesses. Their lack of upward mobility—the challenging return migration story that is told here—evolved from circumstances unique to not only emigration to and return from the United States during the Policy Trap but also the Mexico City labor market, including the invisibility of migrants and the relative importance of formal work for securing higher wages.

Table 6.1 *Work Experiences in Mexico City of the Thirty-Four Return Migrants in 2019*

	Work in Mexico City (current work in bold)		Previous Work Experience
Age		Premigration	Work in the United States
Women			
35	**Informal sales**		Domestic work
38	**Informal sales; manufacturing**	Informal sales	Cashier
41	**Informal sales; domestic work**	Informal sales; domestic work	Domestic work
43	**Cleaning; boardinghouse**	Administrative	
43	**Craft production; education; informal sales**	Informal sales	Retail; manufacturing
48	**Volunteer; education**	Research	Volunteer
58	**Craft production**	Informal sales	Manufacturing
60	**Out of labor market**		Cleaning
66	**Out of labor market**	Hairstylist	Restaurant; informal sales; care
Men			
24	**Call center; military; restaurant**		
26	**Repairs; social services**		Restaurant; manufacturing
29	**Call center; construction; security**		Illicit (forgery)
31	**Real estate; construction**		Lifeguard; construction; marketing
33	**Driver; security**	Manufacturing; transport	Construction

34	**Web developer**; informal sales; call center	Informal sales	Construction; manufacturing
36	**Call center**; repairs		Restaurant; transport
36	**Social services**; manufacturing	Skilled trades; restaurant	Construction
37	**Craft production**	Craft production	Landscaping; manufacturing; shipping
38	**Craft production**; sales	Skilled trades	Manufacturing; shipping
38	**Hairstylist**	Hairstylist	Restaurant; manufacturing
40	**Construction**	Skilled trades	Restaurant; construction; illicit (forgery)
40	**Construction**; landscaping	Transport; sales; skilled trades	Landscaping; snowplowing
43	**Maintenance**	Marketing	Clerk; painter
43	**Unemployed**; retail; security	Skilled trades	Dishwasher
44	**Unemployed**; informal sales	Manufacturing; skilled trades	Skilled trades; construction; transport
44	**Printing**; retail; informal sales	Retail	Agriculture; construction; restaurant
45	**Printing**	Maintenance	Agriculture; construction
45	**Maintenance**; cleaning; construction	Distributor; packer; tinsmith	Skilled trades; construction
47	**Cleaning**	Construction	Landscaping; construction; cleaning
49	**Construction; gig driver**	Administrative	Restaurant
53	**Unemployed**; printing		Call center; recreation
55	**Cleaning**; informal sales; printing	Manufacturing	Agriculture
57	**Maintenance**	Skilled trades	Construction; skilled trades
67	**Small-scale manufacturing**	Transport; printing	Manufacturing

Source: Authors' compilation.

In this chapter, we first discuss how scholars have viewed the relationship between migration, return, and economic outcomes. We then illustrate four pathways into employment taken by return migrants in Mexico City.

Understanding Economic Integration and Return

Common explanations of economic outcomes upon return migration focus on motivations for emigration, conditions in the destination country, and the social and economic contexts of reintegration after return.[2] Previous research has highlighted that theories of migration imply an association between return migration and distinct economic experiences.[3] For instance, the "new economics of labor migration" theory explains that target migration is moving to earn money that one intends to use for business or capital investments upon return.[4] In this theory, migrants are prompted to return by their economic success in the destination country, marked by the completion of their earnings goals.[5] On the other hand, neoclassical theories of migration, by suggesting that migrants return because they have failed to achieve their goals and to become integrated in the destination country, imply that economic prospects are more limited upon return.[6]

Other theories have shifted from a success-versus-failure dichotomy and toward elaborating how returnees plan for their return by mobilizing networks, savings, and skills in the origin economy. In a sweeping review of theories of return, Cassarino argues that preparedness is key to understanding the return experience.[7] Involuntary return upends the planning process, leading to difficulty in the labor market for those deported or otherwise compelled to leave. Sociologist Jacqueline Hagan and others point to nuanced pathways of resource mobilization to support economic integration in the return process; they have documented how skill formation—including language, business know-how, and familiarity with novel manufacturing or agricultural processes—combined with preparedness, may translate into upward mobility as migrants integrate over time.[8] Our analysis builds on previous work that highlights how returnees activate both networks and capital upon return, but we reveal the limits of these resources for migrants in Mexico City.

Indeed, the experiences of the migrants we interviewed in Mexico City were distinct from earlier scholarly narratives of the return migration of labor migrants to the Traditional Region of central-western Mexico. This prior work revealed a pattern of return as success: migrants return to areas where emigration has been common for decades, is socially acceptable and even esteemed, and often translates into remittances, investment, and business formation upon return in everything from new housing to agricultural endeavors to small-scale manufacturing.[9] Those with limited financial capital accumulation abroad may still find success through skill accumulation abroad, and even those who are not necessarily prepared to return could integrate with time.[10]

Beyond the Traditional Region, and in the more recent context of heightened involuntary return, the "return as success" model is less dominant. A wide range of case studies and ethnographic and qualitative work in different locales have uncovered diverse outcomes for returnees.[11] For instance, in a study of returnees in rural Yucatán, business formation was rare and often accomplished only by relying on premigration networks, not skills acquired abroad.[12] Instead, many returnees were stuck in less than ideal employment, in part because of the limited opportunities for investment and market expansion in the origin community. Research from a small town in Veracruz similarly revealed that returnees faced precarity and lack of opportunity upon return.[13]

In both cases, small place size is seen as a key barrier, but evidence from much larger cities hints at similar difficulties. Research on business formation in urban areas shows that U.S. migration experience is associated with informal entrepreneurship, which may be insecure and lower-quality than formal paid work or self-employment.[14] In Rivera's study of Nezahualcóyotl, a municipality in the State of Mexico that is well integrated into the Mexico City metropolitan area, she found that some returnees didn't experience upward mobility, working the same jobs they had before emigrating.[15] Along Mexico's northern border, evidence indicates that returnees have varied experiences: some are channeled into lower-paying construction and service work, and others are able to integrate into better-paying manufacturing jobs or niche employment that relies on English skills.[16] For instance, call centers uniquely capitalize on English language skills, offer relatively higher wages given job requirements, and provide an environment that is ostensibly supportive of people with varied histories in the United

States, including deportation.[17] At the same time, call center jobs might not offer much mobility, trapping people in one industry or employer.[18] Call centers are not limited to border cities; they have emerged as niche employment for returnees in some large cities throughout the country, including Mexico City.

Recent research has begun to more systematically consider how and why place shapes returnees' mobilization of the skills and financial resources they accumulated abroad. In our own previous work, we found that the economic integration of recent returnees depends on the region they return to, with fortunes declining the most for those who return to places outside of the Traditional Region, especially in the North.[19] We suggested that regional differences are related to the structure of regional economies and regional histories of emigration and return. Other work has shown that a high community prevalence of emigration is associated with informal business creation in urban areas.[20] Hagan and sociologist Joshua Wassink offer explanations of economic integration being shaped by the size of the locale to which migrants return.[21] Studying the emigrant-sending state of Guanajuato in the Traditional Region, they show that return migrants in León, a large urban area, transferred U.S. human capital into successful entrepreneurship and formal employment, while in urban-adjacent communities (places that are next to urban centers and accessible by paved roads), returnees relied more heavily on accumulated financial capital to make small and profitable capital investments in small businesses. However, returnees to isolated rural areas (those around an hour from an urban area and not accessible by public transit) were cut off and largely either entered lower-wage, informal, and farming work or even stopped working. Hagan and Wassink's research suggests that the characteristics of places shape the meanings of capital, with human capital important in the largest urban areas and financial capital more important in smaller, urban-adjacent areas.

Mexico City is a megalopolis with unique economies within it. Neighborhoods can be economies unto themselves; some have well-developed manufacturing and high-end service sectors, and others support small-scale subsistence agriculture, but all are connected through a dense web of commuter networks across a wider labor market. We anticipate that the types of skills and resources that migrants return with will have a varied impact in a city as vast and diversified as Mexico

City, although earlier work suggests that human capital may be particularly important. Since educational reforms promoting completion of primary and high school in the 1990s and 2000s, average educational attainment in Mexico has increased.[22] As in the United States, wages in Mexico, especially in the formal sector, are responsive to both levels of formal education and work experience.[23] Formal credentials, like educational certification, as well as more informal reference checks are important to securing work and good wages in the city.[24]

Finding work after return migration may also be a gendered process. Men and women often migrate to the United States for different reasons. Much previous work has focused on men as labor migrants and women as migrating for reasons tied to family, even as more women migrate and do so independently.[25] Labor markets in both the United States and Mexico are highly gendered, but in unique ways. The majority of women in the United States participate in the paid workforce in gender-segregated occupations.[26] In Mexico, on the other hand, only around 44 percent of women are in the paid labor market.[27] Besides women's low rates of paid labor force participation, gender norms also lead to the expectation that women will take primary responsibility for unpaid family and domestic labor.[28] As a result, the return experiences of men and women are likely to differ, especially in the context of a vast metropolitan area where commutes are long.[29]

From the work experiences of the return migrants we spoke to, we identified four paths that illustrate how unique barriers combined with returnees' motivations for emigration, their experiences in the United States, and the impact of the conditions they encountered on return on work outcomes in Mexico City. In identifying these paths, we considered previous theories of integration, including preparedness for return, structural barriers in the U.S. and Mexican labor markets, network connections on both sides of the border, education, and skill development over the life course, as well as work experiences and ideal jobs in both countries. The four paths reflect people's mobilization of resources and negotiation of opportunities in the context of Mexico City's labor market. Each path had distinct implications for longer-term labor market engagement and success.

We first discuss the path taken by many returnees who had few contacts or connections in Mexico City, who struggled to find work or to translate their skills into new occupations, and who ended up in survival employment, like Mario. This path usually led to a gen-dered experience, with women more likely to end up in informal craft work. On the second type of path, migrants forged new networks upon return through activism and community organization, which offer dis-tinct forms and meanings of employment. The third path was taken by migrants who mobilized premigration networks and skill sets to rebuild upon return and whose experiences abroad played little role in facilitating upward mobility. And finally, we discuss the more tradi-tional path of return as success, as taken by migrants who, upon return, were able to mobilize the resources produced by their migration tra-jectory. These four paths highlight the diversity of migrant experiences in returning from the United States to Mexico City during this period and the range of resources and varied network ties that shaped their job opportunities.

Survival Employment: Strained Ties, Strained Bodies, Limited Credentials

A common experience for returnees in Mexico City was finding them-selves on a path into employment filled with obstacles, resulting in survival employment.[30] These obstacles were numerous: a mismatch between their skills and the job market, discrimination based on gender and age, struggles to balance work and childcare, limited social net-works in the city, and few economic resources. Lucía's case exemplifies this route to precarity, which she experienced in the United States as well. Lucía was born in Mexico City and migrated to the United States to be with her boyfriend, who became her husband. She worked briefly in the United States as a cashier at a Latin American market, but was forced to stop working by a complicated pregnancy. When she was eight months pregnant, her husband was murdered. Although Lucía wanted to imme-diately leave the United States, she remained to avoid jeopardizing her pregnancy. When she gave birth, the medical team caused birth com-plications that required treatment and rehabilitation, which prolonged her stay another six months. Distraught with grief, disillusioned with the United States, and caring for an infant with health problems, Lucía returned to Mexico City. She struggled to regain contact with her hus-band's family and lived for a while in an apartment owned by her father in a dangerous part of the city, before having a falling-out with him and moving in with her mother's family. Amid a traumatic experience of emigration and return, Lucía struggled to secure formal employment. As she told us, when she sought work in formal employment, for "a business or government," she was turned away for many different reasons:

> I have worked for many things, but when I try to get a job at a company, at the government, or something like that, they start saying, "You can't because you have a daughter, you can't because you're not blond, you can't because we need people full-time, who work more than ten hours, you can't." Our country and the government put many obstacles in the way of single mothers.

Lucía worked briefly in a food processing factory, but the time demands of the factory job interfered with the time needed to care for her child, particularly after her daughter began losing weight in preschool. As a result, she left the factory and began selling toys and painting faces in the park for a couple of hours every day of the week, work that offered little in the way of income but allowed her to care for her daughter and interact with children, which she found rewarding. Operating her small business was challenging, however, even if it offered flexibility. She described the financial insecurity of the job:

> In this park, one needs to pay a monthly bribe, one needs to pay the government for them to let you work there. It is not very much what you need to pay, it is around 500 pesos [US$25] monthly, but for a single mom, well, it's the cost of one week's [work], because there are weeks that are very good and weeks that are very bad. . . . Some weeks I have 500 pesos [US$25] in my pocket, and there are weeks that I have 100 [US$5], and from there I still must invest to buy toys or to buy makeup, so I live on borrowed money.

Even informal self-employment required Lucía to invest in products and entangled her in the institutions of the informal economy with bribes to local officials for a place in the park. She often had to borrow from family members to cover these expenses.

Although Lucía had not worked for very long in the United States, she had a negative view of the value of work there because of barriers to translating work experience and skills gained in the United States to the Mexico City labor market. Her difficulties led her to question the American Dream and whether migration was at all valuable. When asked if she had found any benefits to spending time in the United States, she noted the barriers to realizing any advantages:

> No, you do not have any! Why? Because you have no way to prove your experience over there [in the United States], you do not have a paper, you do not have anything. Here in Mexico, the life is of papers. . . . Verify! Verify where you live, prove what it is that you do, verification of everything. And if you get to travel . . . to the United States, and you work in certain things, you have no way to verify [your past jobs].

The importance in Mexico City of verifying one's education, skills, and experience renders any experience gained abroad invisible; instead, working in the United States creates a hole in an employment record and provides no clear pathway into an occupation.

Lucía was not involved in migrant organizing or targeted programs for returnees, but other women we spoke to, like Carla and Lety, participated in an organization for women returnees that allowed them to care for their children by focusing on selling small handicrafts, goods, and food at open-air markets or out of the home. For women who experienced work challenges because of gender discrimination or childcare responsibilities, this form of more flexible self-employment provided them with income to survive.

Although men also struggled in the labor market, they encountered different types of survival employment, as well as distinct and more curtailed familial and care obligations. Mario's experiences illustrate both these similarities and key differences. As described earlier, Mario's work in the United States in various high-value agricultural harvests for close to twenty years became a source of pride for the myriad skills he developed. During his twenty-year stay in the United States, Mario lost regular contact with his family who remained in Mexico, and he had no intention of ever returning. As described in chapter 3, his life in the United States was upended when a car he had informally sold to a family member was involved in a hit-and-run. Given that his name was still on the car's title, Mario was charged with the crime and eventually deported back to Mexico. He landed at the airport in Mexico City, a place where he had not been in decades.

Upon arrival in Mexico, Mario reconnected with a niece whose husband had a cellophane wrapping paper factory and allowed Mario to take extra cellophane to sell informally to stores. He then sold tamales, but he couldn't consistently make enough money to survive. A chance encounter in the market with a temporary work agency resulted in a cleaning and maintenance job at a bottling plant that offered steady work but low pay. Mario felt lucky to get the job. Initially, they asked for proof of his educational credentials, but eventually they hired him without it. At the same time, his employers cautioned him against talking too much about his U.S. experience, as it would be perceived negatively. He explained that "they helped me quite a lot because they initially wanted me to show a proof of study, and by then I had not recovered the proof of study. . . . Here many times the boss told me not to state that [I emigrated], because here there are many racist people, or to say, that they perceive you were in jail."

Mario planned to continue in this job, even though the income was low. He supplemented it by continuing to sell cellophane paper informally. Ultimately, his goal was to be a chauffeur, a job he had worked in Mexico prior to emigrating, but he had not been able to acquire his military discharge records, which would provide clear proof of his prior work experience in Mexico. He told us:

> I am interested in looking for a job that I like, like being a chauffeur, but for that, I have to get back my papers. There is a discharge that I have from the army. . . . I have not been able to recover my certificate of discharge. . . . But I want to recover it because it is a termination record. If someday I go look for a job, that serves as a reference or to say that proves I was a driver, that I have experience and that is what I want for looking for a driver job.

Mario had set the immediate goal of working as a driver because he perceived other areas of work that interested him as implausible. Given his background, he was interested in security but said that his age would be a problem. Being only in his midfifties, he found Mexican age discrimination shocking. It wouldn't have happened in the United States, he told us:

> This is where one comes to clash with age, because you are in the United States and you say, "I know how to do that, I have capabilities in that," and you arrive here in Mexico and you find a sign that . . . that says, "I am looking for people [workers]," but . . . only twenty and up to forty-five years of age, then. . . . Where does one fit? Yes, yes, despite your age, wherever you want they give you work, but not here anymore, here it's something different.

Mario's and Lucía's experiences highlight how discrimination and lack of credentials funnel returnees into low-wage and informal service work. Women are often compelled by the demands of caregiving to seek informal self-employment, which provides flexibility but little security in terms of income. Men have the option of working in the informal labor market, but seldom in jobs that build from skills they acquired in the United States. Indeed, having some U.S. work experience is considered useless or even a liability for dealing with employers in Mexico City.

Activist Networks and Opportunities

For returnees with few connections in Mexico City and limited resources, organizing with other return migrants offered an avenue to recognize and develop skills and mobilize local financial capital, as discussed in chapter 4. Activist networks in Mexico City were forged out of a need to provide immediate assistance to those deported to one of the largest cities in the world, where many did not have support networks. Some groups formed to greet deported people at the Mexico City airport immediately as they got off the plane and to provide them with transportation and information about identity documentation, housing, and employment. Other groups formed to facilitate longer-term integration and raise awareness about deportation and the circumstances facing return migrants in Mexico City. Many of the work opportunities afforded by activist groups offered only survival employment, but they also provided returnees with community, a sense of political purpose, and connection to civil society and politics in Mexico City.

Roberto's experiences illustrate how activism can shape employment opportunities. Roberto migrated with a group of young men from Jalisco who were recruited by a farmer in the United States. Born in Mexico City, Roberto quickly realized that he was not cut out for farm work and transitioned into restaurant and construction work, the latter an industry in which he envisioned opening a business. In 2016, Roberto was deported after being stopped by ICE on the street. Upon return to Mexico, he had difficulty finding work that related to his experience in the United States or that he found meaningful. He noted that employers saw someone his age as capable only of cleaning or security work, both difficult and low-paid jobs. He told us, "They do not hire me. 'How old are you? Forty-four, oh. . . .' Right? Only cleaning or as a security guard. Then that is a job I do not want to do for survival, right?"

In the late 2010s, Roberto joined with other activists to form a small business to raise awareness of and foster solidarity with deportees, with support from Mexico City's development program, the Secretaría de Desarrollo Rural y Equidad para las Comunidades (Secretariat of Rural Development and Community Equity, or SEDEREC). This was a time of heightened awareness of the difficulties encountered by deportees, many of whom were arriving at the airport in Mexico City with few resources or social connections in the area. Roberto explained that forming this small business in support of deportees was a form of self-expression that allowed for personal reinvention after a range of work experiences:

> I think as long as it's done with love, you have love for what you're doing, I think it's not work, right? It's not work anymore, is it? Work is something that you do by force to survive, that is a job. The going to the office and doing as I am told and I leave. And I am waiting for the weekend to free me from that job. I think what we do here is not a job, it was given. . . . We had to reinvent. I worked in the field, in construction, other coworkers in restaurants. We arrived to the conclusion that creating was a way to express ourselves.

Despite providing opportunities for self-expression and fulfillment of political goals, the business encountered difficulties on the economic side: participants made little money, and the considerable time they spent on organizational goals precluded finding potentially more lucrative work. At the same time, however, working in an artistic and political field garnered visibility that might ultimately open a pathway back to the United States, and starting the business with other activists cultivated a new type of support network for the many deported people who lacked any support network at all.

Roberto's experiences were emblematic of a grassroots approach to gaining employment and work experience through activism, but other organizations and businesses explicitly targeted the unique skills of return migrants for market niches in Mexico, especially the call centers mentioned earlier. In some ways, such work fits the fourth path, taken by migrants who were able to develop and utilize skills across the migration circuit ("migration as success"). We mention them here because call center employers often recruit from within networks of returnees, sometimes in connection with political programs or social innovation initiatives that address the difficulties of returnees. A few studies in Mexico City have documented the efforts of call centers that target migrants for their English by opening facilities in neighborhoods with denser concentrations and networks of returnees.[31] We interviewed one such migrant, a returnee named Reynaldo, who grew up in the United States. His English language skills proved useful to the call center where he worked, but he disliked the treatment he received from some (U.S.) Americans he had to engage with on the phone. He told us about one incident:

> I had a call with a very racist man. He said to me, "Say, I just talked to a woman, she's like some kind of Pakistani or something." He was calling her a witch, witch with a B. And I was like, "Sir, this is inappropriate behavior. You cannot do this." And I think he heard my accent and said to me, "Where do you come from?" "I'm from Mexico City." "Oh my God, I approved that, Trump . . . approved the border, the wall." He says he is going to build the wall, he says we are going to pay for it. I am just like, "Yeah, sir, okay. Yeah." I am not going to fight with him. It's on us. To fight with a person like that is to lower to their level and stay there. So, I am just like, "Okay, okay, anything else I can do for you?" And that made him mad. I think he wanted me to respond to him. It's people like that.

Reynaldo had become tired of dealing with "people like that" on the phone who directed their racist tirades at him, and he no longer worked at the call center.

Other returnees participated in unique programs for returnees that sought to build skills to perform remote work for U.S.-based companies. For instance, Manuel, a thirty-five-year-old returnee who had spent much of his childhood in the United States, worked in a call center for many years using his English skills. Eventually, through a migrant-serving organization, he found a program that taught coding skills and helped match people with U.S. technology companies that hired foreign coders. This unique opportunity to upskill was predicated on both U.S. experiences and economic development initiatives spearheaded by migrant-serving organizations and some resettlement policies. It is unclear how widespread involvement in these types of opportunities is among returnees, but for this group in Mexico City, connecting with other migrants, support networks, and policy initiatives proved important to their reintegration.

Mobilizing Premigration Networks and Skills

Osmundo's migration experience in many ways is emblematic of the pattern of emigration from and return to the Traditional Region, except that he returned to Mexico City and his successful reintegration relied on mobilizing premigration resources, networks, and skills. We learned a little about Osmundo's experience resettling in Mexico City in chapter 3, but here we focus on his work history. At the age of fourteen, Osmundo migrated to California from Guerrero, where his family had a successful, critically acclaimed handicraft business. Many of his siblings were already in California, and emigration was common in his community, so pursuing opportunity and adventure in the United States seemed a natural part of growing up. When Osmundo arrived, he quickly secured a job in a nursery and then moved on to manufacturing work in factories. He worked manufacturing car parts and assembling computer parts, eventually moving up to quality control before making a move into warehousing and shipping. He regularly sent money home to his parents, helping them build a house and get a truck, but he did not return to visit.

In 2008, at the height of the Great Recession, work in the United States began to slow down, and Osmundo began to worry about his family's business and well-being. He decided to return to Guerrero to help his parents, who had worked thirty-five years in their family business. He stayed a while in Guerrero, but when he had a falling-out with his family, he decided to move to Mexico City, near his wife's family. As it turned out, his father had been traveling to the city every weekend to sell their artwork in markets, and Osmundo proposed that he take over the market business. Eventually he ended up owning the business.

Osmundo and his children expanded the business and were featured in art books and invited with some frequency to present work in shows in the United States. The success of the family business was enhanced by the English skills of Osmundo's children, who could connect with English-speaking tourists in the market and gallery owners in the United States. At the same time, Osmundo's own success reflected his training in his craft and the premigration networks that he mobilized upon return. When asked to reflect on the skills or advantages he gained from working in the United States, he noted that they were minimal, given that the owners and managers of large companies determine how things are done in their business and their ways don't necessarily translate to small businesses or entrepreneurship.

Preexisting Mexico City connections could also ameliorate the process of finding work upon return to the city. Emblematic of this route were Paolo and Rocío, reluctant international migrants who held Mexico close. As discussed in the previous chapter, Paolo and Rocío migrated to and from the United States together several times to split time between Ana, Rocío's daughter in California, and her son Ricardo, a hairdresser in Mexico City. Paolo was too young to work in the United States on the first two trips, but on their third trip he worked in various food industry positions, including in fast-food restaurants and food manufacturing. On their last return to Mexico, Paolo followed in his brother Ricardo's footsteps and started his own hairdressing salon, where he still worked while attending college part-time. In some ways, Paolo's trajectory tracked theories of return as success: he secured employment by working in his own business upon return. Yet, for Paolo, the traditional mechanisms were not in play. He migrated to the United States for family reasons, and with little choice, and did not accumulate significant capital there; upon return, he had to relearn a skill (as a hairdresser), and his success in business was predicated on his brother's earlier efforts to establish the business in Mexico City.

Building on Migration Experiences

A small group of people we interviewed, most of whom migrated to the United States as children, were able to translate their U.S. experiences into lucrative small businesses or pathways to stable employment. Even among these returnees, however, a lack of formal educational and occupational credentialing presented barriers that channeled them out of their preferred work.

Julio exemplified a trajectory in which U.S. experience translated into opportunity, albeit opportunity constrained precisely by that same experience. Julio was born in Mexico City to parents who had migrated internally from Guanajuato. In search of better opportunities, the family decided to migrate to the United States when Julio was a child. They lived in New York, in Brooklyn, and then in Queens, where Julio completed high school. While Julio was a good student and held jobs in high school, he realized as he approached graduation how difficult it would be for him to attend university or obtain stable employment without documentation. At the same time, his mother began to have health issues from working in a difficult factory job. The family decided that he, his sister, and his mother would return to Mexico, while his father continued working in the United States. With savings and help from his father, the family constructed a building in the Chalco neighborhood of southeastern Mexico City, and he and his mother started two small businesses. In his business he repaired video game consoles, a skill he learned in a U.S. high school class:

> In my case, I had the idea of having a business, not like my mom's, because hers was to sell a product, which involves her having to go for the product or to lose it, and that is another cost. Then I told my mom, "Why do you not try something that is only a cost-effective service, I mean a cyber-café or some Xbox machines?" and that was my idea. Then, when I spoke to my dad, he said, "Sure, that is okay, your mom has hers, and you have yours." And like, that is what we did.

Although it is clear that migration built both skills and financial capital for the family, Julio did not initially want to start a business; ultimately he wanted to work elsewhere, perhaps in formal paid employment as a teacher. In fact, his goal upon return was to attend university, but this proved challenging. His experience highlights not only how goals shift over time but also the challenges of foreign education and experience recognition. He explained:

> We begin to realize that it is not like in the United States, [where] you go to an office and if you give a complaint, they respond instantly, or to say, there you are treated as a human 100 percent [of the time], and here we realize that, "if you do not stumble, you will not advance." When I did the revalidation of studies . . . it was going to take six months for elementary school. Fortunately, they did it in less time, but middle school and high school was six months [for] one and six months [for] the other. . . . I couldn't even work either, because I did

not have all of my documents. I left high school in the United States
as a technician of tourism, and the truth is, I could not practice here
if I didn't have all my documents. It was a mess of documentation.

Instead of enrolling in university as intended, Julio was lured by a
private technical school that didn't require documents but was very
costly for him. He left the school after three months to contribute to the
family rather than spend his family's money on school. Before starting
his business, he worked a series of jobs that he thought would capitalize
on his English abilities, including work at a call center. He explained
that he learned a lot at the call center, particularly how vulnerable many
other returnees were as a result of their appearance—including tattoos, varied Spanish-language competencies, accents, and styles—and
their presumed association with deportation and crime in the United
States.[32] Although call centers offer the promise of relatively higher pay
to many with limited options, Julio found the job of talking to hostile
and abusive customers difficult and demoralizing, much as Reynaldo
did. His difficult experiences with having his credentials and skills recognized and being channeled into niche employment led Julio to question the entire process of return and his place in Mexican society:

> I realized that the idea of return brutally changed, because my idea
> was to return to my country of origin, that is, the rejection that I felt in
> the United States from not being able to work at McDonald's because
> I was undocumented. I thought, "Here I will achieve," and it was not
> like that. The truth was not like that. A year passed, a year and a half,
> the year of revalidation [of documents], and later the rest, that it was
> the sad truth. Including my mom, for example. When she returns, the
> locals were already there, but she had the idea of returning to work for
> at least a year or a few months to generate more money, and because
> of her age they no longer hired her. In my case, the lack of documen-
> tation, one of the keys, then it was a mental change to have to return
> and to say, "Everything will be better," but it was not like that, and you
> have to find [work] through one form or another.

Even those who found economic stability through self-employment
were not fully able to achieve their goals or capitalize on their full
range of skills. These experiences emphasize the challenges of defining
successful reintegration, as it often involves difficulties, compromises,

and sheer luck. The process is also not necessarily linear or constant as people spend a long time continually strategizing about how to align their experiences with opportunities.

Conclusion

The paths described in this chapter tell us about the barriers, the mechanisms, and the range of outcomes for migrants who returned to Mexico City during the Policy Trap period after years spent building human capital, careers, and businesses in the United States. Examining these paths in light of returnees' migration histories, social connections, and financial resources provides insights into their economic integration upon return, as well as the labor market barriers that often channel returnees into precarious forms of employment. The Mexico City labor market is large, complex, and competitive, and the barriers that our interviewees faced in the labor market were significant: lack of formal credentials, few economic resources, difficulty translating prior work experience, caregiving obligations, and health challenges, as well as discrimination on the basis of age, gender, family, and migration-status. Notably, the work that many of them found didn't fully value or make use of the range of skills they had acquired in the jobs they had held across their lives. For most everyone we spoke to, no matter how successful they had been in the United States, finding meaningful employment in a vastly unequal and credential-based city proved a struggle that helped define their experience of return. Scholars have documented similar returnee struggles in other small towns and large cities throughout Mexico.[33]

For many people, the difficulty of securing work upon return cast doubts on whether their original decision to migrate to the United States had been "worth it," at least in terms of economic security. A large body of work focuses on international migrants' difficulty in translating their skills and credentials in host countries, especially for those who work in occupations that require high levels of education or certification.[34] Credential and skill recognition is also critical for returnees, however, as well as for those working in a wide range of jobs, even those that are unregulated and don't require decades of formal schooling, echoing previous findings from urban areas.[35] In Mexico City, employers often ask for records of work history or recent educational attainment.

Yet many people do not keep records of previous work and schooling in Mexico as they build lives in the United States, or they lose documents during arduous return or deportation experiences. Providing references from the United States is difficult, and because U.S. experience can be stigmatized, returnees sometimes conceal their work history along with their migration history. Other scholars have pointed out that seeking skills and experience recognition is time-consuming and can delay reintegration, block efforts to mobilize resources, and prolong hardship.[36]

Although it may seem that Mexico City would offer more opportunities, especially for those with limited resources, compared to some other parts of Mexico—or even the United States—pay in Mexico City can be very low and opportunities may be limited. At the same time, for those starting anything beyond a survival business, succeeding in the large, stratified economy of Mexico City requires resources, perhaps more so than in smaller cities and rural areas in Mexico. In this context, the return migrants we interviewed creatively strategized to find employment to support themselves and their families and ended up in varied work situations, many far from ideal. The challenges of the city and their feelings of loss compared to their successes in the United States framed not only the paths taken by returnees but also the achievements they secured.

CHAPTER SEVEN

REORIENTING THE COMPASS

When Olivia was deported, U.S. immigration agents delivered her to Ciudad Acuña, a border city in the state of Coahuila. Olivia told us that after she left the U.S. border, ICE officers told her not to look back or move. "They tell you they are going to shoot you if you move, and then you walk, and you get there, and then there is the Mexican police, and they stop you. I even told them, 'I'm already in my country, and now, why are you going to stop me?'" She was then brought to an office of the Instituto Nacional de Migración (INAMI, National Institute of Migration). She was asked where she came from, why she was deported, and how many years she had lived in the United States.

Olivia stayed less than two hours in Ciudad Acuña. She knew no one there and was well aware of how dangerous it was, but two hours gave her enough time to receive the benefits of the Programa de Repatriación Humana (Program of Human Repatriation), which was implemented in 2007, ten years before her deportation. Olivia was critical of the support she received:

> Well, supposedly they give you support, but it's a support that . . . they give you a talk, right? They start saying, "Bienvenido, Paisano" [Welcome, fellow Mexican], and blah blah blah, and they tell you that they are going to give you support of who knows how much money, but they come out and then tell you, "Not right now, we do not have the funds available until the next three or four days." And they give you about 400 pesos [US$20], but one night in a hotel there at the border costs you about 800 [US$40]. The only thing they gave me was the

https://doi.org/10.7758/kokl2957.9171

repatriation paper, and right there I walked to the bus station that was nearby, I bought my ticket, and I came here.

Olivia arrived at her sister's house in Mexico City with a very bad urinary tract infection brought on by the conditions she suffered while in detention, being shuttled from one facility to another. She also arrived depressed. She didn't want to leave her room and cried all day. She didn't know how to start a new life so far from her children, while living with a sister she hadn't seen in almost two decades. Her kidney problems seemed insignificant compared to feeling norteado.

Our interviewees gave us clear descriptions of the social and structural problems affecting their lives, having experienced them firsthand, and we have analyzed many of these experiences in the pages of this book. What should be done with the resulting knowledge? How do we turn it into action, and what sort of action do we pursue?

The purpose of this book has not been to evaluate policy or provide a list of policy recommendations. Other authors have already done so, including scholars who have focused on the implementation of a variety of social policies over time and at different geographical levels, ranging from education policies to work to securing human rights for returnees, as well as on the impact of the relationship between foreign policy and Mexican migration policy on migrant populations.[1] There is also a long-standing debate about how to advance immigration reform in the United States, which of course would impact the families of the people we interviewed on both sides of the border.[2] Reforms to public policy in Mexico to address issues of poverty and decrease social inequality, such as support for the unemployed, work training programs, disability accommodations, and higher-quality, universal health care, would improve the lives of returnees, who tend to be disadvantaged within contemporary Mexican social and economic systems.[3] Instead of describing the rationales, politics, and implementation of these sorts of policies, in this chapter we bring into clear focus the ideas expressed by the return migrants we interviewed about ways to improve their lives.

Throughout our interviews, people reflected on social, economic, and political changes that would allow them to have a better life. Some of these reflections emerged in response to direct questions—for example, when we asked about their ideal jobs, the value of their U.S. work experience to Mexican employers, what it meant to be a parent, or their experiences accessing a given service. People also advocated for change when reflecting on the differences between their life in Mexico and what they experienced in the United States. They sometimes volunteered this sort of information when we asked if they wanted to add anything else before ending the interview. Some returnees, especially those who were active members of migrant organizations, had strong opinions and well-developed ideas about specific policies and their on-ground implementation, and how issues have been addressed by the Mexican and U.S. governments. However, most others suggested only small, practical changes to address their daily needs as returnees, members of binational families, and residents of Mexico City. In other words, they described specific ways to reduce the experience of being norteado. We begin with experiences and reactions to the programs that greet returning migrants upon arrival in Mexico.

Welcome Back: More than "Bienvenido Paisano"

In 2007, the Mexican federal government implemented a program, the Program of Human Repatriation, to welcome return migrants who had been deported. This program started in Tijuana to receive deportees from the United States and offer them immediate aid upon arrival: food and a basic cleaning kit, support in making a phone call to family members, funds for transportation to bus stations or temporary shelters, a paper that certified their arrival, information on shelters and services they could access, and medical and psychological assistance. Over time the program opened offices in other border states, and once deportees started arriving in the interior by plane in 2012, an office was opened in Mexico City. Today other nonborder states (Jalisco, Michoacán, Puebla, Querétaro, and Tabasco) have similar programs.[4]

Since 2007, the Mexican federal government has implemented a series of programs to welcome, upon arrival, not just deportees but returnees in general. For example, the policy called Somos Mexicanos (We Are Mexicans), created in 2016, included a series of programs, both targeted and untargeted, that could help returnees reintegrate. It included information at the consulates abroad for those wanting to return voluntarily; aided returnees upon arrival after deportation by U.S. authorities; and implemented offices of the INAMI to provide general information for accessing health services, finding a job, or starting a business. In 2020, the name was changed under the new administration to the Estrategia Interinstitucional de Atención Integral a Familias Mexicanas Repatriadas y en Retorno (Interinstitutional Strategy for Integral Assistance to Mexican Repatriated and Return Migrant Families), but its nature remained the same.

Although some of our participants found support through special programs put in place by the Mexican government and private organizations focused on helping returnees, as we described in chapters 4 and 6, they also found these programs to have significant limitations and considered them only first steps toward changing conditions for returning migrants. Lety, for example, praised the government's effort to provide an *hoja de repatriación*, a certificate granted by Mexican authorities that eases entry into Mexico when a national is deported by facilitating access to paperwork and identity documents, which are particularly important for deportees who have spent a lot of time in the United States and lost contact with their family members. She told us, "Well, today, I think, there are already more rights. For example, they [deported people] are given the repatriation certificate. Many people who do not have family or who have lost family contact with their family here have had a hard time reintegrating here because they were years living there."

In addition to the repatriation certificate, deported people also receive a small lunch box, a toothbrush and toothpaste, and help with transportation. Like Olivia, Roberto and Antonio were welcomed by people from the Mexican government. Roberto recalled that he was given twenty pesos (one U.S. dollar), a bag with a sandwich and juice, and access to a phone in order to make a call. Roberto also mentioned that groups of returnees met with a psychologist who gave them tips on how to deal with anger: "They tell you, 'Don't feel guilty, get a pillow, hit it and scream loudly.'"

Antonio appreciated this first encounter upon arrival, since he, like many others, had nowhere to spend the first night. He told us that he arrived at the Mexico City airport and was welcomed by government officials dressed in pink vests (the official color of Mexico City when Miguel Angél Mancera was mayor from 2012 to 2018) who gave him a fifty-peso bill (two and a half U.S. dollars). Antonio had no idea how much the bill would buy, but he was able to receive support from a woman from an organization that provided him with shelter for a couple of days. Antonio's experience shows the importance of receiving such aid immediately upon arrival, since it enabled him to avoid sleeping on the street. But others, like Olivia, were critical of the limited effectiveness of Bienvenido Paisano. This support was not enough to enable returnees to start a new life, as discussed in policy reports and academic studies highlighting not only the limited support of both public and private programs but the barriers to accessing this support.[5]

Other returnees highlighted the problem of political change and the interruption of efforts, programs, and organizations over time. For example, Carla had previously received support from a federal program for women from the Instituto Nacional de las Mujeres (INMUJERES, National Institute for Women), but now, she explained, "INMUJERES disappeared and is now the Secretaría de la Mujer [Secretariat for Women]. But I have no idea how it will work out. SEDEREC [the small grants program] also disappeared, and they put a different name, but I am out of the loop and I don't know where to sell my products now." We described how SEDEREC helped Roberto and other deported people start a small business in chapter 6.

Bienvenido Paisano, which is now called Héroes Paisanos (Fellow Mexican Heroes), aims to ease the entry, transit, and return of Mexicans living abroad, mostly in the United States and Canada, by providing information at booths in airports and in border cities.[6] SEDEREC was created in 2007 to generate and implement public policies and programs for rural development and Indigenous populations as well as migrants and their families. Its name was changed in 2018 to Secretaría de Pueblos y Barrios Originarios y Comunidades Indígenas Residentes (Mexico City's Secretariat of Original Towns and Neighborhoods and Indigenous Communities), and its focus narrowed to helping Indigenous communities living in Mexico City, eliminating any support for returnees and other migrants.

Some might argue that regardless of the support provided by governments, people should organize for assistance and recognition. For example, Raúl believed that for big change to happen, people need to mobilize for change: "People say, 'Oh, the new government was going to send some help,' but it's not about what they will give you. I tell people,

'You need to get involved for change to happen.' . . . I know that for this government to work, there needs to be a mobilization, we need to get involved." This was a common belief among many of our interviewees who engaged in activism and volunteer work with other returnees, welcomed returnees at the Mexico City airport, or provided support to fellow returnees by helping them access documentation and information and meet other needs. Still, even the groups that had mobilized were aware of not having enough support. Much of this mobilization involved trying to make visible the often invisible population of returnees in the large metropolis.

How to Make Visible the Invisible Without Creating Harm

Many activist organizations fight to make the needs of the return migrant community visible, but as we argued in previous chapters, returnees' invisibility in Mexico City is due in part to the very nature of the metropolitan area. Moreover, some of our interviewees worried that greater visibility might sometimes bring greater harm than benefit. For example, at the May 2018 presidential debate, Ricardo Anaya (the PAN candidate) drew attention to returnees when he showed the *costal* (bag) that deportees receive with their belongings when they arrive in Mexico, as we described in chapter 4. Many in the community saw this as a political move and opportunistic on his part, and so it also led many to question the benefits of short-term media and political attention without a real change.

Returnees come back to Mexico for a variety of reasons, but the fact that federal programs demand an *hoja de repatriación* to access support programs has led many to conceive of "return" as a synonym for "repatriation," or "deportation." These sorts of targeted programs also raise questions about who deserves support.

Julio poignantly described the importance of differentiating between return, repatriation, and deportation and decried the significant differences in experiences and needs that are overlooked when all returnees are put into a single category. He told us:

Here in Mexico sometimes the people talk about the phenomenon [return migration] and it becomes generalized. The term "Dreamers" is complex. . . . We need to start making distinctions. There are also other young people who also come for a dream, let's say to study. They are looking for a dream that they did not have there [in the United States]. Sometimes the phenomenon is referred to a lot as "repatriation," and it is not the same. All this creates so many stigmas. . . . This distinction must be made not to hurt the communities. Sometimes these young people go back to high school, and they are all seen as cholos, or when you say, "They were studying there [in the United States] and for x reason, they were deported," or "This girl who was deported because she was with her mother in the wrong place."

Julio was referring to people's strong association between deportation and criminal activity, as well as between return and deportation.

Julio brought up another issue that is important for thinking about heightening visibility without creating harm: the complex debate on Dreamers, or those undocumented immigrants who arrived in the United States as children. In the United States, the debate regarding the DREAM Act and DACA can imply that only some immigrants deserve access to U.S. citizenship.[7] The focus on "deserving" youth arrivals suggests that older migrants are not deserving and reveals a broader neglect of older migrants. Similar discourse focusing on youth or bilingual returnees, or so-called Dreamers in Mexico, also risks ignoring older returnees. Evaristo, whose daughters obtained DACA, maintained that he and other returnees "are all dreamers":

In Mexico, the Dreamers are very few. Some organizations refer to Dreamers like those who are young. Me, as an adult, I can also be a dreamer, because I do not need to be eighteen or twenty to dream. At my age, I was a dreamer, and dreamed to make more good things for my family, and you can achieve many things by dreaming. Here many people think a Dreamer is a young person, but no! We are all dreamers.

Our data showcase the heterogeneity of experiences by complex intersections of age, gender, health status, class, family migration, cause of return, as well as time in the United States and time back in Mexico. In other words, the experience of return is not unique or lived in a single way. To this end, Julio explained that someone like him might have needed help accessing higher education, getting an undergraduate degree validated and recognized, while others needed help finding a job or certifying their skills; some needed a secure space where they could meet other fellow returnees and share their experience, while others needed safe shelter.

Recognizing the variety in returnees' needs is particularly important in the face of corruption, police abuse, and insecurity in Mexico, as discussed in chapter 4; as Evaristo and others explained to us, authorities often take advantage of return migrants. Evaristo claimed that return migrants could not achieve their dreams "because Mexico limits you a lot. You receive no support. The government limits you. Why? Because you need to give bribes all the time." Alberto told us that he had become demoralized by age discrimination when trying to access government funds for projects. Raúl also shared with us how tense he had become in the metro after witnessing the police colluding in the theft of a cell phone. Overall, deep-rooted corruption, awareness of the vulnerability of migrants (both Mexican and foreign-born) when people believe they might have money, and their knowledge of repeated (and well-documented) violations of transit migrants' human rights have reduced returnees' trust in authorities.[8]

At the same time, Julio, noting that sadness should not be the only focus when talking about return, highlighted the importance of successful stories. He told us: "We should touch upon all these issues, and make the distinction, but also make sure society does not only put a sad look at it. There are also other parts of the story, and even though these kids returned in this condition, they are also succeeding. Not everything is sad, not all of them were deported and returned to gangs. We must also disseminate positive things." Julio's comment challenged us to think about how to convey positive and successful experiences alongside accounts of hardships.

Here we draw insights from Julio again, to highlight a successful space that he praised: the Universidad Autónoma de la Ciudad de México (UACM, Autonomous University of Mexico City). He noted that the UACM motto is "*Nada humano me es ajeno*" ("Nothing human is foreign to me"). At the UACM, he observed coexisting migrant populations, and also met a fellow student from the state of Oaxaca and another from Honduras. His own migration story became meaningful in a broader sense as he realized "that your reality is part of the reality of others, and that helped me, it helped me think about my situation and realize that my story is one of many," he told us. If more spaces in

Mexico City provided avenues for people to realize the importance of their own migration stories—whether internal, international, or intergenerational—and to make visible their migrant lives in a way that allowed for a celebration of diversity and experiences, nonmigrants and returnees might be better able to coexist while validating their unique experiences.

Julio told us that his family was now not the only family in his neighborhood that had returned from the United States. He felt proud of being a return migrant, and his sister Abril now felt proud of being born in the United States. Julio said that it felt good to support new arrivals as they re-adapted to Mexico:

> There is a lot of stigma and people have created a symbolic burden, so you don't want to expose yourself and better remain silent. . . . I have always told my sister, "Don't be ashamed of your condition, you come from there, so keep speaking English," and that is what has helped her in school. Nowadays they see her as very strange, they tell her, "You were born there, I was born here, wow!" And instead of feeling that rejection that she felt in primary school, she now says, "I feel good, I feel that now, my condition makes me be important." And it is the same thing that I do. Where we live, two people have recently returned, right? And they come up to me and say, "How did you do it?" "Come, I'll help you." Something that was lacking before. So those conditions help us a lot to strengthen ourselves and even more so when you become an activist or see this reality and start to make a change, that is the idea, not to stay all the time in the abyss and in the darkness. Also getting out of there and supporting others is what has motivated me.

Family

Family separation was the most painful—and painfully unsolvable—issue raised by the people we interviewed. As we explained in chapter 5, many of our participants shared how they longed for the family they left behind in the United States. The experience of separation affected not only their everyday life and the support available to them in Mexico but also their sense of identity as a mother, father, daughter, or son. The pain was felt on both sides of the border. Olivia, whose story we recounted at the beginning of this chapter and in chapter 3, described it this way:

> Well, you try to live your life according to the rule of law as much as possible. Like, we pay taxes, we try not to get into trouble with the police, and all that. But at the end of the day, what happens? When they want to, they get rid of you. They give you a kick in the ass and kick you out, over with your life, with your dreams, with your kids' dreams, with your family's. Because, well, now, if you ask my kids what they want to do for Christmas, most likely they tell you, they are not thinking, "Ay, I want Santa Claus to bring me this." No, they are thinking, "I want to see my mom." And that is the most difficult part, because they are stealing the dreams of our children, not just ours, but our children's as well.

Olivia reminded us that her deportation deprived her children of the thing they most desired: to be with their mother. U.S. immigration law separates families through deportation, bars on reentry, and visa rules. Most of the people we spoke with were Policy Trap returnees: they were separated from family and had no legal means of reuniting with them.

Family separation is a major focus of migrant activism in Mexico; the organizations we introduced in chapter 4, including IMUMI and APOFAM, raise awareness of migrant issues, seek policy changes, and provide legal (and other) services to people in Mexico who are separated from their family in the United States. We learned in our exchanges with people involved in these organizations that they struggle to keep up with the demand for their services, fund their efforts, and successfully reform laws and policies that prioritize law enforcement over family and child well-being. Each of these issues suggests a deceptively simple solution: create new legal services for migrant families, fund existing services, and seek legal and policy reform to accommodate family reunification.

Our interviewees argued most forcefully for visas—that is, for permission to travel legally and safely to visit their family members in the United States. Yazmín would have liked to have a visa in order to visit her grandchildren, who were U.S. citizens but too young to travel to Mexico without their parents, who themselves did not have visas. Lety would have liked to accompany her own U.S. citizen children to the United States, but she was denied a visa when she applied because of her prior record of unlawful entry. Most of the people we spoke with believed that they would be denied a visa for that reason. They pointed out that their initial entry was undocumented precisely because no law provided the means for them to immigrate legally in the first place.

Those who were given deportation orders with a specific bar on reentry (a period of time in which they could not apply for lawful reentry) were waiting for the time to pass, as we described in chapter 3. Mario, whose children were in the United States, explained why he had no plan to return to the United States: "Because on my deportation they gave me ten years of punishment. . . . That doesn't mean I can't return . . . but the problem is that if they find me there again, well, I will be sentenced again, and the time will go up. Those ten years mean that you . . . can arrange your papers once you complete the ten years."

Rubén, whose experience of return after deportation as a disabled person we described in chapter 4, was separated from his children and grandchildren in California. When we asked him if he hoped or planned to return, he paused for a long time before answering. Then he said:

> I hope in the future there will be an opportunity to return, because here I don't feel like myself. I don't like it. . . . But you have to request a pardon. And it's a long process. Your family has to support you, I don't know how to explain it, I don't know very much about it. The migration laws are very strict, very different from the laws of other subjects. Like criminal law, they might see things one way, but migration law is stricter.

As Rubén, Mario, Lety, and Yazmín saw it, their basic desire to be with their family members, to feel like themselves as members of a family, was not legally attainable. U.S. immigration law was too strict and complicated and, after separating them from family and home, provided no means for legal reunion.

A few people we spoke to expressed confidence and security in their experience of separation from family. These were migrants who had been separated from other adult family members (parents or adult children) and who felt that they or their family members could travel if they wanted to. Reynaldo, whose father remained in the United States with a new wife and children, was the only person we spoke with who told us that he felt that he could obtain a visa if he wanted one; however, he said, he did not want one. Rocío did not believe she could obtain a visa, but her adult daughter Ana, who resided in California with her U.S. citizen children, was a U.S. permanent resident and made frequent trips to Mexico to visit her mother. At this point in her life, Rocío felt no need to return to the United States.

Work

For many people, securing adequate work after returning to Mexico City was a major challenge, one made all the more frustrating by the loss of careers and opportunities in the United States. Many people commented on the generally poor quality of the Mexico City labor market, especially the low wages, which often felt like exploitation. Evaristo, who had worked in several successful family restaurants in the United States, described the experience of being offered low wages not only to cook but also to develop a menu for a high-end restaurant in a trendy neighborhood that attracted well-off locals and international tourists:

> I felt deceived. There is a place here . . . in Condesa, a restaurant, where they offered me work. They offered me 1,500 pesos [US$75] a week and one day off. They wanted my recipes. I am not a famous chef, but my recipes were a lot of work. I didn't create them overnight. You are not going to arrive to a place where a plate of pasta is 200, 300 pesos [US$10 to US$15] and you basically gift it to them so they can continue to exploit the same workers. I prefer not to work that way. . . . I am not going to loan my labor to a place where they are going to exploit me.

Evaristo's shock at the wages he was offered was shared by many returnees, especially compared with their experiences in the United States. There, they told us, working hard and long hours resulted in more pay, even in the same types of jobs, industries, and market segments. In addition to low pay, many people could only find informal work, in which they were employed without a formal contract, the protections of labor laws, and access to benefit systems. Indeed, scholars, policymakers, workers' organizations, and international development organizations have decried the scale of informality in the Mexican labor market; at around 57 percent of the workforce in 2018, Mexico had the highest share of informal workers among Organization for

Economic Cooperation and Development (OECD) countries.[9] Recent interventions have slowly begun to encourage formalization, but the majority of jobs in the Mexican labor market continue to lack labor protections. Improving minimum wages in Mexico City and formalizing work, while not interventions targeted at returnees, would certainly benefit them.

Many people we interviewed felt that the skills they developed in the United States were wasted in Mexico, and they advocated policies to enhance skill matching, job creation, and entrepreneurship. Manuel described the range of returnees' skills that he didn't see valued in Mexico:

> We build our own apartments, our own houses, our own gardens, do our own cleaning, that is, anything is possible. So it's a different way, and what's left is to simply improve on our own skills. . . . That's what I would like, for them to give us the opportunity to exploit our own knowledge and skills. That these skills not be lost, but used, and used for our benefit. That they take advantage of our English. . . . It is a win-win—you help me, I help you, we all win.

Manuel framed assistance with skill transfer as a potential win-win for migrants, employers, the government, and the economy. Such assistance programs could connect returnees with employers who require English language skills, not just in call centers but also in businesses that cater to English-speaking tourists, engage in cross-national manufacturing, and beyond. They could also help people implement innovative new construction methods or adapt their trade skills to the particularities of the Mexico City construction industry. At the heart of these suggestions is the recognition that returnees have developed unique skills that could benefit the Mexican economy.

Although the Mexican government implemented the strategy Repatriados Trabajando (Deportees Working) in 2010, studies have shown the very limited impact of these programs in helping returnees find good work.[10] Although Repatriados Trabajando is a federal program, support varies by state, with typical programs including orientation to the labor market and modest monetary job search payments. Returnees implement different strategies for accessing this local support. For instance, Humberto confessed to us that he lied about his address to obtain a temporary job provided by the Mexico City government to work in a booth located in a central metro station providing returnees with information about government resettlement services. Although he lived in a municipality of the State of Mexico in the metropolitan area, he provided proof of residence in one of the alcaldías of Mexico City to access the program. "I really liked it," he told us, "because there were people who would get interested in the projects and programs, and different type of aid provided by the government, and I would give them the info and they would enroll."

Coping with a New Life

Many returnees shared with us that they struggled with mental health problems upon return to Mexico. Some people also told us that they had developed substance abuse problems from using alcohol or painkillers to cope with and manage their distress. Others had made suicide attempts.

Manuel told us that returnees need psychological support that is sensitive to their unique needs. His experience is illustrative. Manuel struggled to adjust to life in Mexico after his deportation ten years ago. He perceived the forced return as a loss of life, as though someone close to him had died, except that it was his own life and the future he had imagined for himself. One of his recommendations was to provide returnees with psychological support to help those suffering from the loss of their life as an immigrant:

> A lot of therapy is needed. Psychologists focusing on us. It's not easy to leave a culture, a whole life there. I mean, before leaving [Mexico], you put your life in a suitcase and go to try your luck. You make a life there [in the United States] that you like, and then it is lost. All that is in your mind. People believe they can have those resources again, that life. And the idea would be to guide them with the idea that it is possible, but to detach from there. That they focus for a while on here [Mexico], so that later they can get again what they had there, but in their own country.

Adjustment to life in Mexico for Manuel involved the work of detaching from the idea that his future life was in the United States. He argued for the need to employ mental health professionals who understand and can help return migrants cope with the loss of life and the identity reconciliation that accompanies it.

Although Olivia had received the kind of therapy that Manuel alluded to—that is, through a program created to serve return migrants—the quality of the services left her questioning whether it was worth it. Olivia told us that it was important for mental health professionals to also have training in the kinds of social and legal issues that return migrants regularly face, such as family separation:

> I was in psychological therapy for a long time. These were therapies that you initially get for free because you are deported or returned. But the people who give you the therapies are not really sensitized or really interested in helping you. They say, "If you like the therapy, come back with me," and you have to start paying. I feel like they're not that interested in the topic and they just want to find a solution for you. They tell you, "Oh, you're already here, stay here and live your life," and they don't help me to fight with the fact that my family is elsewhere. But right now, from the therapy I took, it didn't really help me. I think it left me worse.

Even with therapy, readjusting to life in Mexico was difficult for Olivia because her family was left behind in the United States, a problem for which there was no easy solution. Again grief is a relevant concept here: although Olivia's children were alive, living with their father in the United States, she grieved their absence from her daily life. Olivia also pointed out that the program appeared to be a business-building technique for therapists who tried to transform program participants into regular paying clients.

Olivia also explained that returnees' emotional pain is often accompanied by physical pain, especially for those who spent time in detention. As we discussed in chapter 4, many migrants return to Mexico with physical health problems or disabilities. Olivia's kidney problems became much worse during her time in detention. Similarly, while Matías already suffered from knee problems when he was detained, he seriously injured his knee when he fell off his bunk bed in the detention center. He told us about accessing health care while in detention:

> When I fell, I couldn't walk. . . . A man from another prison arrived who was already on his way to Mexico, and I remember the man told me, "You know, I am going to treat you," and he rubs my knee and straightens it . . . and he tells me: "Look, with this you are going to stay [injured] . . .

you are very hurt, you need to take care of this." So I went to see a doctor there on the inside of . . . you can say that it is migration, the prison, and . . . well, the doctor was asleep, he said, "No, you don't have anything wrong." I think he was drunk. . . . So they gave me some crutches and later a wheelchair where the tubes were falling apart, really old. It was horrible treatment. It was impressive how bad it was.

Matías's deportation and return to Mexico were traumatic, and he fell into a deep depression. He told us that in the first few weeks after returning to Mexico, he and his mother fought frequently as they tried to adjust to living together after all of their adult lives apart. He told us about the moment when he started to adjust:

> All of that was depressing me, all of that was like, surrounding me. I remember that one time we [my mother and I] argued and I left walking, and . . . there arrived a time that there in my mind, I didn't think, it was like, all dark. That is to say, I didn't try anything, but I had already decided to do it [suicide], no? So, I remember, my phone rang, and like that, I reacted, no? It was like light again, and it was her [his ex-partner], her, my children were calling me. And in that moment, I understood. I told myself, "Well, if I can't return [to the United States], at least I want for my kids to have a place to sleep when they visit me here."

The phone call from Matías's children motivated him to take action. He talked to a lawyer who guided him to SEDEREC, which gave him a small grant [US$2,000], which he used to fund an operation on his knees. He was now able to walk normally again.

For deported and return migrants like Manuel, Matías, and Olivia, the issues of mental health, physical health, family separation, and adjustment in Mexico were deeply intertwined. Their needs extended across multiple domains, suggesting a role for social workers trained in the services available for return migrants, including legal services, financial aid, mental health services, and physical health services.

Many people we interviewed expressed gratitude to us for listening to their stories, and some who had not previously shared their experiences of returning from the United States with others told us they were relieved to finally have an opportunity to do so. However, we were keenly aware that we are not trained as psychologists or social workers, and that we could not directly provide them with the type of support they needed. Instead, we provided information about resources they might access; however, in the context of their experiences, and as Manuel and Olivia instructed us, we were aware that these resources were often woefully inadequate.

Matías was ultimately able to access in Mexico the health care that he was denied in the U.S. detention center. Others, like Juan, had private health insurance through their employment in the United States, but in Mexico they had to depend on Seguro Popular, the public health insurance program that was terminated in 2020 by President Andrés Manuel López Obrador. Juan shared the experience of many Mexican families who have their medical needs attended to through the private, low-quality health care provided, for example, by Farmacias Similares (or Farmacias del Ahorro), pharmacies that offer low-cost, walk-in medical consultations. Others, like Rubén and Eduardo, whose experiences navigating the city in wheelchairs we described in chapter 4, reflected positively on U.S. laws and infrastructure that enable the mobility of disabled people. Undoubtedly, improving health care access and quality and making the streets of Mexico City more accessible—identified by returnees as important needs—would benefit not only returnees but the general population in Mexico City and beyond.

Conclusion

Returnees' reflections on how their lives could be improved reflect a diversity of experiences, highlighting the reality that no one policy can address everyone's needs. They also speak to how important it is to involve community members who are not returnees to facilitate the understanding of the migrant experience—in other words, to make visible the invisible, but in a way that avoids generalizing and stigma. Seeking the participation of the whole community resonates with what other scholars have found before: the need to involve not only return migrants but also those who stayed behind, community leaders, and service providers in policies that are comprehensive, inclusive, and protective of the needs of returnees and nonmigrants alike.[11] It is organizations like Otros Dreams en Acción, Deportados Unidos en la Lucha, Comunidad en Retorno, and others that are doing this work daily. They are working alongside—and as organized representatives and actors—on behalf of the migrant, deported, returned, and Dreamer communities at the forefront of discussions about policy reform, in both Mexico and the United States.

CHAPTER EIGHT

CONCLUSION

When we caught up with him in 2021, we learned that Evaristo had stopped driving an Uber because his health had been compromised by sitting for long periods. No doubt demand for Uber drivers also declined during the Covid-19 pandemic. The pandemic affected Evaristo in other ways as well. Although he had problems obtaining his medication as the Mexican health and pharmaceutical sectors focused on Covid-19, he still managed to drive around the city to visit ill people in hospitals, bringing them rosaries provided by his local church. He found it fulfilling to be useful to others during the pandemic and told us that he was not afraid to move around the city because God protected him from the coronavirus.

Many things had changed since we carried out fieldwork in 2019. Back then, no one knew that a pandemic would soon impact daily life worldwide. When the pandemic hit, we put aside our plans to continue interviews in 2020 and devoted ourselves instead to analyzing the data we had. We continued our virtual, tri-national weekly meetings, which had brought us in front of screens well before our working lives were transformed by the health crisis. In these discussions, we often wondered how the pandemic had impacted the lives of those who had shared their stories with us the year before.

We checked in with Yazmín and found that she was coping. She remained devoted to her church and was comforted by online sermons posted on Facebook. In 2019, Yazmín had told us that one of her younger daughters was considering moving back to Mexico, but in 2021 the daughter was still in New Jersey. In other news, Yazmín's husband had moved across the United States for a job in California.

https://doi.org/10.7758/kokl2957.2725

Osmundo kept us updated on his life and business. His family took advantage of online platforms to sell their art abroad after the weekend markets were closed by the pandemic. Sales were slow, but online markets allowed them to continue working. They broadened their portfolio to include jewelry, clothes, and even face masks. We learned that Osmundo applied for and was denied a U.S. tourist visa, which he had hoped to use to participate in art fairs in the United States and accompany his children on trips to their birth country.

Paolo and Rocío were two of the millions of people indirectly affected by the tragic accident on the evening of May 3, 2021, when the bridge that supported the Line 12 metro collapsed between the stations of Tezonco and Olivos, killing as many as twenty-six people and wounding more than one hundred. Line 12 of the metro is twenty-five kilometers (fifteen miles) long and connects the alcaldías Benito Juárez, Iztapalapa, and Tláhuac, in the central and southeastern parts of Mexico City, to the rest of the metropolitan area. Olivos is the metro station closest to Paolo's barbershop. We had ridden the Line 12 metro there and descended the station's long escalators to meet him and Rocío for interviews in 2019. Many people had alerted authorities that the bridge was damaged in the earthquake of September 19, 2017, but the authorities did not follow up. On January 30, 2024, the renovated and repaired stations of Line 12 finally reopened.

We lost touch with Mario and Olivia. We do not know whether they remain separated from their families in the United States and wonder if Mario continues to work in janitorial services and what progress Olivia has made toward owning her own home.

The pandemic brought renewed attention to the Mexico-U.S. border. New U.S. policies, such as the Migrant Protection Protocols and Title 42, introduced draconian restrictions on the entry of people seeking asylum in the United States, policies that have since been lifted. The U.S. Customs and Border Protection agency recorded more encounters at the Mexico-U.S. border in 2023 than in any prior year, but that year was also notable because Mexicans accounted for a historically small share—only 37 percent.[1] Mexico's demographic and economic transitions of the last eighty years make it unlikely that levels of emigration will ever again reach those seen in the 1990s and early 2000s. It is increasingly clear that Mexico has transitioned from being a country of emigration to a country of transit migration—a way station for people seeking refuge in the United States from violence and political crises in their homes south of Mexico's southern border. Mexico may have also become a site of immigration, or at least forced displacement, owing to the impossibility of entry to the United States.[2]

Some things have not changed since we carried out our fieldwork. The Policy Trap remains in effect. The Biden administration did not make headway on immigration reform, and the 2024 presidential election had Democratic Party leaders making concessions to Republicans on border policies. The border remains a site of political maneuvering and fearmongering. Trump's rhetoric on immigration on the 2023–2024 presidential campaign trail did not change much from 2015–2016; if anything, it intensified. In some campaign speeches, Trump said that he would introduce more restrictive and aggressive policies of immigration law enforcement if elected president in November 2024. He also said that he would deport almost eleven million migrants from all over the world currently living in the United States with undocumented status. In November 2024, Trump was elected and remained committed to a policy of mass deportations.

On June 2, 2024, Mexico elected Claudia Sheinbaum as president, the first woman and first Jewish person to serve as a president or prime minister in North America. Mexicans may vote from abroad, but only 187,000 Mexican adults living outside the country (out of around ten million) registered to participate in the 2024 election, even though both Sheinbaum and Xóchitl Galvez visited the United States during their campaigns to attract the migrant vote. Migration was discussed in the presidential debates and campaigns mostly as it related to transit migration and immigration control. Issues around emigration or return were seldom discussed, and the role of returnees in politics was not discussed at all.

Why Return Migration?

Return migration has marked the shifting tides of Mexico-U.S. migration and led to profound changes in the binational population of Mexican immigrants and their children in North America. From the middle of the twentieth century through the first decade of the twenty-first, the population of Mexican immigrants living in the United States grew steadily, peaking at 12.8 million in 2007.[3] This massive immigration implied that, by 2007, one out of every ten Mexican-born people resided in the United States.[4] But since 2007, more people have left the United States for Mexico than have entered the United States from Mexico.[5] The population of Mexican immigrants in the United States has declined by two million.[6] At this moment, the pressing questions regarding Mexico-U.S. migration are not why people immigrate to the United States and how they do after immigration, but why immigrants leave and how they do after returning to their home country. Our book answers these questions.

We can offer only a general answer to why immigrants leave based on the sample of thirty-four return migrants to Mexico City we interviewed in 2019. Their experiences are not representative of all returnees to Mexico, and we do not have a non-returnee comparison group. Other data and methods are needed to provide a full answer to this question, and some scholars have already begun to meet this need.[7] In our data, the U.S. immigration regime of mass deportations, particularly during the first six years of Obama's presidency, played an important role. Half of the people we spoke to had been deported, all after long periods of residence in the United States. These sixteen people made up a small share of the 1.8 million Mexican nationals who were deported during the Obama presidency.[8] Two people we spoke to had migrated to accompany a deported family member, which is de facto deportation. The other people we spoke to had returned for a variety of reasons, including family concerns, economic considerations, and health crises. Some returned with little plan or intention. Among the nondeported people who returned after some consideration, all did so having determined that their life would be better upon return to Mexico, whether because work opportunities had dried up in the United States during the Great Recession or because of a strong desire to reunify with family left behind in Mexico.

The question of why people returned to Mexico raises the importance of earlier migrations—especially emigration from Mexico and experiences of immigration in the United States—that set the stage for a later return. Our findings draw attention to the connections between individuals' migrations as well as connections across lives linked by family, as discussed in chapter 5. In analyzing migration histories linked over time and across family ties, conceptual distinctions between migrations—such as whether a migrant is an "economic" or a "family" migrant—become blurry. Many people we interviewed were one or the other at different times in their lives: an economic migrant, for instance, later migrated for family or vice versa. The circumstances leading to a first migration often created the conditions for the next, such as when the economic circumstances motivating migration originated in family transitions, or family transitions evolved from economic migrations.

As economic and family migrations become blurred within the life histories of return migrants in Mexico City, so do the categories of "voluntary" versus "forced" migration. None of the people we interviewed qualified for legal refugee status based on the United Nations High Commissioner for Refugees (UNHCR) definition, but many were forced to migrate to Mexico. They were forced by the U.S. state, which often deported them in spite of their long histories in, connections to, and families left behind in the United States, as we described in Olivia's and Mario's stories in chapter 3. Some were forced to return when they faced the deportation of a family member and had no option to remain together in the United States without the threat of further legal consequences, as happened to Lety, whose story we told in chapter 5. Others were forced to emigrate: the U.S.-born children of deported parents or of return migrants were not themselves returnees when they arrived in a place they had never been before.

One final category of distinction becomes blurry in our analysis—the geographical distinctions commonly drawn to study Mexican migration. Although we focused on return migrants in urban Mexico City, these return migrants had drawn on rural and Traditional Region networks to emigrate abroad, like Osmundo, whose step migration we described in chapter 2. His emigration and that of other Mexico City residents became possible because networks based in rural places and states in the Traditional Region spread beyond the local and operated across the country through internal migration. Urban emigration and return migration cannot be understood without understanding rural migration processes.

The "Integration" of Return Migrants

Although our study allowed us to reflect on why people emigrate or return, our focus was on the experience after return. Immigrant integration theories focus on what happens after people immigrate. In other words, how do immigrants fare at the destination across different dimensions, including economically, socially, and politically? Integration is thought to unfold in stages: from short-term adaptation and acculturation to assimilation—long-term structural integration into dominant social institutions and practices over time and across generations.[9] In some senses, none of these processes apply to returnees; in others, all apply, albeit in messier or more complex ways.

As we relayed in chapters 4 to 7, data from our interviews complicate traditional accounts of adaptation, acculturation, assimilation, incorporation, and integration because traditional accounts do not consider return. Migrants who return from the United States to Mexico "integrate" as Mexican nationals with full rights in their birth country. If they are over eighteen, as soon as they obtain a voting identification they can vote. Political integration: check. Recent research on economic integration has shown that returnee salaries are as low as those of their Mexican nonmigrant counterparts.[10] Economic integration, if integration is wage equality: check. Unless they migrated to the United States as very young children, Spanish proficiency upon return is usually not an issue. Linguistic integration: check. What does adaptation look like for those who are already structurally integrated on these dimensions, or who become so upon arrival?

For some returnees, going to Mexico City is a return home to families who reunite to celebrate goals furthered through migration. But for many others, home is in the United States; now that they are back in Mexico, their families are far away. For some returnees, like Olivia, integrating into the city will never feel complete because the city is no longer their home: their compass points north. Others navigate the city with a compass that points both north and south; for many of them, life unfolds on both sides of the border, *aquí y allá* (here and there), in the streets of both Mexico City and the United States, as it did for Osmundo. Studies of transnationalism have long centered these issues.[11] But what we encounter here is transnationalism with a twist: for migrants in Mexico, integrating in Mexico is also related to their prior integration and their family's integration in the United States.

A unique integration experience of the return migrants we studied was their strong sense of relief upon returning to Mexico after a period of time with noncitizen status in the United States during the Policy Trap. As we discussed in chapter 3, return migrants no longer lived with the threat of immigration enforcement; they were also free of the sense of disempowerment and the focus on work and money that pervaded their experience as noncitizen immigrants in the United States.

While the sense of relief from various systems of U.S. surveillance and control was pervasive among returnees who had settled in Mexico City, this did not necessarily translate into feeling settled, comfortable, or successful upon return. Our participants experienced return migration to Mexico City after a period of residence in noncitizen status in the United States during the Policy Trap as disorienting and characterized by a sense of loss that is best summarized as "norteado," the word that Evaristo used to describe his fellow return migrants.

As we explained in the first pages of the book, the Spanish word *norteado* means "disoriented" or "lost," which captures the experience of returning to a global city after a long period away. In the first place, it is disorienting to return to the city because the city itself is a disorienting place: rapidly evolving, Mexico City is dynamic, unequal, and massive. The return migrants we interviewed disappeared into the city's vast and diverse landscape. The word "norteado" also captures the experience of being disoriented by migration to *el norte* (the north), a Mexican colloquialism for the United States. The return migrants we interviewed had been particularly affected by the Policy Trap: after U.S. immigration laws and policies had made it difficult for them to live in the United States in noncitizen immigrant status, upon their return to Mexico, the Policy Trap also prevented their safe or legal remigration to the United States. Being norteado describes returnees' struggle to reintegrate upon return to Mexico City, that is, to be secure and settled back in Mexico. The Policy Trap, by reinforcing political rhetoric and media that criminalize migrants, plays a significant role in fostering the stigmatization of and discrimination against return migrants in Mexico City.

What is striking is the similarity between the experiences of return migrants in Mexico City and migrants in the United States, in spite of their different migrant trajectories. The return migrants we interviewed were trapped in Mexico, apart from the United States, the same way that undocumented immigrants are trapped in the United States, apart from Mexico. An unknown but presumably large number of families are forced apart in North America by the U.S. Policy Trap. The sociologist Hein de Haas defines human mobility as the "capability (freedom) to choose where to live—including the option to stay—rather than the act of moving itself."[12] The migrants we studied had not all chosen to remain in Mexico City; some aspired to remigrate to the United States, but the Policy Trap undermined their ability to do so.

Although we found that our thirty-four interviewees in Mexico City were deterred from reentering the United States by the costs and risks imposed by the Policy Trap, this is not to say that U.S. policies have entirely succeeded in their intent to control undocumented migration and prevent all unlawful reentry to the United States. We interviewed thirty-four people who had settled in Mexico City, far from the U.S. border. These thirty-four people did not represent the population of return migrants or deported people from the United States to Mexico (or other countries). The many who headed to other destinations, including back into the United States, were not available for recruitment into our sample.

Return migrants across Mexico and in other countries may be norteado by the experience of forced separation from their former lives in the United States. In our study of return migration from the United States to Mexico City, return migrants found themselves integrating back into the place they came from but oriented toward the home that many of them had been forced to leave behind. For many of our respondents, the particular environment of Mexico City heightened their sense of being norteado, as we described in chapter 4. The conditions of the city—its size and dynamism, violence and insecurity, economic vitality and inequality, political barriers and opportunities—made it hard for them to reorient to life in Mexico as a return migrant. These return migrants to Mexico City found themselves disoriented upon arrival as they discovered a city that had expanded and changed since they last lived there. Not only did they need to find housing, schools, and jobs, but some had to learn how to navigate the city after suffering disabling accidents or health crises in the United States that predated or precipitated their return. Learning to navigate the city also involved navigating new political environments, violent and insecure neighborhoods, and institutions marred by corruption. Moreover, these disorienting experiences occurred in a context where the return migration experience went unnoticed in the social environment.

Some of the return migrants we spoke to formed or joined organizations to create the kinds of support that family or the state should typically provide but that were absent for them, such as housing, work, legal assistance, and small loans. In doing the work of activism, return migrants and deported people in the city make themselves known to other actors in civil society and politics, the media, and the public. They draw on the political opportunities of Mexico's capital city to bring attention and resources to return migrants, as well as to argue for substantive change in U.S. and Mexican policies toward immigrants, deported people, return migrants, and the children of migrants.

These conditions—separation from their former lives and disorientation in their new lives—were not conducive to building financial resources or securing desired employment. In Mexico City, the return migrants we interviewed struggled to secure preferred or adequate work and align their migration experiences with their education and work goals. Most of them described their experience in the United States as a time of growth in education, skills, earnings, and assets. Although return migration can fuel local development in some contexts and enable upward mobility for some returnees, the return migrant experiences we have shared in this book paint a less optimistic picture. Rather than experiencing return migration as an engine of local change and individual achievement, unplanned return, precarity in the labor market, and the lack of recognition of their skills and work experience undermined the economic well-being of many of our interviewees. Nevertheless, they contributed to the Mexico City economy by pulling resources together creatively and making use of social networks.

The experience of being norteado after return migration to Mexico City from the United States during the Policy Trap may be familiar to others around the globe whose experience as return migrants is invisible in everyday life. Ideally, the lives of future returnees will unfold with a sense of freedom and security in their birth country, and they will be able to incorporate their migration experiences productively into their lives and communities and live truly binational lives. Today an estimated 10.2 million Mexican-born immigrants live in the United States.[13] An estimated 5.0 million Mexicans live in the United States with undocumented immigrant status, and several million people are the U.S.-born children of undocumented parents.[14] The foreign-born are potential future returnees. If all were to move to Mexico suddenly, regardless of where they arrive, they would be visible in Mexico, and their absence would be felt in the United States. It is highly unlikely that this will happen, but millions of lives could go through similar processes as the ones we have documented here.

Families and Children

U.S.-born children of returnees living in Mexico add a layer of complexity to the discussion of integration, as they are immigrants in their parental homeland.[15] We interviewed the parents and siblings of several U.S.-born children in Mexico, a population estimated to be over half a million.[16] These U.S.-born immigrants in Mexico are not returnees themselves; when they accompany their parents to Mexico, they arrive there for the first time. In the U.S. scholarly literature, children of immigrants are characterized as second-generation migrants and are expected to integrate more easily than their parents. Although foreign-born children of return migrants can be considered first-generation immigrants in Mexico, their generation status is unclear. As Zúñiga and Giorguli-Saucedo have written, the U.S.-born in Mexico are the 0.5 generation, the generational counterpart to the 1.5 generation in the United States, who are Mexican-born in the United States.[17] Such binational citizens could successfully integrate in Mexico or the United States, or even in both.

Some of the 0.5 generation are in Mexico because their parent was deported.[18] In the case of de facto deportation, the U.S. government forced children to emigrate out of the United States if they were to remain with their deported parent. U.S.-born children's status as U.S. citizens gives them the right to travel to and live in the United States, travel to other countries on a U.S. passport, work and obtain social services in the United States, vote and run in U.S. elections, and sponsor family members for immigration. U.S. citizenship rights are not easily acted upon by a person who lives in Mexico, as these children do because their parents are prevented from lawfully entering and residing with their children in the United States. U.S.-born children who grow up in Mexico do so without the socialization that childhood in the United States provides and without learning English as a child, going to U.S. schools, or benefiting from U.S. social programs designed to protect and foster the development of children. We do not mean to imply that childhood in the United States is superior to childhood in Mexico—many families might choose to raise their children in Mexico instead of in the United States for very good reasons. But de facto deportation is not the outcome of choice. It is the outcome of forced migration in a policy context that has eliminated the consideration of children's best interests from the deportation proceedings of their parents.

Many of the people we interviewed in Mexico City were separated from 1.5-generation children who resided in the United States with DACA status. These young adults migrated with their parents as children and lived and grew up in the United States without immigration documents. The 2012 DACA program provided them with protection from deportation and work authorization, but DACA did not guarantee them the right to travel internationally to visit their parents. Moreover, their status was subject to executive discretion and judicial proceedings. Parents in Mexico who cannot reenter the United States legally or safely are separated from their DACA recipient children in the United States by the Policy Trap.

We also interviewed some return migrants who migrated to the United States as children and returned to Mexico as adolescents or adults, people like Julio, Rubén, and Reynaldo. These former 1.5-generation migrants were back in Mexico but had the unique experience of growing up in the United States and being educated in U.S. schools. They were "Dreamers" in Mexico. English language skills gave those who were young and healthy certain advantages in the Mexican labor market. But many of these return migrants felt alienated from the United States. Most of them could not return legally, and being formally excluded from their childhood home undermined their affection for it.

Separated families and de facto deportation are not unique to return migrants in Mexico City—or to return migrants in Mexico, for that matter. A much broader group of migrants and their families have been affected by the Policy Trap.[19] Our study has contributed to a growing body of research that documents the long arm of U.S. immigration policy, which extends beyond the U.S. border to affect migrants and their families after deportation or return.[20] It will be important to study what happens to these families in the future, as bars on legal reentry expire and U.S.-born children in Mexico age into adulthood. In the United States, the future of DACA remains in the hands of the judicial system and future presidential administrations.

Our thirty-four interviewees' memories of returning to Mexico were as vivid and deep as their memories of crossing the border into the

United States. We would argue that returnees will always be returnees. The person we interviewed who spent the least amount of time in the United States, Rodrigo, lived for six months in San José, California, in 1999, and returned to Mexico City with the idea of emigrating again with his wife and young son. But as events unfolded, he ended up staying in Mexico. He told us, "I don't want to go there [to the United States]. I want to be close to my family." Staying in Mexico was a decision he had to make and remake, as other family members and friends who remained in the United States suggested that he remigrate, offered him support in migrating, and told him about their lives in the United States. Even now, he had daily communication with other returnees in Mexico City. The person we interviewed who spent the most time in the United States, Rubén, lived in California for fifty-one years, having moved there as a small boy. Although Rodrigo's and Rubén's migration experiences differed dramatically, they shared the common experience of being a returnee. Their experiences are equally invisible in Mexico City, but emigration was meaningful in both their lives. Both Rodrigo and Rubén had to redefine life upon return, and even as they reoriented their compasses in different ways, both carried with them the experience they had in the United States.

For the return migrants in our study, the end of the Great Mexican Migration is difficult to fathom, as their recent migrations to the United States and the connections they still had there weighed powerfully in their personal histories, current lives, and imagined futures. Their migrant identities—as former U.S. immigrants, as returnees, as deported people, as Dreamers, and as Americans—were indelibly a part of them, however invisible to others. Those migrant identities mixed with their paisano, chilango, Mexican, and Tenochca identities as they redefined themselves as parents, children, grandparents, and partners and carved out their lives on the streets and in the neighborhoods of Mexico City.

METHODOLOGICAL APPENDIX

This methodological appendix describes our research process, including our team approach, the values and goals that directed our work, our positions within Mexican and U.S. societies, and how each of these shaped the project.

Our Team

We adopted a team approach to data collection and analysis that enabled members to draw from their unique academic training and lived experience, challenge each other's understandings of migration and return, and mirror some aspects of the binational and cross-border lives of the people we interviewed. Our decision to collectively discuss the ethics and practice of our research at each stage of the research process required a commitment to frequent, and at times lengthy, meetings and conversations with the entire team. In the end, this approach enabled us to recruit and build rapport with return migrants, carry out various qualitative methodologies and consider their relationship to quantitative research in the social sciences, incorporate unique approaches to research ethics, engage with the community, and gain a richer understanding of language and meaning in translation.

Considering the central goal of our research—to understand return migration from the United States to Mexico City during the Policy Trap period—the diverse experiences of our team of seven researchers were a tremendous asset to the research. Our team included the three authors of this book: Claudia Masferrer, who was born in Mexico City

https://doi.org/10.7758/kokl2957.9958

to Peruvian and Argentinian parents, studied in Mexico, the United States, and Canada, and now lives and works in Mexico City; Erin Hamilton, who was born in Greece to U.S. foreign service officers, spent most of her elementary and middle school years in Latin America, and now lives and works in the United States; and Nicole Denier, a U.S.-born immigrant in Canada who grew up around Washington, D.C. Gabriela Pinillos, who participated in the project during a postdoctoral fellowship at El Colegio de Mexico, is a Colombian immigrant to Mexico who completed a PhD in sociology at El Colegio de la Frontera Norte in Tijuana. The team also hired three research assistants on the project: Francisco Flores Peña, Anilú "Ani" Tomas, and Agnieszka Wieczorek. Francisco and Ani were born and raised in Mexico City and worked with Claudia on their undergraduate theses on migration at the Escuela Nacional de Antropología e Historia (ENAH, National School of Anthropology and History). Agnieszka was a PhD student in sociology at the University of Illinois–Chicago; originally from Poland, she studied and lived for many years in Mexico City.

In addition to our different migration experiences, we brought complementary academic backgrounds and language skills to the team. At the time of the study, we were all academic researchers with affiliations at well-resourced universities in Mexico, the United States, and Canada. We varied in our career stages, from college students to professors, and we brought distinct disciplinary training to the team, from anthropology, sociology, and demography. Because the three authors of this book were trained primarily as social demographers, we relied on our anthropological and sociologically trained collaborators for their expertise in qualitative methods. We also drew heavily on published guides to qualitative research.[1]

Four of us spoke Spanish as a first language, two spoke English as a first language, and one spoke Polish as a first language. Three team members grew up in Mexico City, learned Spanish as a first language, and were familiar with slang and colloquialisms specific to the city. The rest of the team had accents that identified them as foreigners in the country and the city. Those of us who spoke Spanish as a second language learned the language in school or by living in Spanish-speaking countries or households with native Spanish speakers. We conducted our team meetings primarily in Spanish.

As a team, we frequently brought our unique backgrounds as immigrants and scholars of migration to the conversation. We sought to articulate differences in perspectives within the team owing to these backgrounds—for example, what someone who grew up in Mexico City knows, what someone who spent time in the United States as an immigrant knows, or what someone who spoke only halting English or Spanish at one point in their life knows. Our discussions of the project, as filtered through our unique perspectives, deepened our understanding of the topic of our research.

We were acutely aware of our legal privilege as residents of and travelers in Mexico, the United States, and Canada. As far as we discussed, all of us had citizenship or legal status in our countries of residence, and those of us who had traveled internationally had visas to do so. None of us had experienced deportation, but many of us had family members or people close to us who had experienced involuntary or undocumented migrations. We recognize that our legal privilege was granted by the same state policies and laws that exclude and harm the people we interviewed. We therefore approached the field with humility and respect for the return migrant's experiences and knowledge and with the desire to give back in return for the time and energy that we asked of our respondents. We fostered a sense of curiosity about and empathy for their experiences, seeking to connect with them and to learn from what they shared with us.

It was less explicit how other facets of our backgrounds and identities shaped the research. In the United States, discussions of positionality in the field revolve around the power embedded in gender, class, and race, which can define insider and outsider status.[2] We sought to recognize the filters that our positionalities brought to the research and how they shaped what we could see and understand about our respondents and their lives. We also sought to be aware of the power and privilege bestowed on us by our backgrounds and identities vis-à-vis our respondents and to mitigate the possibility of replicating power dynamics within the field. This involved ongoing reflection and discussion within the team, as well as writing and sharing reflection memos. We sought to maintain a strict adherence to research ethics based on respect for the dignity and humanity of our respondents, as well as protecting the confidentiality of our data that sometimes involved changes to identifiable characteristics of respondents.

An interesting point of discussion within the team involved race and racial positionality. In the U.S. context, race is a master status that structures a system of power with relatively well-defined categories. According to U.S. racial categories, our team members were White and/or Latina/o/x/e or Hispanic. None of these racial-ethnic categories transfers exactly to the Mexican context. In Mexico, whiteness proxies for class status and foreignness, and neither Latino/a/x/e nor Hispanic are categories commonly used. In Mexico, scholars understand miscegenation, or *mestizaje,* as a national historical project to create a unifying national identity based on cultural mixing.[3] Today there is an ongoing debate among scholars, activists, and others about whether and how indigeneity, skin color, and ancestry are used to differentiate people in Mexico, but the boundaries between the three major Mexican "race" categories of Indigenous, mestizo, and Afro-descendant are blurry for much of the population.[4] In the context of our multinational team, we discussed these differences, but because we could not rely on a common understanding of their meaning or implications, we ultimately could not agree on how race affected us, our respondents, or the research process. Erin and Nicole are White in the United States and Mexico, but Claudia is unsure whether to select Latino, Hispanic, or mixed race in the United States, given the Chinese, Jewish, and Catalan origins of her Latin American parents. Even if it was unclear how situational dynamics were influenced by unequal racial positions, we were nevertheless aware of class dynamics, particularly as students or faculty working in bilingual and tri-national professional settings.

Our team was also majority women, with just one man among us. Historically, migration and return between the two countries have been dominated by male migrants. The majority of our respondents were men. We were sensitive to ensuring that both team members and interviewees felt comfortable and tried to have mixed-gender research interview teams when possible.

All team members had access to the data and the opportunity to write and publish their work with the data, as well as to coauthor chapters of this book. Agnieszka Wieczorek coauthored chapter 6 of this book. As of early 2024, team members have prepared various publications with these data. In 2020, Gabriela Pinillos and Francisco Flores Peña published an article titled "Migración de retorno y separación familiar: Un estudio de caso en la Ciudad de México" ("Return Migration and Family

Separation: A Case Study of Mexico City") in *Coyuntura Demográfica*.[5] In 2023, Gabriela Pinillos published the article "Reencountering the State: Making the Processes of Return and Post-Return in Mexico City Visible and Invisible" in *Norteamérica*.[6] Claudia Masferrer, Erin Hamilton, and Nicole Denier have a book chapter titled "Adding Return Migration to the Equation: U.S. Immigration Policy and Migrant Families in Mexico" in an edited volume published by Springer and are preparing an article on de facto deportation with Angelita Repetto for the special issue "The Deportation System and Its Aftermath" of the *Russell Sage Foundation Journal of the Social Sciences.*

Writing this book was also a team effort among the three of us. Each of us took the lead on a first draft of different chapters, depending on our expertise and interests, and then we worked from these drafts to find a common voice. We met almost weekly for three years to develop ideas, edit chapters, revise, prepare a book proposal, prepare a first draft for submission, revise the manuscript to address reviewer comments, and refine our arguments. After these years of writing a book together, we understand what many authors explained to us: the process takes much longer than expected, but it is worth it.

Recruiting Participants

Our fieldwork took place in Mexico City mostly in the spring of 2019. In that period, we conducted thirty-two semistructured life history interviews with return migrants in the broader Mexico City metropolitan area. We conducted two additional interviews after this period ended. We had intended to collect more interviews in the spring and summer of 2020 but postponed owing to Covid-19. When the pandemic continued through the beginning of 2021, we decided to abandon additional data collection and focus our efforts on analysis. Appendix table A.1 provides the demographic, economic, and migration characteristics of our interviewees, who had diverse experiences of migration and return.

Because the return migrant population is dispersed throughout Mexico City and not identifiable through public information or in day-to-day interaction, we used a multipronged approach to find return migrants in the city.[7] We advertised the study via social media but did not receive reliable responses through this method. In addition, we do not recommend this method of recruitment for the type of fieldwork

Appendix Table A.1 *Characteristics of Research Sample: Thirty-Four Return (U.S.) Migrants Interviewed in Mexico City in 2019*

	Percent or Mean
Basic demographic characteristics	
Age (range: 24–67)	43
Gender: male/man	74
Education	
Less than high school	21
High school	53
More than high school	26
Partnership status	
Married/coupled	41
Previously married, single	29
Never married	29
Has children	76
Has U.S.-born children	44
Migration	
Migrated internally before U.S. migration	35
Had family in the United States prior to migration	79
Made undocumented crossing of Mexico-U.S. border	82
Deported from the United States	50
Year of first migration to the United States (range: 1968–2008)	1997
Total years in the United States (range: 0.3–50)	14.2
Total migrations to the United States (range: 1–3)	1.8
Year of last return to Mexico (range: 1999–2019)	2013
Years in Mexico since return	7.2

Source: Authors' calculations.

that we did, because advertisement often implies a financial incentive. We used geographic sampling, approaching possible interviewees in places where returnees are known to gather, including in the neighborhood of Santa María la Ribera, known by some as Little L.A., outside call centers that employ English speakers, and on university campuses with active groups of former-migrant students. We also employed our networks and asked respondents to refer us to friends and family members with U.S. migration experience.

We found several interviewees through contacts at organizations created to serve return migrants and deportees. However, we were concerned about relying on migrant organizations as a source of recruitment. These organizations use their members' stories as powerful tools in arguing for support of their pragmatic and political goals. A migrant's story can affect an audience in ways that data, statistics, and policy discussions cannot: stories create connection, empathy, and understanding in an audience, motivating change in ideas and attitudes in unique ways. As such, the migrant's story is a source of power. Well aware of the power of stories, migrant organizations can be wary of the academic researcher's distinct goals and interests in migrants' stories. We sought to respect this important boundary drawn by activists to protect and maintain owner-ship of the power of their own stories.

We were also already familiar with some of the most prominent activists' stories because we had watched and read news accounts that featured them and seen them speak at events in the city. Although we knew that an interview with these individuals would produce original data, we nevertheless wanted to interview migrants who had not told their stories before and whose stories had not been constructed with organizational goals in mind. We sought to tap into the iterative and semi-automatic (or subconscious) process of meaning-making that can unfold as a person seeks to make sense of their life events in conversa-tion with another person.[8]

As a result of recruiting through diverse means, the people we spoke to had varied connections to migrant-serving organizations, activist networks, and neighborhoods and workplaces where returned U.S. migrants concentrate in the city. Some people were tightly connected to these communities, while others had no connections to them at all. We also sought a balanced sample of people who were deported and those who returned for other reasons. Deportation is stigmatized in Mexico, and many people conceal their experience of deportation from strangers. We did not prescreen possible respondents for deportation experience but instead adjusted our sampling procedures along the way; if people chose to reveal why and how they returned, they did so after a discus-sion about privacy and institutional ethics policies and some establish-ment of trust with the research team.

Our recruitment was fundamentally shaped by our decision not to offer money in exchange for participation. In the United States, the use of monetary incentives for research participation is routine; it typ-ically involves small payments or gift cards and is seen as a symbolic but important way to thank and compensate someone for the time that they give to a study. In Mexico, a payment that might seem small or symbolic in the United States, such as $10, can be a substantial incentive. This kind of incentive may exert undue influence on a potential respondent, making them unwilling to decline to participate, even if they would prefer to protect their privacy or to not talk about their lives with a stranger. Undue influence violates the human rights of research subjects and is a key tenet of laws surrounding ethics in research with human subjects.

It is also the case that many Mexican researchers do not have (grant-funded) money to pay cash incentives to participants, as is common in the United States. By bringing this U.S. practice to Mexico, respondents may come to expect payment or else not participate, making research more difficult and expensive for Mexican researchers. We were sensitive to the concern that U.S. researchers could inadvertently displace Mexican researchers by introducing a practice of research payments for participation.

In fact, we encountered this in the field when we attempted to recruit in Santa María la Ribera, near the Monument to the Revolution (in the alcaldía Cuauhtémoc), which is located about two kilometers from the historic center of the city. A call center that employs English-language speakers, including many U.S. returnees, is located at the main plaza of the monument. We approached call center employees leaving their shifts to inquire about an interview, but U.S.-funded researchers had recently recruited at this same location and had paid for participation in their projects. People we approached at this site wanted to know how much we were paying and refused to participate when we told them there was no payment for participation. We later learned that this practice was controversial among returnees. Many returnees disapproved of fellow return migrants accepting payments for participating in studies or organizing and facilitating their participation without being clear about the monetary exchange involved.

We would have liked to pay respondents for several reasons. For one, we wanted to interview people like the call center workers who would not participate without payment. In their case, we did not see payment as a form of undue influence but rather as a rightful demand to be compensated for their time. We also wanted to pay the people we interviewed, who were willing to give their time and share their experiences with us without payment, often inviting us into their homes.

We built rapport and trust without financial incentives, but we know that the people we spoke to could have used the money. Our decision not to pay was based on respect for Mexican norms of field research and an intent to avoid disrupting those norms, but it was not an easy decision to make.

Although we still think that not paying participants was the best decision, we wondered often how different our fieldwork and subsequent analysis would have been if we had decided otherwise. Recruiting participants in a huge metropolis, aiming for diverse perspectives and returnees living off the radar of organizations, was hard. As we have argued in the book, one of the characteristics of returnees to Mexico City is their invisibility as returnees, and we certainly struggled to find them.

We received few outright refusals to participate, but some refusals were indirect. For example, we learned that the young daughter of an acquaintance had a U.S.-born friend at school, and we were told that one of the child's parents was deported. We tried to get a hold of the mother, without success; we suspect that she was not interested in participating in our study and preferred to ignore our inquiries rather than directly refuse them. This is, of course, normal when carrying fieldwork in any context, but we realized through the recruitment process that returnees do not often define themselves as returnees. Some returnees hide this status. When we asked people to refer us to others, we had to explain that we wanted to talk to people who had been in the United States for a while and then returned for different reasons. The concept of "return migrant"—*migrante de retorno*, or *migrante en retorno*—is often used by academics, policymakers, and activists, but the term is not widely used in everyday life in Mexico City. This lack of presence in everyday vocabulary reflects the invisibility of returnees.

Asking about Migration

We conducted semistructured interviews to gain insight into the complexities of people's migrations and how they related to broader policy, economic, and social contexts. Semistructured interviews allow researchers to ask about interviewees' experiences, using concepts from existing theories, but provide flexibility that allows interviewees to introduce novel insights outside of a predetermined set of questions.

We devised an open-ended interview guide, provided at the end of this appendix, that began by asking about broad life and migration histories and then focused on life experiences, particularly around themes of work and family. We asked about each of these themes at key times: before migration to the United States, while in the United States, and after return to Mexico. Our interviews thus generated detailed life and family histories, which allowed us to analyze multiple migrations within Mexico and back and forth across the U.S. border within a single person's life.

We followed a single interview guide that we developed as a team. As is apparent from the guide, we built in some repetition to enable us to be comprehensive on a variety of topics and across various moments in the interviewee's life. We discovered that the guide was occasionally cumbersome and inefficient for our conversation, and we frequently departed from it, only returning to it to introduce new topics at moments of pause or transition. Other interviews stuck strictly to the guide's structure. We conducted all interviews in Spanish, although some respondents sometimes used English. We interviewed people in their homes and workplaces, as well as in public spaces such as plazas and cafés. Interviews lasted between sixty minutes and three hours and were audio-recorded with respondents' permission. We changed all names of the interviewees, their family members' names, and some key details to protect their privacy. The protocol for our study was reviewed and approved by the UC Davis Institutional Review Board.

Most of the interviews were carried out in pairs, by a Mexican member and a foreign-born member of the team. This arrangement addressed our safety concerns about moving around alone in the city, especially when visiting unsafe neighborhoods. Interviewing in pairs also helped us build rapport and trust with interviewees, making the social interaction a bit less uncomfortable than it could have been with only two people, as the two interviewers could each relate in unique ways to each respondent, helping to create connection and get the conversation flowing. We also learned that interviewing in teams gave us the opportunity to conduct interview debriefings: the two team members would discuss and analyze the interviews immediately afterward, confirming some details, reviewing key insights, and clarifying points of confusion. This was particularly useful when respondents referred to local places or policies, used slang, or made cultural references in one or the other country. Plus, the time together commuting through the city created stronger bonds between team members.

Making Sense of Return Migration

Working as a team, the seven of us transcribed, coded, and analyzed the interviews. One person wrote a biographical memo for each respondent, summarizing the key details of their life. Later, the three of us translated all the quotes that appear in this book from Spanish to English to ensure that our translations reflect the original meaning and intent.

We developed a unique multi-stage coding process that combined independent and collective insights and applied it to the analysis of our data. We first followed the guidelines laid out by the sociologists Nicole Deterding and Mary Waters to develop a large coding tree with seventeen index (or "mother") codes, such as family, work, human capital, transnationalism, and health.[9] We wrote thematic memos to describe our understanding of and expectations regarding each of the codes. We used MaxQDA software to code all interviews for index themes. Two coders coded each interview during this first round. We also linked statistical codes to each transcript, including gender, age at first migration, year of first migration, year of last return to Mexico City, whether deported on last return, current marital status, and number of children.

At the end of this first stage, we each had a copy of an extensively coded set of interview transcripts linked to statistical codes and biographical memos about each interviewee, and we began analytical coding. We used the coded transcripts to code subindexes within each index. Most of us found it difficult to code only within one theme, since many of the ideas we develop in this book focus on processes that evolve across the life course and through other themes (for example, how family life shapes work opportunities). Many of us therefore started anew, coding entire interviews as we read them again, one by one, with our questions and theoretical perspectives in mind. This round of coding involved abductive analysis, which allowed surprising or theoretically unexpected findings to emerge, pushing us to create new codes.[10]

Inspired by the feminist approach to qualitative research taken by the sociologist Neda Maghbouleh and her colleagues, we used the analysis as an opportunity to discuss our interpretations, understandings, and the nuances of the language in the interviews.[11] In dedicated weekly meetings to discuss a specific interview, our conversations were animated by the interviewee's story, the interviewer's field experience with the interviewee, discussions of cultural references, coding breakthroughs or dilemmas, and confusion about the meaning of particular words or passages—all of which proved analytically productive. Differing language abilities among team members sparked many of these discussions as we sought clarification on the meaning of specific words or their different uses in context. For instance, when Paolo used the Spanish adjective *muégano* to describe how his mother thinks of family, the native English speakers among us were confused. Definitions of *muégano* often include pictures of gooey dough, at times in packages. In this context, Paolo used the word to indicate the closeness of individual members of the family, describing them as "stuck together." In other weekly meetings, team members who did not participate in the interview under discussion could ask about styles of dress and ways of interacting. In these conversations, we uncovered deeper meanings of language and the presentation of self as the interviewers shared their perceptions of the respondent and each of us contributed what we thought was interesting, important, useful, and relevant.

Data We Wish We Had

As expected in fieldwork, not everything went as smoothly as we planned or hoped. In retrospect, we are now attuned to several issues we would have liked to explore more or differently. Beyond listing these issues here as potential limitations, we hope that sharing our experiences motivates others to explore these issues in future studies.

Most basically, we would have liked to conduct more interviews. Trained as demographers, we had trouble coping with an *n* of thirty-four. That being said, we also found it difficult to manage the sheer amount of data we collected in in-depth interviews, even with only thirty-four people! We remarked on the amount of time we spent reading, coding, discussing, writing memos, rereading, and recoding interviews. We would frequently return to interviews with people whose stories we thought we knew well only to discover something new and important. We would occasionally realize that we did not remember a person very well, or that we remembered different things about them.

Although thirty-four still seems to us like a paltry number, we have trouble imagining how we would have managed to understand and present people's complex narratives and life histories with many more participants than that.

Second, there were some details we did not gather in the interviews that we wish we had. Drawing on a technique common in anthropological studies, we decided to map genograms that showed where people's families resided and their migration histories. The idea was to help us understand whether the migrations of those we interviewed were unique within their networks. We began the process with the richest interviews, the ones in which we both covered all the questions on the guide and heard much more from our respondents. These sorts of interviews yielded detailed, thick genograms. It was through them that we began to see, to visibly chart, the experience of being Policy Trapped. Our respondents were in Mexico, their families were in the United States, and some, like Yazmín, were separated from every member of their nuclear family by the border.

Figure A.1 shows an example of one of these genograms. In her genogram, Rocío (ego) is represented by the gray circle marked "ego." Two of her children—a daughter (Ana, represented by the light gray–outlined, black-filled circle under Rocío) and a son (Paolo, the light gray–outlined, gray-filled triangle on the right)—also immigrated to the United States, as indicated by the small dashed boundary around them. Ana still resides in the United States as a U.S. permanent resident, as indicated by the black filling in her circle, and Ana's three children, the dark gray–outlined, black-filled circles under Ana, are Rocío's U.S.-born grandchildren. Rocío and Paolo are former (that is, returned) U.S. migrants who now reside in Mexico City. They were undocumented in the United States and do not have visas for reentry. Ramón, Rocío's son who was tragically killed, never emigrated, nor did her ex-husband. While Rocío and Paolo live in Mexico as Mexican citizens and lack U.S. legal documents for entry, residence, or work in the United States, Rocío's daughter Ana is a U.S. permanent resident with Mexican citizenship. Ana can travel between the two countries with minimal restrictions. Ana's children (Rocío's grandchildren) are U.S. citizens who can travel to Mexico without limits for short visits and tourism; because of their parents' Mexican citizenship, they could apply for Mexican citizenship as well. The differences in these legal

Appendix Figure A.1 *Rocío's Genogram*

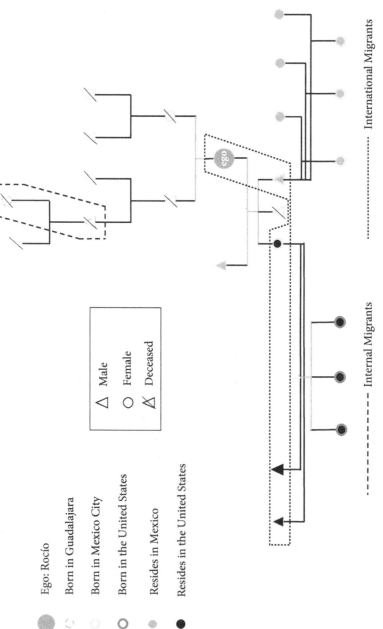

Ego: Rocío

Born in Guadalajara

Born in Mexico City

Born in the United States

Resides in Mexico

Resides in the United States

Male

Female

Deceased

International Migrants

Internal Migrants

Source: Authors' diagram.

statuses bestow unique rights on each member of Rocío's family within the binational context.

We were excited by the analytical potential of these data visualizations, but as we created more genograms, the fact that we had not collected consistent data about the place of birth and migration history of each family member of each of our respondents limited our ability to use them systematically. As a result, we mainly used genograms to complement our understanding of the interview data on an ad hoc basis.

We were fortunate that both Rocío and Paolo accepted our invitation to participate. Their interviews became richer as we were able to triangulate and understand better some events from the perspectives of a mother and son. Something similar happened with Marco Antonio and his brother Eduardo, who provided us with very interesting insights and complementary perspectives on events. Although our focus was on people who returned, we often hypothesized what other family members would tell us about events or about being away and separated from their returned family members. In a bigger project, we would like to interview Mexican immigrants in the United States who may have considered returning to Mexico in order to understand their choice to stay. With this recommendation in mind, Alejandra Santiago, a doctoral candidate from COLMEX, carried out fieldwork in both the United States and Mexico to inform her analysis of return, settlement, remigration, and circularity.

Presenting Challenges and Successes

Our interview guide included questions on familiarity with policies and programs upon return, participation in migrant-serving organizations, and the role of institutions in the migration process. We aimed to allow people to discuss what would improve their lives without formulating specific policy recommendations or evaluating existing policies and programs. However, our analysis did not happen in a void. Because we participated in policy forums on the challenges that returnees faced and ways to alleviate them, we had a vision of the policies and their efficacy. Activists have long called for action to bring an end to the challenges faced by deported and returned people, as well as for U.S. immigration reform, including putting a stop to deportations and ending family separation. They have long criticized the Mexican government for the limited support it provides not only to deported and returned people but also to other migrants. Our data featured the migrants' perspectives, but these academic, policy, and government discourses surely shaped our interpretation of their perspectives.

Although returnees in Mexico faced numerous challenges, many of the people we talked to remarked that they felt relief, a sort of freedom, being back in their home country. We struggled with how to represent returnees' experiences in the book. How would we present these freedoms and successes alongside the difficulties? Our discussion about this issue was motivated by our interview with Julio, who emphasized the importance of recounting successful stories to avoid stigmatization and criminalization, even as we also needed to address returnees' challenges. At the end of his interview, he told us, "Society should not see everything with a sad look, because there are other aspects, and despite some youth who were deported, some are triumphing. Not everything is sad, and not all of those deported returned to gangs. We need to tell these stories." We aimed to treat our respondents and their experiences with respect, and so we considered Julio's point in deciding how we would present our findings. As the previous chapters have revealed, many people felt that there had been little improvement in their lives since returning and were not optimistic about the chances of future change at the institutional level. However, we invite readers to consider the balance that Julio advocates, and we hope that in telling the stories of some of the people we interviewed in depth, that balance emerges in the book.

Finally, we also contemplated the definition and use of the concepts of "return migrant" or "returnee," "voluntary" versus "involuntary" return, "deportation" and "de facto deportation," "repatriated" (*repatriado*), and "Dreamers." Language matters, and Julio also made us think about this, as we discussed in chapter 7 when we explained the dilemma of making visible the invisible without creating harm. At the end of the interview, after we asked him if he felt we had missed something he would have liked to discuss, Julio replied:

> Maybe only the distinction between the conditions of the deportee and the returnee. This is something that has started to be discussed in Mexico. Truly, we cannot deny that some people who were deported committed violent acts in the United States. But here in Mexico sometimes it gets generalized. Also, discussing Dreamers in Mexico, there is no such thing. It is complex, but we cannot talk about a Dreamer here, since "the

Mexican Dream" does not exist. We need to start making distinctions, think of managing different physical spaces, for example, for those who were deported and spent time in prisons and they need other things. But there are also young people who also came following a dream, to study. It's true. Some came because they were looking for a dream they didn't have there. The Mexican dream. But the issue is often discussed a lot around repatriation, and it is not the same, truly. Sometimes so many stigmas are created upon us. For example, on my neighborhood, some say, "Oh, he came back, maybe he was in a gang," and no, it's not the same. In other words, we need to make a distinction not to hurt those in the communities.

We do not use the term "repatriation" owing to its legal connotation, association with deportation, and potential stigmatization of the returnee community. In fact, we prefer to use the term "return migrant," as it captures diverse experiences and heterogeneous profiles. However, returnees do not necessarily call themselves "returnees," except if they are involved with migrant organizations or aware of academic, policy, activist, or government discussions. We understand that our book, with its own small impact, is part of this discourse.

Interview Guide

BACKGROUND

- Tell me a little about yourself: Where are you from? Where were you born? (*Probe:* I don't know that place—could you tell me a little more about what your community is like?)
- How many years of school have you completed? (What is your degree of study?)
- If you are not from Mexico City, how did you come to live in Mexico City? How many years have you been in Mexico City?
- How many years did you live in the United States?
- What do you do now?

FAMILY

- Can you tell me a little about your family?
- Who do you live with currently?

· Where is your family from, and where do they live now?
· How many siblings do you have? Where do they live?
· Do you have a spouse/partner? Where do they live? How long have you lived together?
· Do you have any children? How old are they? Where were they born? Where do they live?

LIFE BEFORE MIGRATING

· Before migrating, what was happening in your life? Where did you live? Who did you live with? (*Probe:* How many children did you have at that time?)
· What did you do? Did you study? If you worked . . . what did you do at work?
· Before you migrated to the United States, what did you know about the United States or immigration? What did you think about this topic?
· Did you know people who migrated before you? Who? Can you tell me a little about their stories?
· Thinking about the first time you went to the United States, can you tell me a little about what you know or remember about the process of leaving? How was the travel process?
  · [*parents only*] Before going to the United States, did you talk to your children about migration? What did you talk about? What did your children think of migration?

THE EXPERIENCE OF MIGRATION

· Where in the United States did you go the first time you went? Who did you go with? How long were you there?
· Where in the United States did you live? (*Probe if changed place of residence:* Tell me about moving within the United States.)
· Who did you live with in the United States? (*Probe:* Other people in your community? Did you have contact with migrants from other communities or states or other countries?)
· How much contact did you have with people in Mexico? (*Probe:* By phone, by Skype) Did you send money to Mexico? How often did you send money and to whom?

- What was it like for you to work in the United States? How did you find work? What was your job? What did you do at that job?
- What trades or skills did you learn in the United States? (*Probe:* Did you learn English?)
- How often did you go back and forth from the United States to Mexico? How did you do it?
  - [*If not . . .*] Would you have liked to come more? Why didn't you come back more often?
- What is life like in the United States? How is it similar or different from what you thought before migrating?
- What is life like in the United States for people who do not have papers [residency documents]?
  - Do you know any of your family or friends who have papers [residency documents]?
- Has life in the United States changed for migrants since you first arrived? How?

RETURN

- Can you tell me the story of how you returned to Mexico [*most recently*]? How did you decide to return? To what extent did you plan the return? (*Probe:* What did you do or what happened to the things you had there—your money, your car, your house?)
- Who did you return to? Did anyone else from your family return after you? Did anyone stay there? [*If yes*] Do they plan to join you?
- How much contact do you maintain with friends, family, or acquaintances in the United States? With employers?
- How did you decide to live in Mexico City? Do you like it? Why? Where would you like to live instead of Mexico City? Have you thought about moving?
- What is the experience of being Mexican after having been in the United States[*returnee or deportee*]?
- Are there certain advantages to having immigration experience? Any problems you have encountered?
- Do you think other people know that you were in the United States here in Mexico? Can you tell when someone else has been in the United States? How?
- Have you used services dedicated to returning migrants [*or deportees*]?

- Have you been able to access official documents you need, including the INE [voter credential], license, or CURP [unique identification number]? What has the process of accessing them been like? (*Probe:* What difficulties or support have you had?)
- How has the process of accessing social services or rights been? [*e.g., work, housing, education, or health*]
- Do you have family in the United States now? If yes, who is in the United States? Where are they? How long have they been in the United States?
- Do you hope to return to the United States? Tell me a little about that idea. (*Probe:* When? How? Why? With whom? Where to? Who would you like to go with? If your children wanted to stay in Mexico, what would you do? Who would you leave them with? What is your strategy? How would you prepare to go? How do you plan to get a visa? What type of visa? If the visa doesn't work, how would you do it? Have you thought about going to other countries . . . like Canada?)

WORK

- How many jobs have you had in your life? (*Probe:* How much did they pay you?)
- Where do you currently work? Who is your employer?
- What exactly do you do? What sorts of tasks do you do?
- Do you go to this job every day? How many hours do you work a day?
- What type of contract do you have? Does the salary seem good to you? How often do you get paid? (*Probe:* So it's not a fixed amount?) Do you have insurance or any other benefits? And how do you negotiate vacations? Are you in the IMSS or the ISSSTE?
- How did you find your job? What other options did you look for? What other jobs did you have before?
- Where is your work located?
- And do you only work in [. . .] or somewhere else as well?
- If you didn't work in [. . .] what would you do?
- What do you like about your job? And dislike?
- Have you thought about opening your own business?
- What is your ideal job? Is it the same for you in Mexico as in the United States?

- Is it difficult to find work in Mexico? In the United States? (*Probe:* Why do you think there is no work?)
- If you don't have a job . . .
  - What do you do for a living? Do you have any business or independent activity? (Do you sell a product? Do you have a stall somewhere?)
  - Are you looking for work? What kind?
  - What do you think is the reason [that you can't find work]?
- What does your partner do?
- Other household income? [*If there are no others*) Then they are only supported by your salary?
- Do you think the employment situation is different for migrants in the United States than for native-born Hispanics or other U.S. natives? (*Probe:* Why do you think that is like this?)
- Is the employment situation different for return migrants (or deported people) in Mexico?
- Where do you see yourself working, or hope to work, in ten or fifteen years?

FAMILY AND MIGRATION

- What does it mean to you to be a mom/dad?
- How did the return affect the plans you had for your children?
- What are your children's perceptions of Mexico? What are your children's perceptions of the United States?
- Is parenting in the United States different from parenting in Mexico? How?
- If they have children . . .
  - If you left children here when you went to the United States, tell me about that experience.
  - If the children went to the United States later, how was the transition for your children in the United States?
  - Did you have children in the United States?
- The process of returning to Mexico if they have children . . .
  - Did you return to Mexico with the children?
  - How did you bring them? Did you think about them staying in the United States with friends and family?
  - How have they adapted to life back in Mexico? How has school been for them?

- What languages do your children speak among themselves or with their friends? What languages do they speak with you? (*Probe:* If they speak both, which one do they prefer?]
- Do you think your children will migrate during their lives?
- If the children are in the United States . . .
  - Can you tell me a little about the situation with your children who stayed in the United States?
  - Who do they live with? Who takes care of your children?
  - How often are you in contact with them?
  - Can you tell me about the decision for them to stay in the United States?
  - Would they like to move to Mexico? Would you like them to move?

CONCLUDING

- Could you tell me more about . . . [anything requiring more explanation]
  - *Check demographic information: age, gender*
- Is there any other topic, problem, or experience that is important to you but we haven't talked about yet?
- Do you have any questions for me?

NOTES

Chapter 1: Introduction

1. Escobar Latapí and Masferrer 2022; Masferrer 2021a; Masferrer and Prieto 2019.
2. Gonzalez-Barrera 2021.
3. We use the terms "emigration," "migration to the United States," and "U.S.-bound migration" interchangeably to refer to international migration departures from Mexico to the United States. In other contexts, the more general term "migration" is used to refer to any movements across geopolitical boundaries—including international boundaries or municipal, state, or metropolitan boundaries within Mexico—that involve a longer-term relocation of residence, typically of one year or longer. "Return migration" refers to migration to Mexico following emigration to the United States (King and Kuschminder 2022). We use the term "immigration" to refer to international migration from the perspective of the destination; this could be immigration to Mexico from the United States, such as by the U.S.-citizen children of return migrants, who themselves are not returnees.
4. Garip 2016.
5. From our analysis of the 2000 Mexican census.
6. Durand, Massey, and Zenteno 2001.
7. Our analysis of the 2000 Mexican census.
8. Our analysis of the 2000 Mexican census. The Traditional Region includes the Mexican states of Durango, Zacatecas, San Luis Potosí, Nayarit, Aguascalientes, Jalisco, Guanajuato, Querétaro, Colima, and Michoacán (Durand, Massey, and Zenteno 2001).
9. Hamilton and Villarreal 2011.
10. Andrews 2018; Durand, Kandel, et al. 1996; Massey et al. 1987; Smith 2006.
11. U.S. Department of Homeland Security 2009, 2022; for data on U.S. immigration actions, see also Syracuse University's Transactional Records Access Clearinghouse at https:/trac.syr.edu/.

12. Hamilton, Masferrer, and Langer 2023; Masferrer, Hamilton, and Denier 2019.
13. We use the term *norteado*, which is the form of the word used most commonly in the Spanish language, and it was the form used by our respondents. However, we recognize that the word—in ending in "*o*"—implies a masculine gender. We do not intend to impose a gendered meaning on this term, nor do we intend to impose ideas about the gender binary on the experience of our respondents, who varied in their gender identities, gender expression, and ideas about gender.
14. The film *Norteado* (*Northless*) (2009) captures this exact experience.
15. King and Kuschminder 2022.
16. Escobar Latapí and Masferrer 2022; Hanson and McIntosh 2010; Riosmena, Nawrotzki, and Hunter 2018.
17. Durand 2016; Escobar Latapí and Masferrer 2022; Hanson and McIntosh 2010; Riosmena, Nawrotzki, and Hunter 2018.
18. Gonzalez-Barrera 2015.
19. Passel, Cohn, and Gonzalez-Barrera 2012.
20. Alba 1978; Durand and Massey 2019; Hanson and McIntosh 2010.
21. Lee 2002; Zavala 1993, 2014.
22. Durand, Massey, and Zenteno 2001.
23. Hatton and Williamson 1994; Martin and Taylor 1996; Massey 1988; Sassen 2000; Taylor et al. 1996.
24. World Bank 2023.
25. UN-Habitat 2023.
26. Consejo Nacional de Población 2024.
27. Passel, Cohn, and Gonzalez-Barrera 2012.
28. Gonzalez-Barrera 2015.
29. Masferrer, Hamilton, and Denier 2019; Zúñiga and Giorguli-Saucedo 2020.
30. Garip 2016; Masferrer and Roberts 2012; Massey, Durand, and Riosmena 2006; Riosmena and Massey 2012; Roberts and Hamilton 2007.
31. Chávez 2012; Fussell 2004; King and Skeldon 2010; Lozano Ascencio, Roberts, and Bean 1997; Roberts, Frank, and Lozano-Ascencio 1999; Villarreal and Hamilton 2012.
32. Masferrer 2021a; Masferrer and Roberts 2012.
33. Cornelius 1992; Massey 1986; Reichert 1981.
34. Durand and Massey 2019.
35. Massey et al. 1987.
36. Asad and Garip 2019; Curran and Rivero-Fuentes 2003; Davis, Stecklov, and Winters 2002; Denier and Masferrer 2019; Donato 1993; Donato et al. 1992; Donato, Wagner, and Patterson 2008; Durand and Arias 1997; Durand and Massey 1992, 2003, 2004; Durand, Massey, and Zenteno 2001; Durand, Parrado, and Massey 1996; Frank and Wildsmith 2005; Gandini, Lozano Ascencio, and Gaspar Olvera 2015; Garip 2016; Garip and Asad 2016; Glick and Yabiku 2016; Hamilton and Villarreal 2011; Hanson and McIntosh 2010; Kanaiaupuni 2000; Kanaiaupuni and Donato 1999; Kandel and Kao 2001; Kandel and Massey 2002; Lindstrom 1996; Lindstrom and Giorguli-Saucedo 2002, 2007; Lindstrom and López Ramírez 2010;

Lozano Ascencio, Roberts, and Bean 1997; Masferrer, Hamilton, and Denier 2019; Masferrer and Roberts 2012; Massey and Espinosa 1997; Massey and Gentsch 2014; Massey, Goldring, and Durand 1994; Massey and Parrado 1994; Nobles 2013; Palloni et al. 2001; Papail 2002; Parrado and Gutierrez 2016; Rendall and Parker 2014; Riosmena 2009; Riosmena, González González, and Wong 2012; Riosmena and Massey 2012; Roberts, Frank, and Lozano-Ascencio 1999; Stecklov et al. 2005; Villarreal 2014; Wassink and Massey 2022. For a full list of MMP studies, see the MMP website at: https://mmp.opr.princeton.edu/research/publications-en.aspx.

37. Ariza and D'Aubeterre 2009; Cavalcanti and Parella 2013; Cruz-Manjarrez 2013, 2016; Cruz-Manjarrez and Baquedano-López 2020; D'Aubeterre Buznego 2007, 2012; Durand, Kandel, et al. 1996; Durand, Parrado, and Massey 1996; Flores Garrido 2010; Flores-Hernández et al. 2012; Franco 2017; García Castro and Burgueño Angulo 2017; Kanaiaupuni and Donato 1999; Li, Sadowski, and Wan 2016; Lindstrom 1996; Martínez Díaz 2012; Massey and Parrado 1994; Ocampo Marín 2016; Parrado and Gutierrez 2016; Sandoval-Cervantes 2022; Smith 2006; Tinajero Vega 2015; Vega Briones 2004; Viera 2020; Woo Morales 2019.

38. Durand, Parrado, and Massey 1996.

39. Delgado Wise and Marquez 2008.

40. de Haas 2021; de Haas and Fokkema 2011.

41. Cornelius 2001; Massey, Durand, and Malone 2002.

42. Donato and Massey 1993; Massey and Gentsch 2014; Phillips and Massey 1999.

43. Massey, Durand, and Malone 2002.

44. Gándara 2020; Ojeda 2009; Vargas-Valle and Camacho Rojas 2015; Vargas-Valle, Glick, and Orraca-Romano 2022.

45. Gil-Everaert, Masferrer, and Rodríguez Chávez 2023; Meneses 2005, 2012; Slack 2019; Slack and Campbell 2016; Slack and Whiteford 2011.

46. Andrews 2023.

47. Townsend 2019.

48. King 1986; King and Kuschminder 2022; Kuschminder 2017.

49. Cassarino 2004. Another useful reference is Kuschminder 2017.

50. Garip 2012, 2016.

51. Hagan, Hernández-León, and Demonsant 2015; Hagan and Wassink 2016.

52. Masferrer, Hamilton, and Denier 2019; Waldinger 2023; Zúñiga and Giorguli-Saucedo 2020.

53. Zúñiga and Giorguli-Saucedo 2020. Zúñiga and Giorguli-Saucedo also include in this category the 1.5 generation (Mexican-born child migrants to the United States) who return to Mexico.

54. Hamilton, Masferrer, and Langer 2023.

55. Amuedo-Dorantes and Juárez 2022; Barros Nock 2019; Borja et al. 2021; Hamann, Zúñiga, and Sánchez Garcia 2008; Herrera García and Montoya Zavala 2019; Jacobo-Suárez 2017; Sánchez 2007; Zayas 2015; Zúñiga and Carrillo Cantú 2020; Zúñiga and Giorguli-Saucedo 2020; Zúñiga and Hamann 2014, 2020.

56. Acosta García 2016; Bojórquez Chapela et al. 2015; Bojórquez Chapela et al. 2014; Bórquez et al. 2019; Brouwer et al. 2009; Fernández-Niño et al. 2014;

Martinez-Donate et al. 2015; Peláez Rodríguez and París Pombo 2016; Pinedo, Burgos, and Ojeda 2014; Pinedo et al. 2018.

57. Andrews 2023.

58. Irwin and Meneses 2023.

59. Hernández-León 2008, 2012.

60. Guzmán Elizalde 2022.

61. Rivera Sánchez 2013a, 2015a, 2015b, 2016; see also Mendoza 2015.

62. Andrews 2023.

63. Masferrer 2021a.

64. King 1986, 4; King and Kuschminder 2022.

65. Masferrer 2021a.

Chapter 2: Mexico City: A Migrant Metropolis

1. Townsend 2019.

2. Sobrino 2008, 2020.

3. Sobrino 2020.

4. Tuirán 2002.

5. Consejo Nacional de Población 2024.

6. Garza and Schteingart 1978.

7. Ward 1998.

8. Connolly 2012; Duhau 1991; Garza and Damián 1991; Ward 1998.

9. Aguilar, Ward, and Smith 2003; Delgado 1990; Ward 1998.

10. Izazola 2004; Villarreal and Hamilton 2009.

11. Allier Montaño 2018.

12. Nájar 2017.

13. Sobrino 2022.

14. Hanson 1998.

15. Escobar Latapí et al. 1997; Villarreal and Hamilton 2012.

16. Gilbert and de Jong 2015.

17. Mendoza 2015.

18. Hiernaux 1995.

19. Secretaría de Movilidad 2020.

20. Secretaría de Turismo 2019.

21. Gonzalez-Barrera 2015; Passel, Cohn, and Gonzalez-Barrera 2012.

22. Gonzalez-Barrera 2015; Passel, Cohn, and Gonzalez-Barrera 2012.

23. Canales 1999; Durand, Massey, and Zenteno 2001; Papail 2002.

24. Chávez 2012; Fussell 2004; Garip 2016; Guzmán Elizalde 2022; King and Skeldon 2010; Lozano Ascencio, Roberts, and Bean 1997; Lozano Ascencio 2002; Marcelli and Cornelius 2001; Masferrer and Roberts 2012; Massey, Durand, and Riosmena 2006; Meza González 2017; Riosmena and Massey 2012; Roberts and Hamilton 2007; Villarreal and Hamilton 2012.

25. Hernández-León 2008; Riosmena and Massey 2012; Roberts and Hamilton 2007.

26. Garip 2016.

27. Our analysis of 1995 Mexican count data. See Lozano Ascencio 2004 for an analysis using 2000 Mexican census data.
28. Our analysis of 1995 Mexican count data.
29. Our analysis of 2000 Mexican census data.
30. Our analysis of 2000 Mexican census data.
31. Garip 2016; Hernández-León 2008.
32. Flores-Yeffal and Aysa-Lastra 2011; Fussell and Massey 2004; cf. Paredes-Orozco 2019.
33. Flores-Yeffal and Aysa-Lastra 2011; Flores-Yeffal, Hernández-León, and Massey 2004; Mendoza 2009; Roberts, Frank, and Lozano-Ascencio 1999.
34. Hernández-León 2008.
35. Rivera Sánchez 2013a.
36. Rivera Sánchez 2013a, 2015a, 2015b, 2016.
37. Mendoza 2015.
38. In fact, one in six is similar to the share that has been observed in studies of migrants with internal and U.S. migration experience at the national level; see Masferrer 2014.
39. Conway 1980; see also Carling and Schewel 2018.
40. Paul 2011.
41. Ibid.
42. Conway 1980.
43. See the definition of "cholo" in the *Dictionary of Mexican Spanish* at https://dem.colmex.mx/Ver/cholo.
44. Rivera Sánchez 2015c.
45. Brown and Bean 2016; King and Skeldon 2010; Lozano Ascencio, Roberts, and Bean 1997; Roberts, Frank, and Lozano-Ascencio 1999.
46. See definitions of these terms in the *Dictionary of Mexican Spanish* (https://dem.colmex.mx/).
47. Sabates and Pettirino 2007.
48. Toluca is the capital city of the State of Mexico.

Chapter 3: The Policy Trap

1. Given our focus on people who were in the United States with noncitizen status (and thus were at risk of deportation) and our interest in speaking to both returnees who were deported and those who returned for other reasons, it is no surprise that half of our interviewees had been deported. The true rate of deportation among return migrants is unknown, owing to data limitations. In the 2020 Mexican census, which reports on recent migrants' reasons for migrating to Mexico, 14 percent of people who had migrated to Mexico from the United States since 2015 cited deportation as their reason for migrating (Masferrer and Pedroza 2021). In addition to the fact that return migrants in the census include people who are not at risk of deportation, such as naturalized U.S. citizens, causing an underestimate of the rate of deportation, we also suspect that deportation is underreported as a reason for return in survey data.

2. Bean, Telles, and Lowell 1987; Bean, Edmonston, and Passel 1990; Massey, Pren, and Durand 2016; Massey and Pren 2012.

3. Massey, Durand, and Malone 2002; Massey, Pren, and Durand 2016; Massey and Pren 2012.

4. Bean, Edmonston, and Passel 1990; Massey, Durand, and Malone 2002; Massey, Pren, and Durand 2016.

5. Chávez 2016.

6. U.S. Customs and Border Protection 2024.

7. Cornelius 2001; Massey, Durand, and Malone 2002; Massey, Pren, and Durand 2016.

8. Cornelius 2001; Massey, Pren, and Durand 2016.

9. Hamilton and Hale 2016.

10. Massey, Pren, and Durand 2016.

11. Macías-Rojas 2018.

12. Ibid.

13. Pedroza 2013.

14. Asad 2023; Hagan, Rodriguez, and Castro 2011; Prieto 2018.

15. Martínez, Slack, and Martínez-Schuldt 2018.

16. Menjívar and Abrego 2012.

17. Asad 2020a; Asad 2020b.

18. U.S. Citizenship and Immigration Services 2021 (see "Deferred Action for Childhood Arrivals [DACA] Quarterly Report [Fiscal Year 2021, Q1])."

19. Passel, Cohn, and Gonzalez-Barrera 2012.

20. Warren 2021.

21. Passel and Cohn 2019; Warren 2021.

22. We note that if they had qualified for DACA, it is unlikely that we would have interviewed them, given our focus on returnees in Mexico City.

23. See general advice on travel for DACA recipients from the Immigrant Legal Resource Center at https://www.ilrc.org/sites/default/files/documents/advance _parole_guide.pdf.

24. For example, Abrego 2011, 2014; Abrego et al. 2017; Asad 2020a, 2020b, 2023; Barros Nock 2019; Bean et al. 2015; Berger Cardoso et al. 2018; Boehm 2008, 2016; Brown and Sanchez 2017; Caldwell 2019; Castañeda 2019; Cervantes et al. 1995; Enriquez 2015, 2020; Fenton, Catalano, and Hargreaves 1996; Golash-Boza 2015; Irwin and Meneses 2023; Lopez 2019; Martínez-Aranda 2022; Menjívar 2006; Menjívar and Abrego 2012; Patler 2014, 2015, 2017; Patler and Golash-Boza 2017; Patler, Hamilton, and Savinar 2021; Pedroza 2012, 2013, 2022; Perreira and Pedroza 2019; Saadi et al. 2020; Saadi, Patler, and De Trinidad Young 2022; Slack et al. 2015; Suárez-Orozco et al. 2011; Torche and Sirois 2019; Valdivia 2019, 2021; Yoshikawa 2011; Yoshikawa, Suárez-Orozco, and Gonzales 2017.

25. An estimated one-third of immigrants who entered the United States and became undocumented in 2014 were visa overstayers (Warren and Kerwin 2017).

26. Asad 2023.

27. Many people do reenter, in spite of the legal consequences if they are caught (Amuedo-Dorantes and Juárez 2022; Martínez, Slack, and Martínez-Schuldt

2018; Torre Cantalapiedra and Calva Sánchez 2021; Vargas Valle, Hamilton, and Orraca Romano 2022). We did not interview those people, since we were focused on return migrants living in Mexico City.
28. Menjívar 2014.
29. Massey, Durand, and Pren 2015.
30. Fullerton Rico 2023.

Chapter 4: Settling Back in the City

1. Pedersen 1994; Ward, Bochner, and Furnham 2020.
2. Balistreri and Van Hook 2004.
3. Macías-Rojas 2018.
4. Abrego and Lakhani 2015; Asad 2020a; Martínez, Slack, and Martínez-Schuldt 2018.
5. Asad 2020a.
6. Arenas et al. 2015; Davies et al. 2011; Pedroza and Chung 2021.
7. See Observatorio Nacional Ciudadano, "Interactive Observatory of Crime Incidence," https://delitosmexico.onc.org.mx/.
8. Chort and de la Rupelle 2016; Rodríguez Chávez 2021.
9. Lomnitz-Adler 2000; Morris 2013; Sarsfield 2012.
10. Medina and Menjívar 2015.
11. For a study on bribes in Mexico City in particular and in Mexico in general, see Sarsfield 2012.
12. Chávez 2016; Irwin and Meneses 2023; Pinillos Quintero and Velasco Ortiz 2021.
13. Pinillos Quintero 2023; Pinillos Quintero and Velasco Ortiz 2021.

Chapter 5: Family

1. Berumen Sandoval, Frías Valle, and Santiago Hernández 2012; Garip 2016.
2. Ariza and D'Aubeterre 2009; D'Aubeterre Buznego 2007; Dreby 2010; Mummert 2010a, 2010b, 2012a; Nobles 2011.
3. See, for example, Massey et al. 1993.
4. Massey et al. 1993; Massey and Espinosa 1997; Stark and Bloom 1985.
5. Boehm 2016; Hamilton, Masferrer, and Langer 2023; Kanstroom 2007; Zayas 2015.
6. Hamilton, Masferrer, and Langer 2023.
7. Masferrer, Hamilton, and Denier 2024.
8. Masferrer, Hamilton, and Denier 2019; see Zúñiga and Giorguli-Saucedo 2020 for more on this population.
9. Hamilton, Masferrer, and Langer 2023.
10. Masferrer, Hamilton, and Denier 2019.
11. Zayas 2015.
12. Aguilar Zepeda 2018; Borjian et al. 2016; Medina and Menjívar 2015; Meza González and Pederzini Villarreal 2018; Ruiz Peralta and Valdéz Gardea 2012;

Román González and Carrillo Cantú 2017; Valdéz Gardea et al. 2018; Vargas Valle and Camacho Rojas 2015; Vázquez Vázquez 2011; Woo Morales and Ortiz Rangel 2019; Zúñiga and Hamann 2014.

13. Orraca, Rocha, and Vargas 2017; Vargas-Valle and Glick 2021.

14. Bean et al. 2015; Dreby 2015a; Yoshikawa 2011.

15. Zúñiga and Giorguli-Saucedo 2020.

16. Dreby 2010, 2015a; Massey, Durand, and Malone 2002.

17. For an excellent and updated review of theories of international migration, see Riosmena 2024.

18. Ariza 2007; Donato and Gabaccia 2015; Donato et al. 2006; Hondagneu-Sotelo 1994, 1999, 2003; Mahler and Pessar 2006; Mummert 2012b; Pedraza 1991; Pessar 2003.

19. Berumen Sandoval and Santiago Hernández 2012. Another area of feminist research on Mexico-U.S. migration has focused on how gender is experienced and changed through the process of migration (Ariza 2007, 2014). Much of this work focuses on the gendered experiences and family dynamics of separation (and reunion) as a result of migration (Ariza 2012; Ariza and D'Aubeterre 2009; Asakura 2011, 2012; Carling, Menjívar, and Schmalzbauer 2012; Dreby 2006, 2010; Hondagneu-Sotelo and Avila 1997; Mummert 2009, 2010a, 2010b; Salas Alfaro, Baca Tavira, and Alcántara Quintana 2013). Our interest in how family and gender manifest in the decision to migrate is similar to the theoretical work that explains how economic motivations and contexts play out in the decision to migrate. Most of the work on gender (and family) in this vein has been quantitative. For three exceptions, see the excellent qualitative work on gender and the process of migration in Hondagneu-Sotelo 1992, 1994; Ruehs 2017).

20. Cerrutti and Massey 2001; Donato 1993; Hondagneu-Sotelo 1994; Riosmena 2010.

21. Ariza 2007; D'Aubeterre Buznego 2012; Hondagneu-Sotelo 1994.

22. Garip 2016.

23. Pinillos Quintero and Flores Peña 2020.

24. Andrews 2023; Andrews and Khayar-Cámara 2022.

25. Bean et al. 2015; Dreby 2015a; Yoshikawa 2011.

Chapter 6: Work

1. Anderson 2015; Caldwell 2019; Cassarino 2004; Golash-Boza 2015; Hagan, Rodriguez, and Castro 2011; Roberts, Menjívar, and Rodríguez 2017; Silver and Manzanares 2023.

2. Cassarino 2004.

3. de Haas, Fokkema, and Fihri 2015; Parrado and Gutiérrez 2016.

4. de Haas, Fokkema, and Fihri 2015; Stark and Bloom 1985.

5. Cassarino 2004; de Haas and Fokkema 2011.

6. de Haas, Fokkema, and Fihri 2015.

7. Cassarino 2004.

8. Hagan, Hernández-León, and Demonsant 2015; Hagan and Wassink 2016, 2020; Hagan, Wassink, and Castro 2019; Wassink and Hagan 2018.

9. Denier and Masferrer 2019; Durand, Kandel et al. 1996; Durand, Parrado, and Massey 1996; Hagan, Hernández-León, and Demonsant 2015; Lindstrom 1996; Massey and Parrado 1998; Papail 2002; Parrado and Gutiérrez 2016.

10. Cruz Vásquez and Salas Alfaro 2018; Hagan, Hernández-León, and Demonsant 2015; Hagan and Wassink 2016, 2020; Hagan, Wassink, and Castro 2019; Salas Alfaro 2013; Salas Alfaro and Cruz Vázquez 2013.

11. Franco Sánchez and Granados Alcantar 2018; Garbey Burey 2012; Hualde Alfaro and París Pombo 2019; Masferrer 2021a; París Pombo, Hualde Alfaro, and Woo Morales 2019; Prieto and Koolhaas 2013; Ramírez Armas 2018; Rivera Sánchez 2013b; Salas Alfaro and Román Reyes 2017; Solís Martínez 2019; Tinajero Vega 2015; Valenzuela Camacho and Medina 2015; Woo Morales and Ortiz Rangel 2015.

12. Solís Lizama 2018.

13. Anguiano-Téllez, Cruz-Piñeiro, and Garbey-Burey 2013.

14. Cuecuecha Mendoza, Cruz Vásquez, and Tapia Mejía 2022; Sheehan and Riosmena 2013.

15. Rivera Sánchez 2013b, 2015a.

16. Hualde Alfaro and Ibarra 2019; Hualde Alfaro and París Pombo 2019; París Pombo, Hualde Alfaro, and Woo Morales 2019; Valenzuela Camacho and Medina 2015.

17. Anderson 2015; Caldwell 2019; Da Cruz 2018; Guzmán Elizalde 2022; Hualde Alfaro 2017; Hualde Alfaro and Ibarra 2019; Hualde Alfaro and París Pombo 2019; Rivera Sánchez 2013b; Silver and Manzanares 2023.

18. Da Cruz 2018; Silver and Manzanares 2023.

19. Denier and Masferrer 2019.

20. Sheehan and Riosmena 2013.

21. Wassink and Hagan 2022.

22. Organization for Economic Cooperation and Development 2022; Ordaz Díaz 2008; Wassink and Hagan 2018.

23. Cuecuecha Mendoza, Cruz Vásquez, and Tapia Mejía 2022; García and Pacheco 2000; López and Nieto 2011; Rodríguez Pérez 2019; Varela Llamas et al. 2010.

24. Ruiz Soto et al. 2019.

25. Cerrutti and Massey 2001; Donato et al. 2006; Donato and Gabaccia 2015; Pedraza 1991; Massey, Fischer, and Capoferro 2006.

26. England 2010.

27. World Bank 2024.

28. Braun et al. 2008; García and Pacheco 2014.

29. Woo Morales 2019.

30. Creese and Wiebe 2012; Wassink and Hagan 2018. Survival employment typically refers to employment that helps people meet their basic needs but does not match their qualifications or desire for long-term work in terms of pay, working conditions, and other aspects of job quality.

31. Anderson 2015; Da Cruz 2018, 2019.

32. Anderson 2015; Hagan and Wassink 2016; Silver and Manzanares 2023.

33. Gomberg-Muñoz 2021; Hualde Alfaro and Ibarra 2019; Rivera Sánchez 2013b; Solís Lizama 2018.

34. Hualde Alfaro and París Pombo 2019.
35. Akresh 2007; Chiswick and Miller 2009; Damelang, Ebensperger, and Stumpf 2020; Duleep and Regets 1997; Guzmán Elizalde 2022; Sweetman, McDonald, and Hawthorne 2015.
36. Gomberg-Muñoz 2021.

Chapter 7: Reorienting the Compass

1. Giorguli-Saucedo, Angoa, and Villaseñor 2014; Giorguli-Saucedo and Bautista León 2022; Hernández Hernández and Cruz Piñeiro 2019; Jacobo-Suárez 2017; Jacobo-Suárez and Cárdenas Alaminos 2018; Masferrer and Pedroza 2021; Ruiz Soto et al. 2019.
2. Hunt 2022; Johnson 2014, 2021; Migration Policy Institute 2019; Orrenius and Zavodny 2017. Also see https://www.chirla.org/registry/.
3. Altamirano and Flamand 2018.
4. Secretaría de Gobernación 2022a.
5. Álvarez Diez et al. 2018; Jacobo-Suárez and Cárdenas Alaminos 2020; Padilla Flores and Jardón Hernández 2015.
6. Secretaría de Gobernación 2022b.
7. Abrego and Negrón-Gonzales 2020; Monico 2020.
8. Aikin-Araluce and Anaya Muñoz 2013; Díaz de León 2021.
9. Altamirano and Flamand 2018; Organization for Economic Cooperation and Development 2020; Tinoco 2014.
10. Secretaría del Trabajo y Previsión Social 2017; Zárate Gutiérrez 2017.
11. Fernández-Sánchez et al. 2023.

Chapter 8: Conclusion

1. Gramlich and Scheller 2021.
2. Álvarez Diez et al. 2018; Giorguli-Saucedo, García-Guerrero, and Masferrer 2016; Masferrer 2021b; Masferrer and Pedroza 2021.
3. Gonzalez-Barrera 2021.
4. Mexico's population in 2007 was 108.3 million; see World Bank, "World Development Indicators," https://datatopics.worldbank.org/world-development-indicators/.
5. Gonzalez-Barrera 2021.
6. Rosenbloom and Batalova 2022.
7. Chort and de la Rupelle 2016; Masferrer and Roberts 2012.
8. See Syracuse University's Transactional Records Access Clearinghouse at https://trac.syr.edu/.
9. Berry 1997; Gordon 1964; Portes and Zhou 1993.
10. Denier and Masferrer 2019.
11. Waldinger 2023.
12. de Haas 2021, 31.

13. Gonzalez-Barrera 2021.
14. Capps, Fix, and Zong 2016; Moslimani 2022; Van Hook, Gelatt, and Ruiz Soto 2023.
15. Martínez, Slack, and Martínez-Schuldt 2018; Masferrer, Hamilton, and Denier 2019.
16. Masferrer, Hamilton, and Denier 2019; Zúñiga and Giorguli-Saucedo 2020.
17. Zúñiga and Giorguli-Saucedo 2020.
18. Hamilton, Masferrer, and Langer 2023.
19. For example, see Abrego 2014; Berger Cardoso et al. 2016; Masferrer, Hamilton, and Denier, 2024.
20. Andrews 2023; Caldwell 2019; Dreby 2015b; Masferrer, Hamilton, and Denier 2019; Silver 2018; Zayas 2015.

Methodological Appendix

1. Especially Ariza and Velasco 2015; Deterding and Waters 2021; González-López 2011; Lareau 2021; Luker 2009; Maghbouleh et al. 2019; Timmermans and Tavory 2012; Weiss 1995.
2. Recent discussions problematize these categories; see, for example, Merriam et al. 2001; Reich 2021; Reyes 2020.
3. Daniel 2022; Gall 2021; Moreno Figueroa 2022.
4. Sue, Riosmena, and Telles 2024; Velázquez Gutiérrez 2011; Villarreal 2010.
5. Pinillos Quintero and Flores Peña 2020.
6. Pinillos Quintero 2023.
7. Masferrer 2021a.
8. Pugh 2013.
9. Deterding and Waters 2021.
10. Timmermans and Tavory 2012.
11. Maghbouleh et al. 2019.

REFERENCES

Abrego, Leisy J. 2011. "Legal Consciousness of Undocumented Latinos: Fear and Stigma as Barriers to Claims-Making for First- and 1.5-Generation Immigrants." *Law and Society Review* 45(2): 337–70. https://doi.org/10/cpgt9d.

———. 2014. *Sacrificing Families: Navigating Laws, Labor, and Love across Borders.* Stanford University Press.

Abrego, Leisy J., Mat Coleman, Daniel E. Martínez, Cecilia Menjívar, and Jeremy Slack. 2017. "Making Immigrants into Criminals: Legal Processes of Criminalization in the Post-IIRAIRA Era." *Journal on Migration and Human Security* 5(3, September): 694–715. https://doi.org/10.1177/233150241700500308.

Abrego, Leisy J., and Sarah M. Lakhani. 2015. "Incomplete Inclusion: Legal Violence and Immigrants in Liminal Legal Statuses." *Law and Policy* 37(4, October): 265–93. https://doi.org/10.1111/lapo.12039.

Abrego, Leisy J., and Genevieve Negrón-Gonzales. 2020. *We Are Not Dreamers: Undocumented Scholars Theorize Undocumented Life in the United States.* Duke University Press.

Acosta García, César Martín. 2016. "Relatos de vida de veteranos deportados de Estados Unidos en Tijuana: Masculinidades y roles familiares en transformación." Master's thesis, El Colegio de la Frontera Norte.

Aguilar, Adrián G., Peter M. Ward, and C. B. Smith Sr. 2003. "Globalization, Regional Development, and Mega-City Expansion in Latin America: Analyzing Mexico City's Peri-Urban Hinterland." *Cities* 20(1, February): 3–21. https://doi.org/10.1016/S0264-2751(02)00092-6.

Aguilar Zepeda, Rodrigo. 2018. "¿Y si quiero regresar a mi país? Niños estadounidenses en escuelas de Cuernavaca." *Carta Económica Regional* 121(June): 173–92. https://doi.org/10.32870/cer.v0i121.7105.

Aikin-Araluce, Olga, and Alejandro Anaya Muñoz. 2013. "Crisis de derechos humanos de las personas migrantes en tránsito por México: Redes y presión trasnacional." *Foro Internacional* 53(1): 143–81.

Akresh, Ilana Redstone. 2007. "U.S. Immigrants' Labor Market Adjustment: Additional Human Capital Investment and Earnings Growth." *Demography* 44(4, November 1): 865–81. https://doi.org/10.1353/dem.2007.0034.

Alba, Francisco. 1978. "Mexico's International Migration as a Manifestation of Its Development Pattern." *International Migration Review* 12(4, December): 502–13. https://doi.org/10.1177/019791837801200403.

Allier Montaño, Eugenia. 2018. "Memorias imbricadas: Terremotos en México, 1985 y 2017." *Revista Mexicana de Sociología* 80: 9–40. https://www.scielo.org.mx/scielo.php?script=sci_arttext&pid=S0188-25032018000500009.

Altamirano, Melina, and Laura Flamand, eds. 2018. *Inequalities in Mexico in 2018.* El Colegio de México.

Álvarez Diez, Rubén Carlos, Víctor Hugo Bañuelos García, Flor de María García Martínez, and Blanca Isabel Llamas Félix. 2018. "Efectividad de programas federales de fomento al empleo para repatriados mexicanos en 2017." *Opción: Revista de Ciencias Humanas y Sociales*, 18 (extra): 536–53. https://dialnet.unirioja.es/servlet/articulo?codigo=8369862.

Amuedo-Dorantes, Catalina, and Laura Juárez. 2022. "Health Care and Education Access of Transnational Children in Mexico." *Demography* 59(2): 511–33. https://doi.org/10.1215/00703370-9741101.

Anderson, Jill. 2015. "'Tagged as a Criminal': Narratives of Deportation and Return Migration in a Mexico City Call Center." *Latino Studies* 13(1): 8–27. https://doi.org/10.1057/lst.2014.72.

Andrews, Abigail. 2018. *Undocumented Politics: Place, Gender, and the Pathways of Mexican Migrants.* University of California Press.

———. 2023. *Banished Men: How Migrants Endure the Violence of Deportation.* University of California Press.

Andrews, Abigail, and Fátima Khayar-Cámara. 2022. "Forced Out of Fatherhood: How Men Strive to Parent Post-deportation." *Social Problems* 69(3): 699–716. https://doi.org/10.1093/socpro/spaa061.

Anguiano-Téllez, María Eugenia, Rodolfo Cruz-Piñeiro, and Rosa María Garbey-Burey. 2013. "Migración internacional de retorno: Trayectorias y reinserción laboral de emigrantes veracruzanos." *Papeles de Población* 19: 115–47.

Arenas, Erika, Noreen Goldman, Anne R. Pebley, and Graciela Teruel. 2015. "Return Migration to Mexico: Does Health Matter?" *Demography* 52(6, December 1): 1853–68. https://doi.org/10.1007/s13524-015-0429-7.

Ariza, Marina. 2007. "Itinerario de los estudios de género y migración en México." In *El país transnacional: Migración mexicana y cambio social a través de la frontera*, edited by Marina Ariza and Alejandro Portes. Instituto de Investigaciones Sociales–UNAM.

———. 2012. "Vida familiar transnacional en inmigrantes de México y República Dominicana en dos contextos de recepción." *Si Somos Americanos: Revista de Estudios Transfronterizos* 12(1): 17–47. https://doi.org/10.4067/S0719-09482012000100002.

———. 2014. "Migration and Family in Mexican Research: A Recent Appraisal." *Migraciones Internacionales* 7(4): 9–37.

Ariza, Marina, and María Eugenia D'Aubeterre. 2009. "Contigo en la distancia: Dimensiones de la conyugalidad en migrantes mexicanos internos e

internacionales." In *Tramas familiares en el México contemporáneo*, edited by
Cecilia Rabell. Instituto de Investigaciones Sociales–UNAM/El Colegio de
México.

Ariza, Marina, and Laura Velasco, eds. 2015. *Métodos cualitativos y su aplicación
empírica: Por los caminos de la investigación sobre migración internacional*.
Universidad Nacional Autónoma de México, Instituto de Investigaciones
Sociales; El Colegio de la Frontera Norte A.C.

Asad, Asad L. 2020a. "Latinos' Deportation Fears by Citizenship and Legal Status,
2007 to 2018." *Proceedings of the National Academy of Sciences* 117(16):
8836–44. https://doi.org/10.1073/pnas.1915460117.

———. 2020b. "On the Radar: System Embeddedness and Latin American
Immigrants' Perceived Risk of Deportation." *Law and Society Review* 54(1):
133–67. https://doi.org/10.1111/lasr.12460.

———. 2023. *Engage and Evade: How Latino Immigrant Families Manage Surveillance
in Everyday Life*. Princeton University Press.

Asad, Asad L., and Filiz Garip. 2019. "Mexico-U.S. Migration in Time: From Economic
to Social Mechanisms." *Annals of the American Academy of Political and Social
Science* 684(1, July): 60–84. https://doi.org/10.1177/0002716219847148.

Asakura, Hiroko. 2011. "Reorganización y reacomodos afectivos en familias
trasnacionales: Estudio de caso con migrantes de Santa Cecilia (Oaxaca)
en Seattle (Washington)." *Especialidades* 1(1): 45–71.

———. 2012. "Maternidad a distancia: Cambios y permanencias en las prácticas y
las representaciones de las madres migrantes centroamericanas." In *Género y
migración*, edited by Esperanza Tuñón Pablos and Martha Luz Rojas Wiesner.
El Colegio de la Frontera Sur/El Colegio de la Frontera Norte/El Colegio de
Michoacán/CIESAS.

Balistreri, Kelly Stamper, and Jennifer Van Hook. 2004. "The More Things Change
the More They Stay the Same: Mexican Naturalization before and after Welfare
Reform." *International Migration Review* 38(1): 113–30. https://doi.org/10.1111
/j.1747-7379.2004.tb00190.x.

Barros Nock, Magdalena. 2019. "Familias mixtecas fracturadas por las deportaciones
en Estados Unidos." In *¿Volver a casa? Migrantes de retorno en América Latina:
Debates, tendencias, y experiencias divergentes*, edited by Liliana Rivera Sánchez.
El Colegio de México.

Bean, Frank D., Susan K. Brown, James D. Bachmeier, Susan Brown, and James
Bachmeier. 2015. *Parents without Papers: The Progress and Pitfalls of Mexican
American Integration*. Russell Sage Foundation.

Bean, Frank D., Barry Edmonston, and Jeffrey S. Passel. 1990. *Undocumented
Migration to the United States: IRCA and the Experience of the 1980s*.
Urban Institute.

Bean, Frank D., Edward E. Telles, and B. Lindsay Lowell. 1987. "Undocumented
Migration to the United States: Perceptions and Evidence." *Population and
Development Review* 13(4, December): 671–90. https://doi.org/10.2307
/1973027.

Berger Cardoso, Jodi, Erin R. Hamilton, Nestor Rodriguez, Karl Eschbach, and Jacqueline Hagan. 2016. "Deporting Fathers: Involuntary Transnational Families and Intent to Remigrate among Salvadoran Deportees." *International Migration Review* 50(1, March): 197–230. https://doi.org/10.1111/imre.12106.

Berger Cardoso, Jodi, Jennifer L. Scott, Monica Faulkner, and Liza Barros Lane. 2018. "Parenting in the Context of Deportation Risk." *Journal of Marriage and Family* 80(2, April): 301–16. https://doi.org/10.1111/jomf.12463.

Berry, John W. 1997. "Immigration, Acculturation, and Adaptation." *Applied Psychology* 46(1): 5–34. https://doi.org/10.1111/j.1464-0597.1997.tb01087.x.

Berumen Sandoval, Salvador, Nina Frías Valle, and Julio Santiago Hernández, eds. 2012. *Migración y familia: Una mirada más humana para el estudio de la migración internacional.* Centro de Estudios Migratorios/Unidad de Política Migratoria/SPMAR/SEGOB.

Berumen Sandoval, Salvador, and Julio Santiago Hernández. 2012. "Las mujeres en el proceso migratorio México-Estados Unidos: ¿Hacia una feminización de la migración?" In *Migración y familia: Una mirada más humana para el estudio de la migración internacional.* Centro de Estudios Migratorios/Unidad de Política Migratoria/SPMAR/SEGOB.

Boehm, Deborah A. 2008. "'For My Children': Constructing Family and Navigating the State in the U.S.-Mexico Transnation." *Anthropological Quarterly* 81(4, Fall): 777–802. https://doi.org/10.1353/anq.0.0037.

———. 2016. *Returned: Going and Coming in an Age of Deportation.* University of California Press.

Bojórquez Chapela, Ietza, Rosa M. Aguilera, Jacobo Ramírez, Diego Cerecero, and Silvia Mejía. 2015. "Common Mental Disorders at the Time of Deportation: A Survey at the Mexico–United States Border." *Journal of Immigrant and Minority Health* 17(6): 1732–38. https://doi.org/10.1007/s10903-014-0083-y.

Bojórquez Chapela, Ietza, Silvia Mejía, Rosa M. Aguilera, Diego Cerecero, and Sandra Albicker. 2014. "Problemas de salud mental en migrantes de retorno en situación de calle en Tijuana, Baja California." *Coyuntura Demográfica* 6: 91–97.

Borja, Sharon, Jodi Berger Cardoso, Pedro Isnardo De La Cruz, Krista M. Perreira, Natalia Giraldo-Santiago, and Martha Virginia Jasso Oyervides. 2021. "Health Insurance Access among U.S. Citizen Children in Mexico: National and Transborder Policy Implications." *Health Affairs* 40(7, July): 1066–74. https://doi.org/10.1377/hlthaff.2021.00087.

Borjian, Ali, Luz María Muñoz de Cote, Sylvia van Dijk, and Patricia Houde. 2016. "Transnational Children in Mexico: Context of Migration and Adaptation." *Diaspora, Indigenous, and Minority Education* 10(1): 42–54. https://doi.org/10.1080/15595692.2015.1084920.

Bórquez, A., R. S. Garfein, D. Abramovitz, L. Liu, L. Beletsky, D. Werb, S. R. Mehta, et al. 2019. "Prevalence and Correlates of Injecting with Visitors from the United States among People Who Inject Drugs in Tijuana, Mexico." *Journal of Immigrant and Minority Health* 21(6): 1200–1207. https://doi.org/10.1007/s10903-019-00868-8.

Braun, Michael, Noah Lewin-Epstein, Haya Stier, and Miriam K. Baumgärtner. 2008. "Perceived Equity in the Gendered Division of Household Labor." *Journal of Marriage and Family* 70(5, December): 1145–56. https://doi.org/10.1111 /j.1741-3737.2008.00556.x.

Brouwer, K. C., R. Lozada, W. A. Cornelius, M. Firestone Cruz, C. Magis-Rodríguez, M. L. Zúñiga de Nuncio, and S. A. Strathdee. 2009. "Deportation along the U.S.-Mexico Border: Its Relation to Drug Use Patterns and Accessing Care." *Journal of Immigrant and Minority Health* 11(1): 1–6. https://doi.org/10.1007 /s10903-008-9119-5.

Brown, Susan, and Frank Bean. 2016. "Conceptualizing Migration: From Internal/International to Kinds of Membership." In *International Handbook of Migration and Population Distribution*, edited by Michael White. Springer.

Brown, Susan, and Alejandra Jazmin Sanchez. 2017. "Parental Legal Status and the Political Engagement of Second-Generation Mexican Americans." *RSF: The Russell Sage Foundation Journal of the Social Sciences* 3(4, July): 136–47. https://doi.org/10.7758/RSF.2017.3.4.08.

Caldwell, Beth C. 2019. *Deported Americans: Life after Deportation to Mexico*. Duke University Press.

Canales, Alejandro. 1999. "Periodicidad, estacionalidad, duración, y retorno: Los distintos tiempos en la migración México–Estados Unidos." *Papeles de Población* 5(22): 11–41.

Capps, Randy, Michael Fix, and Jie Zong. 2016. "A Profile of U.S. Children with Unauthorized Immigrant Parents." Migration Policy Institute, January 11. https://www.migrationpolicy.org/research/profile-us-children-unauthorized -immigrant-parents.

Carling, Jørgen, Cecilia Menjívar, and Leah Schmalzbauer. 2012. "Central Themes in the Study of Transnational Parenthood." *Journal of Ethnic and Migration Studies* 38(2): 191–217. https://doi.org/10.1080/1369183X.2012.646417.

Carling, Jørgen, and Kerilyn Schewel. 2018. "Revisiting Aspiration and Ability in International Migration." *Journal of Ethnic and Migration Studies* 44(6): 945–63. https://doi.org/10.1080/1369183X.2017.1384146.

Cassarino, Jean-Pierre. 2004. "Theorising Return Migration: The Conceptual Approach to Return Migrants Revisited." *International Journal on Multicultural Societies* 6(2): 253–79. https://papers.ssrn.com/sol3/papers.cfm?abstract _id=1730637.

Castañeda, Heide. 2019. *Borders of Belonging: Struggle and Solidarity in Mixed-Status Immigrant Families*. Stanford University Press.

Cavalcanti, Leonardo, and Sònia Parella. 2013. "El retorno desde una perspectiva transnacional." *REMHU* (*Revista Interdisciplinar da Mobilidade Humana*) 21(41): 9–20. https://doi.org/10.1590/S1980-85852013000200002.

Cerrutti, Marcela, and Douglas S. Massey. 2001. "On the Auspices of Female Migration from Mexico to the United States." *Demography* 38(2, May 1): 14. https://doi.org/10.1353/dem.2001.0013.

Cervantes, Nancy, Sasha Khokha, and Bobbie Murray. 1995. "Hate Unleashed: Los Angeles in the Aftermath of Proposition 187." *Chicano-Latino Law Review* 17: 1–23.

Chávez, Sergio. 2012. "The Sonoran Desert's Domestic Bracero Programme: Institutional Actors and the Creation of Labour Migration Streams." *International Migration* 50(2, April): 20–40. https://doi.org/10.1111/j.1468-2435.2009.00544.x.

———. 2016. *Border Lives: Fronterizos, Transnational Migrants, and Commuters in Tijuana*. Oxford University Press.

Chiswick, Barry R., and Paul W. Miller. 2009. "The International Transferability of Immigrants' Human Capital." *Economics of Education Review* 28(2, April): 162–69. https://doi.org/10.1016/j.econedurev.2008.07.002.

Chort, Isabelle, and Maëlys de la Rupelle. 2016. "Determinants of Mexico-U.S. Outward and Return Migration Flows: A State-Level Panel Data Analysis." *Demography* 53(5, October 1): 1453–76. https://doi.org/10.1007/s13524-016 -0503-9.

Connolly, Priscilla. 2012. "La urbanización irregular y el orden urbano en la Zona Metropolitana del Valle de México de 1990 a 2005." In *Irregular: Suelo y mercado en América Latina*, edited by Clara Eugenia Salazar. El Colegio de México.

Consejo Nacional de Población (CONAPO). 2024. "Conciliación Demográfica de México, 1950–2020." Government of Mexico.

Conway, Dennis. 1980. "Step-Wise Migration: Toward a Clarification of the Mechanism." *International Migration Review* 14(1): 3–14. https://doi.org/10.1177 /019791838001400101.

Cornelius, Wayne A. 1992. "From Sojourners to Settlers: The Changing Profile of Mexican Labor Migration to California in the 1980s." In *U.S.-Mexico Relations: Labor Market Interdependence*, edited by Jorge A. Bustamante, Clark W. Reynolds, and Raul A. Hinojosa Ojeda. Stanford University Press.

———. 2001. "Death at the Border: Efficacy and Unintended Consequences of U.S. Immigration Control Policy." *Population and Development Review* 27(4, December): 661–85. https://doi.org/10.1111/j.1728-4457.2001.00661.x.

Creese, Gillian, and Brandy Wiebe. 2012. "'Survival Employment': Gender and Deskilling among African Immigrants in Canada." *International Migration* 50(5): 56–76. https://doi.org/10.1111/j.1468-2435.2009.00531.x.

Cruz-Manjarrez, Adriana. 2013. *Zapotecs on the Move: Cultural, Social, and Political Processes in Transnational Perspective*. Rutgers University Press.

———. 2016. "Transnacionalismo y migración de retorno en una comunidad zapoteca." In *Nuevas experiencias de la migración de retorno*, edited by Elaine Levine, Silvia Núñez, and Mónica Verea. UNAM, CISAN, Instituto Matías Romero.

Cruz-Manjarrez, Adriana, and Patricia Baquedano-López. 2020. "Los nuevos retornados de la migración maya yucateca en Estados Unidos." *Estudios Fronterizos* 21. https://doi.org/10.21670/ref.2012054.

Cruz Vásquez, Miguel, and Renato Salas Alfaro. 2018. "Algunos casos de emprendimiento de migrantes retornados." In *Emprendimiento y migración de retorno:*

Raíces y horizontes, edited by Miguel Cruz Vásquez and Alfredo Cuecuecha Mendoza. Universidad Popular Autónoma del Estado de Puebla, El Colegio de Tlaxcala, Miguel Ángel Porrúa.

Cuecuecha Mendoza, Alfredo, Miguel Cruz Vásquez, and Erik Tapia Mejía. 2022. "Capital humano, experiencia laboral, ahorro e intención emprendedora: El caso de los migrantes retornados a la Mixteca poblana." *Estudios Demográficos y Urbanos* 37(2): 553–601. https://doi.org/10.24201/edu.v37i2.2083.

Curran, Sara R., and Estela Rivero-Fuentes. 2003. "Engendering Migrant Networks: The Case of Mexican Migration." *Demography* 40(2): 289–307. https://doi.org/10.1353/dem.2003.0011.

Da Cruz, Michaël. 2018. "Offshore Migrant Workers: Return Migrants in Mexico's English-Speaking Call Centers." *RSF: The Russell Sage Foundation Journal of the Social Sciences* 4(1, January): 39–57. https://doi.org/10.7758/RSF.2018.4.1.03.

———. 2019. "El retorno como estrategia para romper el techo de cristal: Trayectorias migratorias y profesionales de los jóvenes mexicanos de la generación 1.5 en los call centers bilingües de la Ciudad de México." In *Experiencias de retorno de migrantes mexicanos en contextos urbanos*, edited by María Dolores París Pombo, Alfredo Hualde Alfaro, and Ofelia Woo Morales. El Colegio de la Frontera Norte.

Damelang, Andreas, Sabine Ebensperger, and Felix Stumpf. 2020. "Foreign Credential Recognition and Immigrants' Chances of Being Hired for Skilled Jobs—Evidence from a Survey Experiment among Employers." *Social Forces* 99(2, December): 648–71. https://doi.org/10.1093/sf/soz154.

Daniel, G. Reginald. 2022. "From Multiracial to Monoracial: The Formation of Mexican American Identities in the U.S. Southwest." *Genealogy* 6(2): 28. https://doi.org/10.3390/genealogy6020028.

D'Aubeterre Buznego, María Eugenia. 2007. "Aquí respetamos a nuestros esposos: Migración masculina y trabajo femenino en una comunidad de origen nahua del estado de Puebla." In *El país transnacional: Migración mexicana y cambio social a través de la frontera*, edited by Marina Ariza and Alejandro Portes. Instituto de Investigaciones Sociales–UNAM.

———. 2012. "Empezar de nuevo: Migración femenina a Estados Unidos. Retornos y reinserción en la Sierra Norte de Puebla, México." *Norteamérica: Revista Académica del CISAN–UNAM* 7: 149–80.

Davies, Anita A., Rosilyne M. Borland, Carolyn Blake, and Haley E. West. 2011. "The Dynamics of Health and Return Migration." *PLoS Medicine* 8(6): e1001046. https://doi.org/10.1371/journal.pmed.1001046.

Davis, Benjamin, Guy Stecklov, and Paul Winters. 2002. "Domestic and International Migration from Rural Mexico: Disaggregating the Effects of Network Structure and Composition." *Population Studies* 56(3): 291–309. https://doi.org/10.1080/00324720215936.

de Haas, Hein. 2021. "A Theory of Migration: The Aspirations-Capabilities Framework." *Comparative Migration Studies* 9(1): 8. https://doi.org/10.1186/s40878-020-00210-4.

de Haas, Hein, and Tineke Fokkema. 2011. "The Effects of Integration and Transnational Ties on International Return Migration Intentions." *Demographic Research* 25(24): 755–82. https://doi.org/10.4054/DemRes.2011.25.24.

de Haas, Hein, Tineke Fokkema, and Mohamed Fassi Fihri. 2015. "Return Migration as Failure or Success?" *Journal of International Migration and Integration* 16(2): 415–29. https://doi.org/10.1007/s12134-014-0344-6.

Delgado, Javier. 1990. "De los anillos a la segregación: La Ciudad de México, 1950–1987." *Estudios Demográficos y Urbanos* 5(2, May–August): 237–74. https://doi.org/10.24201/edu.v5i2.771.

Delgado Wise, Raúl, and Humberto Marquez. 2008. "Migration and Development in Mexico: Toward a New Analytical Approach." *Journal of Latino/Latin American Studies* 2(3): 101–19. https://doi.org/10.18085/llas.2.3.2545272831756836.

Denier, Nicole, and Claudia Masferrer. 2019. "Returning to a New Mexican Labor Market? Regional Variation in the Economic Incorporation of Return Migrants from the U.S. to Mexico." *Population Research and Policy Review* 39(August): 617–41. https://doi.org/10.1007/s11113-019-09547-w.

Deterding, Nicole M., and Mary C. Waters. 2021. "Flexible Coding of In-Depth Interviews: A Twenty-First-Century Approach." *Sociological Methods and Research* 50(2, May): 708–39. https://doi.org/10.1177/0049124118799377.

Díaz de León, Alejandra. 2021. "Why Do You Trust Him? The Construction of the Good Migrant on the Mexican Migrant Route." *European Review of Latin American and Caribbean Studies* 111(March 3): 1–117. https://doi.org/10.32992/erlacs.10645.

Donato, Katharine M. 1993. "Current Trends and Patterns of Female Migration: Evidence from Mexico." *International Migration Review* 27(4, Winter): 748. https://doi.org/10.2307/2546911.

Donato, Katharine M., Jorge Durand, and Douglas S. Massey. 1992. "Stemming the Tide? Assessing the Deterrent Effects of the Immigration Reform and Control Act." *Demography* 29(2): 139–157. https://doi.org/10.2307/2061724.

Donato, Katharine M., and Donna Gabaccia. 2015. *Gender and International Migration.* Russell Sage Foundation.

Donato, Katharine M., Donna Gabaccia, Jennifer Holdaway, Martin Manalansan IV, and Patricia R. Pessar. 2006. "A Glass Half Full? Gender in Migration Studies." *International Migration Review* 40(1, March): 3–26. https://doi.org/10.1111/j.1747-7379.2006.00001.x.

Donato, Katharine M., and Douglas S. Massey. 1993. "Effect of the Immigration Reform and Control Act on the Wages of Mexican Migrants." *Social Science Quarterly* (September 1): 523–41.

Donato, Katharine M., Brandon Wagner, and Evelyn Patterson. 2008. "The Cat and Mouse Game at the Mexico-U.S. Border: Gendered Patterns and Recent Shifts." *International Migration Review* 42(2, June): 330–59. https://doi.org/10.1111/j.1747-7379.2008.00127.x.

Dreby, Joanna. 2006. "Honor and Virtue: Mexican Parenting in the Transnational Context." *Gender and Society* 20(1, February): 32–59. https://doi.org/10.1177/0891243205282660.

———. 2010. *Divided by Borders: Mexican Migrants and Their Children.* University of California Press.

———. 2015a. *Everyday Illegal: When Policies Undermine Immigrant Families.* University of California Press.

———. 2015b. "U.S. Immigration Policy and Family Separation: The Consequences for Children's Well-being." *Social Science and Medicine* 132(May): 245–51. https://doi.org/10.1016/j.socscimed.2014.08.041.

Duhau, Emilio. 1991. "Urbanización popular y políticas de suelo en la Ciudad de México." In *Espacio y vivienda en la Ciudad de México*, edited by Martha Schteingart. El Colegio de México.

Duleep, Harriet Orcutt, and Mark C. Regets. 1997. "The Decline in Immigrant Entry Earnings: Less Transferable Skills or Lower Ability?" *Quarterly Review of Economics and Finance* (special issue) 37(January): 189–208. https://doi.org/10.1016/S1062-9769(97)90065-X.

Durand, Jorge. 2016. *Historia mínima de la migración México–Estados Unidos.* El Colegio de México.

Durand, Jorge, and Patricia Arias. 1997. "Las remesas: ¿Continuidad o cambio?" *Revista Ciudades* 35: 3–11.

Durand, Jorge, William Kandel, Emilio A. Parrado, and Douglas S. Massey. 1996. "International Migration and Development in Mexican Communities." *Demography* 33(2, May): 249–64. https://doi.org/10.2307/2061875.

Durand, Jorge, and Douglas S. Massey. 1992. "Mexican Migration to the United States: A Critical Review." *Latin American Research Review* 27(2): 3–42. https://doi.org/10.1017/S0023879100016770.

———. 2003. *Clandestinos: Migración México–Estados Unidos en los albores del siglo XXI.* Miguel Ángel Porrúa y Universidad Autónoma de Zacatecas.

———. 2004. *Crossing the Border: Research from the Mexican Migration Project.* Russell Sage Foundation.

———. 2019. "Evolution of the Mexico-U.S. Migration System: Insights from the Mexican Migration Project." *Annals of the American Academy of Political and Social Science* 684(1, July): 21–42. https://doi.org/10.1177/0002716219857667.

Durand, Jorge, Douglas S. Massey, and René M. Zenteno. 2001. "Mexican Immigration to the United States: Continuities and Changes." *Latin American Research Review* 36(1, October 5): 107–27. https://doi.org/10.1017/S0023879100018859.

Durand, Jorge, Emilio A. Parrado, and Douglas S. Massey. 1996. "Migradollars and Development: A Reconsideration of the Mexican Case." *International Migration Review* 30(2, June): 423–44. https://doi.org/10.1177/019791839603000202.

England, Paula. 2010. "The Gender Revolution: Uneven and Stalled." *Gender and Society* 24(2, April): 149–66. https://doi.org/10.1177/0891243210361475.

Enriquez, Laura E. 2015. "Multigenerational Punishment: Shared Experiences of Undocumented Immigration Status within Mixed-Status Families." *Journal of Marriage and Family* 77(4, August): 939–53. https://doi.org/10.1111/jomf.12196.

———. 2020. *Of Love and Papers: How Immigration Policy Affects Romance and Family.* University of California Press.

Escobar Latapí, Agustín, Philip Martin, Gustavo López Castro, and Katharine Donato. 1997. "Factors That Influence Migration." In Binational Study on Migration Project, *Migration between Mexico and the United States: Binational Study.* Commission on Immigration Reform, USA, and Secretaría de Relaciones Exteriores.

Escobar Latapí, Agustín, and Claudia Masferrer. 2022. *Migration between Mexico and the United States: IMISCOE Reader.* Springer.

Fenton, Joshua J., Ralph Catalano, and William A. Hargreaves. 1996. "Effect of Proposition 187 on Mental Health Service Use in California: A Case Study." *Health Affairs* 15(1, Spring): 182–90. https://doi.org/10.1377/hlthaff.15.1.182.

Fernández-Niño, Julián Alfredo, Carlos Jacobo Ramírez-Valdés, Diego Cerecero-Garcia, and Ietza Bojorquez-Chapela. 2014. "Deported Mexican Migrants: Health Status and Access to Care." *Revista de Saúde Pública* 48(3, June): 478–85. https://doi.org/10.1590/S0034-8910.2014048005150.

Fernández-Sánchez, Higinio, Jordana Salma, Sara Dorow, and Bukola Salami. 2023. "A Multi-Scalar Critical Analysis of Return Migration Policies in Mexico." *International Migration* 61(6, December): 175–92. https://doi.org/10.1111/imig.13157.

Flores Garrido, Natalia. 2010. "Cambios en la dinámica identitaria de género y en la división del trabajo en hombres y mujeres migrantes de retorno." Master's thesis, FLACSO México.

Flores-Hernández, Aurelia, Landy Cuatepotzo-Cortés, and Adelina Espejel-Rodríguez. 2012. "Manejo, control del dinero y otros logros: Mujeres migrantes de retorno en Tlaxcala, México." *Revista Agricultura, Sociedad y Desarrollo* 9(3): 271–95.

Flores-Yeffal, Nadia Y., and Maria Aysa-Lastra. 2011. "Place of Origin, Types of Ties, and Support Networks in Mexico-U.S. Migration." *Rural Sociology* 76(4, December): 481–510. https://doi.org/10.1111/j.1549-0831.2011.00060.x.

Flores-Yeffal, Nadia Y., Rubén Hernández-León, and Douglas S. Massey. 2004. "Social Capital and Emigration from Rural and Urban Communities." In *Crossing the Border: Research from the Mexican Migration Project*, edited by Jorge Durand and Douglas S. Massey. Russell Sage Foundation.

Franco Aguilar, José. 2017. "Experiencia migratoria, retorno e inserción: Mujeres en zonas rurales de Jalisco." Master's thesis, Universidad Nacional Autónoma de México.

Franco Sánchez, Laura Myriam, and José Aurelio Granados Alcantar. 2018. "Migración de retorno y el empleo en México." In *Desigualdad regional, pobreza, y migración.* UNAM, Asociación Mexicana de Ciencias para el Desarrollo Regional A.C.

Frank, Reanne, and Elizabeth Wildsmith. 2005. "The Grass Widows of Mexico: Migration and Union Dissolution in a Binational Context." *Social Forces* 83(3, March): 919–47. https://doi.org/10.1353/sof.2005.0031.

Fullerton Rico, Kristina. 2023. "Grieving in the 'Golden Cage': How Unauthorized Immigrants Contend with Death and Mourn from Afar." *Social Problems* (May 6): spad023. https://doi.org/10.1093/socpro/spad023.

Fussell, Elizabeth. 2004. "Sources of Mexico's Migration Stream: Rural, Urban, and Border Migrants to the United States." *Social Forces* 82(3, March): 937–67. https://doi.org/10.1353/sof.2004.0039.

Fussell, Elizabeth, and Douglas S. Massey. 2004. "The Limits to Cumulative Causation: International Migration from Mexican Urban Areas." *Demography* 41(1, February 1): 151–71. https://doi.org/10.1353/dem.2004.0003.

Gall, Olivia. 2021. "Mestizaje y racismo en México." *Nueva Sociedad* 292: 53–64. https://nmx.conapred.org.mx/materiales_consulta/descarga/material_18.pdf.

Gándara, Patricia. 2020. "The Students We Share: Falling through the Cracks on Both Sides of the U.S.-Mexico Border." *Ethnic and Racial Studies* 43(1): 38–59. https://doi.org/10.1080/01419870.2019.1667514.

Gandini, Luciana, Fernando Lozano Ascencio, and Selene Gaspar Olvera. 2015. *El retorno en el nuevo escenario de la migración entre México y Estados Unidos.* Consejo Nacional de Población.

Garbey Burey, Rosa María. 2012. "Retorno y reinserción laboral de emigrantes internacionales en Monte Blanco, Veracruz." Master's thesis, El Colegio de la Frontera Norte.

García, Brígida, and Edith Pacheco. 2000. "Esposas, hijos e hijas en el mercado de trabajo de la Ciudad de México en 1995." *Estudios Demográficos y Urbanos* 15(1): 35–63. https://doi.org/10.24201/edu.v15i1.1066.

———, eds. 2014. *Uso del tiempo y trabajo no remunerado en México.* ONU-Mujeres/ El Colegio de México/Inmujeres.

García Castro, Ismael, and Nayeli Burgueño Angulo. 2017. "Menores transnacio-nales: El proceso de incorporación sociocultural en el espacio educativo. El Caso de la comunidad de Cosalá, Sinaloa." In *Tránsito y retorno de la niñez migrante: Epílogo en la administración Trump*, edited by Gloria Ciria Valdéz Gardea and Ismael García Castro. El Colegio de Sonora.

Garip, Filiz. 2012. "Discovering Diverse Mechanisms of Migration: The Mexico–US Stream 1970–2000." *Population and Development Review* 38(3): 393–433. https://doi.org/10.1111/j.1728-4457.2012.00510.x

———. 2016. *On the Move: Changing Mechanisms of Mexico-U.S. Migration.* Princeton University Press.

Garip, Filiz, and Asad L. Asad. 2016. "Network Effects in Mexico-U.S. Migration: Disentangling the Underlying Social Mechanisms." *American Behavioral Scientist* 60(10, September): 1168–93. https://doi.org/10.1177/0002764216643131.

Garza, Gustavo, and Araceli Damián. 1991. "Ciudad de México: Etapas de crecimiento, infraestructura, y equipamiento." In *Espacio y vivienda en la Ciudad de México*, edited by Martha Schteingart. El Colegio de Mexico.

Garza, Gustavo, and Martha Schteingart. 1978. "Mexico City: The Emerging Megalopolis." *Latin American Urban Research* 6: 69.

Gil-Everaert, Isabel, Claudia Masferrer, and Oscar Rodríguez Chávez. 2023. "Concurrent Displacements: Return, Waiting for Asylum, and Internal Displacement in Northern Mexico." *Journal on Migration and Human Security* 11(1): 125–48. https://doi.org/10.1177/23315024231158559.

Gilbert, Liette, and Feike de Jong. 2015. "Entanglements of Periphery and Informality in Mexico City." *International Journal of Urban and Regional Research* 39(3, May): 518–32. https://doi.org/10.1111/1468-2427.12249.

Giorguli-Saucedo, Silvia, Adela Angoa, and Rodrigo Villaseñor. 2014. "Los retos ante el nuevo escenario migratorio entre México y Estados Unidos: Patrones regionales y políticas locales." In *Gobierno territorio y población: Las políticas públicas en la mira*, edited by Silvia Giorguli-Saucedo and Vicente Ugalde. El Colegio de México.

Giorguli-Saucedo, Silvia, and Andrea Bautista León. 2022. *Derechos fragmentados: Acceso a derechos sociales y migración de retorno a México*. El Colegio de México.

Giorguli-Saucedo, Silvia E., Victor M. García-Guerrero, and Claudia Masferrer. 2016. *A Migration System in the Making: Demographic Dynamics and Migration Policies in North America and the Northern Triangle of Central America.*" El Colegio de Mexico.

Glick, Jennifer E., and Scott T. Yabiku. 2016. "Migrant Children and Migrants' Children: Nativity Differences in School Enrollment in Mexico and the United States." *Demographic Research* 35(8): 201–28. https://doi.org/10.4054/DemRes.2016.35.8.

Golash-Boza, Tanya Maria. 2015. *Deported: Immigrant Policing, Disposable Labor, and Global Capitalism.* New York University Press.

Gomberg-Muñoz, Ruth. 2021. "The Mexico City Runaround: Temporal Barriers to Rebuilding Life after Deportation." In *Stealing Time*, edited by Monish Bhatia and Victoria Canning. Springer International Publishing.

Gonzalez-Barrera, Ana. 2015. "More Mexicans Leaving than Coming to the U.S." Pew Research Center, November 19. https://www.pewresearch.org/hispanic/2015/11/19/more-mexicans-leaving-than-coming-to-the-u-s/.

———. 2021. "Before COVID-19, More Mexicans Came to the U.S. than Left for Mexico for the First Time in Years." Pew Research Center, July 9. https://www.pewresearch.org/short-reads/2021/07/09/before-covid-19-more-mexicans-came-to-the-u-s-than-left-for-mexico-for-the-first-time-in-years/.

González-López, Gloria. 2011. "Mindful Ethics: Comments on Informant-Centered Practices in Sociological Research." *Qualitative Sociology* 34(3): 447–61. https://doi.org/10.1007/s11133-011-9199-8.

Gordon, Milton M. 1964. *Assimilation in American Life: The Role of Race, Religion and National Origins.* Oxford University Press.

Gramlich, John, and Alissa Scheller. 2021. "What's Happening at the U.S.-Mexico Border in 7 Charts." Pew Research Center, November 9. https://www.pewresearch.org/fact-tank/2021/11/09/whats-happening-at-the-u-s-mexico-border-in-7-charts/.

Guzmán Elizalde, Lorena. 2022. "Return to Mexico: Exploring Reintegration Experiences." *Journal of International Migration and Integration* 24: 465–83. https://doi.org/10.1007/s12134-022-00962-1.

Hagan, Jacqueline, Rubén Hernández-León, and Jean-Luc Demonsant. 2015. *Skills of the Unskilled: Work and Mobility among Mexican Migrants.* University of California Press.

Hagan, Jacqueline, Nestor Rodriguez, and Brianna Castro. 2011. "Social Effects of Mass Deportations by the United States Government, 2000–10." *Ethnic and Racial Studies* 34(8): 1374–91. https://doi.org/10.1080/01419870.2011.575233.

Hagan, Jacqueline, and Joshua Wassink. 2016. "New Skills, New Jobs: Return Migration, Skill Transfers, and Business Formation in Mexico." *Social Problems* 63(4, November): 513–33. https://doi.org/10.1093/socpro/spw021.

———. 2020. "Return Migration around the World: An Integrated Agenda for Future Research." *Annual Review of Sociology* 46(1, July): 533–52. https://doi.org/10.1146/annurev-soc-120319-015855.

Hagan, Jacqueline, Joshua Wassink, and Brianna Castro. 2019. "A Longitudinal Analysis of Resource Mobilisation among Forced and Voluntary Return Migrants in Mexico." *Journal of Ethnic and Migration Studies* 45(1): 170–89. https://doi.org/10.1080/1369183X.2018.1454305.

Hamann, Edmund T., Víctor Zúñiga, and Juan Sánchez Garcia. 2008. "From Nuevo León to the USA and Back Again: Transnational Students in Mexico." *Journal of Immigrant and Refugee Studies* 6(1): 60–84. https://doi.org/10.1080/15362940802119245.

Hamilton, Erin R., and Jo Mhairi Hale. 2016. "Changes in the Transnational Family Structures of Mexican Farm Workers in the Era of Border Militarization." *Demography* 53(5, October 1): 1429–51. https://doi.org/10.1007/s13524-016-0505-7.

Hamilton, Erin R., Claudia Masferrer, and Paola Langer. 2023. "U.S. Citizen Children De Facto Deported to Mexico." *Population and Development Review* 4 (1, March): 175–203. https://doi.org/10.1111/padr.12521.

Hamilton, Erin R., and Andrés Villarreal. 2011. "Development and the Urban and Rural Geography of Mexican Emigration to the United States." *Social Forces* 90(2, December): 661–83. https://doi.org/10.1093/sf/sor011.

Hanson, Gordon. 1998. "Regional Adjustment to Trade Liberalization." *Regional Science and Urban Economics* 28(4, July): 419–44. https://doi.org/10.1016/S0166-0462(98)00006-4.

Hanson, Gordon, and Craig McIntosh. 2010. "The Great Mexican Emigration." *Review of Economics and Statistics* 92(4, November): 798–810. https://doi.org/10.1162/REST_a_00031.

Hatton, Timothy J., and Jeffrey G. Williamson. 1994. "International Migration and World Development: A Historical Perspective." In *Economic Aspects of International Migration*, edited by Herbert Giersch. Springer Berlin Heidelberg.

Hernández Hernández, Alberto, and Rodolfo Cruz Piñeiro, eds. 2019. *Políticas multinivel para el retorno y la (re)inserción de migrantes mexicanos y sus familias.* Comisión Nacional de los Derechos Humanos and El Colegio de la Frontera Norte. https://www.colef.mx/wp-content/uploads/2019/04/Informe-Politicas-Multinivel.pdf.

Hernández-León, Rubén. 2008. *Metropolitan Migrants: The Migration of Urban Mexicans to the United States.* University of California Press.

———. 2012. "Conceptualizing the Migration Industry." In *The Migration Industry and the Commercialization of International Migration*, edited by Thomas Gammeltoft-Hansen and Nina Sorenson. Routledge.

Herrera García, Martha Cecilia, and Erika Cecilia Montoya Zavala. 2019. "Menores migrantes de retorno en Culiacán, Sinaloa, México: Un reto familiar, educativo y binacional." *Ánfora* 26(46): 137–62.

Hiernaux, Daniel. 1995. *Nueva periferia, vieja metrópoli: El Valle de Chalco, Ciudad de México.* Universidad Autónoma Metropolitana-Xochimilco.

Hondagneu-Sotelo, Pierrette. 1992. "Overcoming Patriarchal Constraints: The Reconstruction of Gender Relations among Mexican Immigrant Women and Men." *Gender and Society* 6(3, September): 393–415. https://doi.org/10.1177 /089124392006003004.

———. 1994. *Gendered Transitions.* University of California Press.

———. 1999. "Introduction: Gender and Contemporary U.S. Immigration." *American Behavioral Scientist* 42(4, January): 565–76. https://doi.org/10.1177 /00027649921954363.

———. 2003. "Gender and Immigration: A Retrospective and Introduction." In *Gender and U.S. Immigration*, edited by Pierrette Hondagneu-Sotelo. University of California Press.

Hondagneu-Sotelo, Pierrette, and Ernestine Avila. 1997. "'I'm Here, but I'm There': The Meanings of Latina Transnational Motherhood." *Gender and Society* 11(5, October): 548–71. https://doi.org/10.1177/089124397011005003.

Hualde Alfaro, Alfredo. 2017. *Más trabajo que empleo: Trayectorias laborales y precariedad en los call centers de México.* El Colegio de la Frontera Norte.

Hualde Alfaro, Alfredo, and Israel J. Ibarra. 2019. "La reinserción laboral de los deportados y retornados en Guadalajara y Tijuana: ¿Empleos sostenibles o empleos precarios?" In *Experiencias de retorno de migrantes mexicanos en contextos urbanos*, edited by María Dolores París Pombo, Alfredo Hualde Alfaro, and Ofelia Woo Morales. El Colegio de la Frontera Norte.

Hualde Alfaro, Alfredo, and María Dolores París Pombo. 2019. "Mercados de trabajo y reinserción laboral de deportados en Tijuana, Baja California." In *¿Volver a casa? Migrantes de retorno en América Latina: Debates, tendencias, y experiencias divergentes*, edited by Liliana Rivera Sánchez. El Colegio de México.

Hunt, Jennifer. 2022. "Renewing America, Revamping Immigration." Brookings Institution, December 7. https://www.brookings.edu/research/renewing -america-revamping-immigration/.

Irwin, Robert, and Guillermo Alonso Meneses, eds. 2023. *Humanizando la deportación: Narrativas digitales desde las calles de Tijuana.* El Colegio de la Frontera Norte.

Izazola, Haydea. 2004. "Migration to and from Mexico City, 1995–2000." *Environment and Urbanization* 16(1, April): 211–30. https://doi.org/10.1177 /095624780401600117.

Jacobo-Suárez, Mónica. 2017. "De regreso a 'casa' y sin apostilla: Estudiantes mexicoamericanos en México." *Sinéctica* 48.

Jacobo-Suárez, Mónica, and Nuty Cárdenas Alaminos. 2018. *Los retornados: ¿Cómo responder a la diversidad de migrantes mexicanos que regresan de*

Estados Unidos? Centro de Investigación y Docencia Económicas (CIDE), Programa Interdisciplinario en Estudios Migratorios (CIDE-MIG).

———. 2020. "Back on Your Own: Return Migration and the Federal Government Response in Mexico." *Migraciones Internacionales* 11(July 15). https://doi.org/10.33679/rmi.v1i1.1731.

Johnson, Kevin R. 2014. "Possible Reforms of the U.S. Immigration Laws." *Chapman Law Review* 18(2): 315.

———. 2021. "Bringing Racial Justice to Immigration Law." *Northwestern University Law Review Online* 116(1). https://doi.org/10.2139/ssrn.3771006.

Kanaiaupuni, Shawn Malia. 2000. "Reframing the Migration Question: An Analysis of Men, Women, and Gender in Mexico." *Social Forces* 78(4, June): 1311. https://doi.org/10.2307/3006176.

Kanaiaupuni, Shawn Malia, and Katharine M. Donato. 1999. "Migradollars and Mortality: The Effects of Migration on Infant Survival in Mexico." *Demography* 36(3): 339–53. https://doi.org/10.2307/2648057.

Kandel, William, and Grace Kao. 2001. "The Impact of Temporary Labor Migration on Mexican Children's Educational Aspirations and Performance." *International Migration Review* 35(4, December): 1205–31. https://doi.org/10.1111/j.1747-7379.2001.tb00058.x.

Kandel, William, and Douglas S. Massey. 2002. "The Culture of Mexican Migration: A Theoretical and Empirical Analysis." *Social Forces* 80(3, March): 981–1004. https://doi.org/10.1353/sof.2002.0009.

Kanstroom, Dan. 2007. *Deportation Nation: Outsiders in American History.* Harvard University Press.

King, Russell. 1986. "Return Migration and Regional Economic Development: An Overview." In *Return Migration and Regional Economic Problems*, edited by Russell King. Croom Helm.

King, Russell, and Katie Kuschminder. 2022. "Introduction: Definitions, Typologies, and Theories of Return Migration." In *Handbook of Return Migration*, edited by Russell King and Katie Kuschminder. Edward Elgar Publishing.

King, Russell, and Ronald Skeldon. 2010. "'Mind the Gap!' Integrating Approaches to Internal and International Migration." *Journal of Ethnic and Migration Studies* 36(10): 1619–46. https://doi.org/10.1080/1369183X.2010.489380.

Kuschminder, Katie, ed. 2017. *Reintegration Strategies: Conceptualizing How Return Migrants Reintegrate.* Springer International Publishing.

Lareau, Annette. 2021. *Listening to People: A Practical Guide to Interviewing, Participant Observation, Data Analysis, and Writing It All Up.* University of Chicago Press.

Lee, Ronald. 2002. "The Demographic Transition: Three Centuries of Fundamental Change." *Journal of Economic Perspectives* 17(4, Fall): 167–90. https://doi.org/10.1257/089533003772034943.

Li, Wei, Claudia Sadowski, and Yu Wan. 2016. "La migración de retorno y el transnacionalismo: La evidencia en la migración altamente calificada." In *Nuevas experiencias de la migración de retorno*, edited by Elaine Levine, Silvia Núñez, and Mónica Verea. UNAM-CISAN-Instituto Matías Romero.

Lindstrom, David P. 1996. "Economic Opportunity in Mexico and Return Migration from the United States." *Demography* 33(3): 357–74. https://doi.org/10.2307 /2061767.

Lindstrom, David P., and Silvia E. Giorguli-Saucedo. 2002. "The Short-and Long-Term Effects of US Migration Experience on Mexican Women's Fertility." *Social Forces* 80(4): 1341–68. https://doi.org/10.1353/sof.2002.0030.

———. 2007. "The Interrelationship of Fertility, Family Maintenance, and Mexico-U.S. Migration." *Demographic Research* 17(December): 821–58. https://doi.org /10.4054/DemRes.2007.17.28.

Lindstrom, David P., and Adriana López Ramírez. 2010. "Pioneers and Followers: Migrant Selectivity and the Development of U.S. Migration Streams in Latin America." *Annals of the American Academy of Political and Social Science* 630(1, July): 53–77. https://doi.org/10.1177/0002716210368103.

Lomnitz-Adler, Claudio, ed. 2000. *Vicios públicos, virtudes privadas: La corrupción en México.* CIESAS.

López, Marcos Valdivia, and Mercedes Pedrero Nieto. 2011. "Segmentación laboral, educación, y desigualdad salarial en México." *Revista Mexicana de Sociología* 73(1): 139–75.

Lopez, William D. 2019. *Separated: Family and Community in the Aftermath of an Immigration Raid.* Johns Hopkins University Press.

Lozano Ascencio, Fernando. 2002. "Migrantes de las ciudades: Nuevos modelos de la migración mexicana a Estados Unidos." *Población y sociedad al inicio del siglo,* edited by Brígida García, vol. 21. El Colegio de México.

———. 2004. "Migration Strategies in Urban Contexts: Labor Migration from Mexico City to the United States." *Migraciones Internacionales* 2(3): 34–59. http://www .scielo.org.mx/scielo.php?script=sci_abstract&pid=S1665-89062004000100002&l -ng=es&nrm=iso&tlng=en.

Lozano Ascencio, Fernando, Bryan Roberts, and Frank Bean. 1997. "The Inter-connectedness of Internal and International Migration: The Case of the United States and Mexico." *Soziale Welt* (special issue) 12: 8–9.

Luker, Kristin. 2009. *Salsa Dancing into the Social Sciences.* Harvard University Press.

Macías-Rojas, Patricia. 2018. "Immigration and the War on Crime: Law and Order Politics and the Illegal Immigration Reform and Immigrant Responsibility Act of 1996." *Journal on Migration and Human Security* 6(1, January): 1–25. https://doi.org/10.1177/233150241800600101.

Maghbouleh, Neda, Laila Omar, Melissa A. Milkie, and Ito Peng. 2019. "Listening in Arabic: Feminist Research with Syrian Refugee Mothers." *Meridians* 18(2, October 1): 482–507. https://doi.org/10.1215/15366936-7789739.

Mahler, Sarah J., and Patricia R. Pessar. 2006. "Gender Matters: Ethnographers Bring Gender from the Periphery toward the Core of Migration Studies." *International Migration Review* 40(1, March): 27–63. https://doi.org/10.1111 /j.1747-7379.2006.00002.x.

Marcelli, Enrico A., and Wayne A. Cornelius. 2001. "The Changing Profile of Mexican Migrants to the United States: New Evidence from California and

Mexico." *Latin American Research Review* 36(3): 105–31. https://doi.org/10.1017/S0023879100019191.

Martin, Philip L., and J. Edward Taylor. 1996. "The Anatomy of a Migration Hump." In *Development Strategy, Employment, and Migration: Insights from Models*. Organization for Economic Cooperation and Development, Publications and Information Center.

Martínez, Daniel E., Jeremy Slack, and Ricardo D. Martínez-Schuldt. 2018. "Repeat Migration in the Age of the 'Unauthorized Permanent Resident': A Quantitative Assessment of Migration Intentions Postdeportation." *International Migration Review* 52(4, December): 1186–1217. https://doi.org/10.1177/0197918318767921.

Martínez-Aranda, Mirian G. 2022. "Extended Punishment: Criminalising Immigrants through Surveillance Technology." *Journal of Ethnic and Migration Studies* 48(1): 74–91. https://doi.org/10.1080/1369183X.2020.1822159.

Martínez Díaz, Dulce Paulina. 2012. "¿De vuelta al campo? El destino de las remesas al retorno de los migrantes en el escenario neo-rural de tres comunidades del centro de Veracruz." Universidad Veracruzana.

Martínez-Donate, Ana P., Melbourne F. Hovell, María Gudelia Rangel, Xiao Zhang, Carol L. Sipan, Carlos Magis-Rodríguez, and J. Eduardo González-Fagoaga. 2015. "Migrants in Transit: The Importance of Monitoring HIV Risk among Migrant Flows at the Mexico-U.S. Border." *American Journal of Public Health* 105(3, March): 497–509. https://doi.org/10.2105/AJPH.2014.302336.

Masferrer, Claudia. 2014. "De regreso a otro lugar: La relación entre la migración interna y la migración de retorno en 2005." In *Análisis espacial de las remesas, migración de retorno, y crecimiento regional en Mexico*, edited by Marcos Valdivia López and Fernando Lozano Ascencio. CRIM, UNAM, Plaza y Valdés.

———. 2021a. *Atlas of Return Migration from the United States to Mexico*. El Colegio de México AC.

———. 2021b. "Efectos de Covid-19 en los flujos migratorios desde y hacia México." *Coyuntura demográfica* 19: 45–52.

Masferrer, Claudia, Erin R. Hamilton, and Nicole Denier. 2019. "Immigrants in Their Parental Homeland: Half a Million U.S.-Born Minors Settle throughout Mexico." *Demography* 56(4): 1453–61. https://doi.org/10.1007/s13524-019-00788-0.

———. 2024. "Adding Return Migration to the Equation: U.S. Immigration Policy and Migrant Families in Mexico." In *Immigration Policy and Immigrant Families*, edited by Jennifer van Hook and Valarie King. Penn State National Symposium on Family Issues, vol. 31. Springer. https://doi.org/10.1007/978-3-031-66679-7_2.

Masferrer, Claudia, and Luicy Pedroza, eds. 2021. *The Intersection of Foreign Policy and Migration Policy in Mexico Today*. El Colegio de México. https://migdep.colmex.mx/publicaciones/foreign-migration-policy-report.pdf.

Masferrer, Claudia, and Victoria Prieto. 2019. "El perfil sociodemográfico del retorno migratorio reciente: Diferencias y similitudes entre contextos de procedencia y de acogida en América Latina." In *Volver a casa? Migrantes de retorno en América Latina: Debates, tendencias y experiencias divergentes*, edited by Liliana Rivera. El Colegio de México.

Masferrer, Claudia, and Bryan R. Roberts. 2012. "Going Back Home? Changing Demography and Geography of Mexican Return Migration." *Population Research and Policy Review* 31(4): 465–96. https://doi.org/10.1007/s11113-012-9243-8.

Massey, Douglas S. 1986. "The Settlement Process among Mexican Migrants to the United States." *American Sociological Review* 51(5, October): 670–84. https://doi.org/10.2307/2095492.

———. 1988. "Economic Development and International Migration in Comparative Perspective." *Population and Development Review* 14(3, September): 383–413. https://doi.org/10.2307/1972195.

Massey, Douglas S., Rafael Alarcón, Jorge Durand, and Humberto González. 1987. *Return to Aztlan: The Social Process of International Migration from Western Mexico*, vol. 1. University of California Press.

Massey, Douglas S., Joaquin Arango, Graeme Hugo, Ali Kouaouci, Adela Pellegrino, and J. Edward Taylor. 1993. "Theories of International Migration: A Review and Appraisal." *Population and Development Review* 19(3, September): 431–66. https://doi.org/10.2307/2938462.

Massey, Douglas S., Jorge Durand, and Nolan J. Malone. 2002. *Beyond Smoke and Mirrors: Mexican Immigration in an Era of Economic Integration.* Russell Sage Foundation.

Massey, Douglas S., Jorge Durand, and Karen A. Pren. 2015. "Border Enforcement and Return Migration by Documented and Undocumented Mexicans." *Journal of Ethnic and Migration Studies* 41(7): 1015–40. https://doi.org/10.1080/1369183X.2014.986079.

Massey, Douglas S., Jorge Durand, and Fernando Riosmena. 2006. "Capital social, política social y migración desde comunidades tradicionales y nuevas comunidades de origen en México." *Revista Española de Investigaciones Sociológicas (REIS)* 116(1): 97–121.

Massey, Douglas S., and Kristin E. Espinosa. 1997. "What's Driving Mexico-U.S. Migration? A Theoretical, Empirical, and Policy Analysis." *American Journal of Sociology* 102(4, January): 939–99. https://doi.org/10.1086/231037.

Massey, Douglas S., Mary J. Fischer, and Chiara Capoferro. 2006. "International Migration and Gender in Latin America: A Comparative Analysis." *International Migration* 44(5, December): 63–91. https://doi.org/10.1111/j.1468-2435.2006.00387.x.

Massey, Douglas S., and Kerstin Gentsch. 2014. "Undocumented Migration to the United States and the Wages of Mexican Immigrants." *International Migration Review* 48(2, June): 482–99. https://doi.org/10.1111/imre.12065.

Massey, Douglas S., Luin Goldring, and Jorge Durand. 1994. "Continuities in Transnational Migration: An Analysis of Nineteen Mexican Communities." *American Journal of Sociology* 99(6, May): 1492–1533. https://doi.org/10.1086/230452.

Massey, Douglas S., and Emilio Parrado. 1994. "Migradollars: The Remittances and Savings of Mexican Migrants to the USA." *Population Research and Policy Review* 13(1): 3–30. https://doi.org/10.1007/BF01074319.

———. 1998. "International Migration and Business Formation in Mexico." *Social Science Quarterly* 79(1, March): 1–20.

Massey, Douglas S., and Karen A. Pren. 2012. "Unintended Consequences of U.S. Immigration Policy: Explaining the Post-1965 Surge from Latin America." *Population and Development Review* 38(1, March): 1–29. https://doi.org/10.1111/j.1728-4457.2012.00470.x.

Massey, Douglas S., Karen A. Pren, and Jorge Durand. 2016. "Why Border Enforcement Backfired." *American Journal of Sociology* 121(5, March): 1557–1600. https://doi.org/10.1086/684200.

Medina, Dulce, and Cecilia Menjívar. 2015. "The Context of Return Migration: Challenges of Mixed-Status Families in Mexico's Schools." *Ethnic and Racial Studies* 38(12): 2123–39. https://doi.org/10.1080/01419870.2015.1036091.

Mendoza, Cristóbal. 2009. "La emergencia de la migración internacional en la periferia empobrecida de la Ciudad de México: Valle de Chalco-Solidaridad, Estado de México." *Migraciones Internacionales* 5(2): 5–37.

———. 2015. "Explaining Urban Migration from Mexico City to the USA: Social Networks and Territorial Attachments." *International Migration* 53(5, October): 69–83. https://doi.org/10.1111/imig.12050.

Meneses, Guillermo Alonso. 2005. "Violencias asociadas al cruce indocumentado de la frontera México-Estados Unidos." *Nueva Antropología* 20(65): 113–29.

———. 2012. "Recesión económica, reflujos migratorios, y violencia antiinmigrante entre México y Estados Unidos." *Norteamérica* 7(2): 221–51.

Menjívar, Cecilia. 2006. "Liminal Legality: Salvadoran and Guatemalan Immigrants' Lives in the United States." *American Journal of Sociology* 111(4, January): 999–1037. https://doi.org/10.1086/499509.

———. 2014. "Immigration Law beyond Borders: Externalizing and Internalizing Border Controls in an Era of Securitization." *Annual Review of Law and Social Science* 10(November): 353–69. https://doi.org/10.1146/annurev-lawsocsci-110413-030842.

Menjívar, Cecilia, and Leisy J. Abrego. 2012. "Legal Violence: Immigration Law and the Lives of Central American Immigrants." *American Journal of Sociology* 117(5, March): 1380–1421. https://doi.org/10.1086/663575.

Merriam, Sharan B., Juanita Johnson-Bailey, Ming-Yeh Lee, Youngwha Kee, Gabo Ntseane, and Mazanah Muhamad. 2001. "Power and Positionality: Negotiating Insider/Outsider Status within and across Cultures." *International Journal of Lifelong Education* 20(5): 405–16. https://doi.org/10.1080/02601370120490.

Meza González, Liliana. 2017. "Migrantes retornados en la Ciudad de México: Es más fácil irse que regresar." In *Emigración, tránsito, y retorno en México*, edited by Liliana Meza González, Carla Pederzini, and Magdalena Sofía de la Peña. ITESO, Universidad Iberoamericana.

Meza González, Liliana, and Carla Pederzini Villarreal. 2018. "Migración internacional y escolaridad como medios alternativos de movilidad social: El caso de México." *Estudios Económicos* (December): 163–206. https://doi.org/10.24201/ee.v0i0.385.

Migration Policy Institute. 2019. "Rethinking U.S. Immigration Policy: Building a Responsive, Effective Immigration System." https://www.migrationpolicy.org /multimedia/rethinking-us-immigration-policy-building-responsive-effective-immigration-system.

Monico, Gabriela. 2020. "Contesting 'Citizenship': The Testimonies of Undocumented Immigrant Activist Women." In *We Are Not Dreamers: Undocumented Scholars Theorize Undocumented Life in the United States*, edited by Leisy J. Abrego and Genevieve Negron-Gonzales. Duke University Press.

Moreno Figueroa, Mónica G. 2022. "Entre confusiones y distracciones: Mestizaje y racismo anti-negro en México." *Estudios Sociológicos* 40(February): 87–118. https://doi.org/10.24201/es.2022v40.2084.

Morris, Stephen D. 2013. "Drug Trafficking, Corruption, and Violence in Mexico: Mapping the Linkages." *Trends in Organized Crime* 16(2): 195–220. https:// doi.org/10.1007/s12117-013-9191-7.

Moslimani, Mohamad. 2022. "Around Four-in-Ten Latinos in U.S. Worry That They or Someone Close to Them Could Be Deported." Pew Research Center, February 14. https://www.pewresearch.org/short-reads/2022/02/14/around-four -in-ten-latinos-in-u-s-worry-that-they-or-someone-close-to-them-could -be-deported/.

Mummert, Gail. 2009. "Siblings by Telephone: Experiences of Mexican Children in Long-Distance Childrearing Arrangements." *Journal of the Southwest* 15(4, Winter). https://doi.org/10.1353/jsw.2009.0001.

———. 2010a. "La crianza a distancia: Representaciones de la maternidad y paternidad transnacionales en México, China, Filipinas, y Ecuador." In *Procreación, crianza y género: Aproximaciones antropológicas a la parentalidad*, edited by Virginia Fons, Anna Piella Vila, and María Valdés. Promociones y Publicaciones Universitarias.

———. 2010b. "La reinvención de lazos familiares en contextos migratorios." In *Familia y tradición: Herencias tangibles e intangibles en escenarios cambiantes*, edited by Nora Edith Jiménez. El Colegio de Michoacán.

———. 2012a. "Pensando las familias transnacionales desde los relatos de vida: Análisis longitudinal de la convivencia intergeneracional." In *Métodos cualitativos y su aplicación empírica: Por los caminos de la migración internacional*, edited by Marina Ariza and Laura Velasco, Instituto de Investigaciones Sociales, UNAM and El Colegio de la Frontera Norte.

———. 2012b. "Synergies between Feminist Thought and Migration Studies in Mexico (1975–2010)." In *Feminism and Migration: Cross-Cultural Engagements*, edited by Glenda Tibe Bonifacio. Springer Netherlands.

Nájar, Alberto. 2017. "Terremoto en México: Por qué la historia del edificio que se desplomó en tres segundos revivió el fantasma de las costureras muertas en el sismo de 1985." *BBC Mundo*, September 21. https://www.bbc.com/mundo /noticias-america-latina-41345526.

Nobles, Jenna. 2011. "Parenting from Abroad: Migration, Nonresident Father Involvement, and Children's Education in Mexico." *Journal of Marriage and*

Family 73(4, August): 729–46. https://doi.org/10.1111/j.1741-3737.2011
.00842.x.

———. 2013. "Migration and Father Absence: Shifting Family Structure in Mexico."
Demography 50(4): 1303–14. https://doi.org/10.1007/s13524-012-0187-8.

Norteado (Northless). 2009. Directed by Rigoberto Pérezcano, written by Edgar
San Juan and Rigoberto Pérezcano. https://www.imdb.com/title/tt1331320/.

Ocampo Marín, Luis Fernando. 2016. "Estudiantes y familias transnacionales en
México." *Tlamati* 7(1): 48–51.

Ojeda, Norma. 2009. "Reflexiones acerca de las familias transfronterizas y las
familias transnacionales entre México y Estados Unidos." *Frontera Norte*
21(42): 7–30.

Ordaz Díaz, Juan Luis. 2008. "The Economic Returns to Education in Mexico:
A Comparison between Urban and Rural Areas." *Cepal Review* 2008
(96, December): 265–82. https://doi.org/10.18356/665c1845-en.

Organization for Economic Cooperation and Development (OECD). 2020.
"Labour Market Inclusion: Promoting Good Jobs for All in Mexico."
ttps://www.oecd.org/mexico/Policy-Brief-Mexico-Labour-market
-inclusion-EN.pdf.

———. 2022. *Education at a Glance 2022: OECD Indicators*. October 3. https://
www.oecd-ilibrary.org/education/education-at-a-glance-2022_3197152b-en.

Orraca, Pedro, David Rocha, and Eunice Vargas. 2017. "Cross-Border School
Enrolment: Associated Factors in the U.S.-Mexico Borderlands." *Social Science
Journal* 54(4): 389–402. https://doi.org/10.1016/j.soscij.2017.07.008.

Orrenius, Pia M., and Madeline Zavodny. 2017. "Creating Cohesive, Coherent
Immigration Policy." *Journal on Migration and Human Security* 5(1, March):
180–93. https://doi.org/10.1177/233150241700500109.

Padilla Flores, Juan Manuel, and Ana Elizabeth Jardón Hernández. 2015.
"Migración y empleo: Reinserción de los migrantes de retorno al mercado
laboral nacional." Instituto de Estudios y Divulgación sobre Migración.
http://ri.uaemex.mx/handle/20.500.11799/65207.

Palloni, Alberto, Douglas S. Massey, Miguel Ceballos, Kristin Espinosa, and
Michael Spittel. 2001. "Social Capital and International Migration: A Test
Using Information on Family Networks." *American Journal of Sociology*
106(5, March): 1262–98. https://doi.org/10.1086/320817.

Papail, Jean. 2002. "De asalariado a empresario: La reinserción laboral de los
migrantes internacionales en la región centro-occidente de México."
Migraciones Internacionales 1(3): 79–102.

Paredes-Orozco, Guillermo. 2019. "The Limits to Cumulative Causation
Revisited: Urban-Origin Mexico-U.S. Migration in an Era of Increased
Immigration Restrictions." *Demographic Research* 41(October): 815–46. https://
doi.org/10.4054/DemRes.2019.41.28.

París Pombo, María Dolores, Alfredo Hualde Alfaro, and Ofelia Woo Morales. 2019.
Experiencias de retorno de migrantes mexicanos en contextos urbanos. El Colegio
de la Frontera Norte.

Parrado, Emilio A., and Edith Y. Gutiérrez. 2016. "The Changing Nature of Return Migration to Mexico, 1990–2010: Implication of Labor Market Incorporation and Development." *Sociology of Development* 2(2, Summer): 93–118. https://doi.org/10.1525/sod.2016.2.2.93.

Passel, Jeffrey S., and D'Vera Cohn. 2019. "Mexicans Decline to Less than Half the U.S. Unauthorized Immigrant Population for the First Time." Pew Research Center, June 12. https://www.pewresearch.org/fact-tank/2019/06/12/us-unauthorized-immigrant-population-2017/.

Passel, Jeffrey S., D'Vera Cohn, and Ana González-Barrera. 2012. "Net Migration from Mexico Falls to Zero-and Perhaps Less." Pew Hispanic Center, April 23. https://www.pewresearch.org/race-and-ethnicity/2012/04/23/net-migration-from-mexico-falls-to-zero-and-perhaps-less/.

Patler, Caitlin. 2014. "Young and Undocumented: The Impacts of Legal Status on the Incorporation of Immigrant Young Adults in California." PhD. diss., University of California at Los Angeles. https://escholarship.org/uc/item/8pr58321.

———. 2015. "The Economic Impacts of Long-Term Immigration Detention in Southern California." University of California at Los Angeles, Institute for Research on Labor and Employment, September. https://escholarship.org/uc/item/23h0r12q.

———. 2017. "Citizen Advantage, Undocumented Disadvantage, or Both? The Comparative Educational Outcomes of Second and 1.5-Generation Latino Young Adults." *International Migration Review* 52(4, December): 1080–1110. https://doi.org/10.1111/imre.12347.

Patler, Caitlin, and Tanya Maria Golash-Boza. 2017. "The Fiscal and Human Costs of Immigrant Detention and Deportation in the United States." *Sociology Compass* 11(11, November): e12536. https://doi.org/10.1111/soc4.12536.

Patler, Caitlin, Erin R. Hamilton, and Robin Savinar. 2021. "The Limits of Gaining Rights While Remaining Marginalized: The Deferred Action for Childhood Arrivals (DACA) Program and the Psychological Wellbeing of Latina/o Undocumented Youth." *Social Forces* 100(1, September) 246–72. https://doi.org/10.1093/sf/soaa099.

Paul, Anju Mary. 2011. "Stepwise International Migration: A Multistage Migration Pattern for the Aspiring Migrant." *American Journal of Sociology* 116(6, May): 1842–86. https://doi.org/10.1086/659641.

Pedersen, Paul. 1994. *The Five Stages of Culture Shock: Critical Incidents around the World*. ABC-CLIO.

Pedraza, Silvia. 1991. "Women and Migration: The Social Consequences of Gender." *Annual Review of Sociology* 17(1, August): 303–25. https://doi.org/10.1146/annurev.so.17.080191.001511.

Pedroza, Juan. 2012. "Mass Exodus from Oklahoma? Immigrants and Latinos Stay and Weather a State of Capture." *Journal of Latino/Latin American Studies* 4(1, April 1): 27–41. https://doi.org/10.18085/llas.4.1.1g7521874u06g160.

———. 2013. "Removal Roulette: Secure Communities and Immigration Enforcement in the United States (2008–2012)." In *Outside Justice: Immigration and the Criminalizing Impact of Changing Policy and Practice*, edited by David C. Brotherton, Daniel L. Stageman, and Shirley P. Leyro. Springer.

———. 2022. "Housing Instability in an Era of Mass Deportations." *Population Research and Policy Review* (May): 2645–81. https://doi.org/10.1007/s11113 -022-09719-1.

Pedroza, Juan, and Pil H. Chung. 2021. "Death and Disabilities in Divergent Deportation Contexts." In *Migration and Mortality: Social Death, Dispossession, and Survival in the Americas*, edited by Jamie Longazel and Miranda Cady Hallett. Temple University Press.

Peláez Rodríguez, Diana Carolina, and María Dolores París Pombo. 2016. "Deportación femenina y separación familiar: Experiencias de mexicanas deportadas a Tijuana." In *Nuevas experiencias de la migración de retorno*, edited by Elaine Levine, Silvia Núñez, and Mónica Verea. UNAM-CISAN, SRE.

Perreira, Krista M., and Juan Pedroza. 2019. "Policies of Exclusion: Implications for the Health of Immigrants and their Children." *Annual Review of Public Health* 40: 147–66. https://doi.org/10.1146/annurev-publhealth-040218-044115.

Pessar, Patricia. 2003. "Engendering Migration Studies: The Case of New Immigrants in the United States." In *Gender and U.S. Immigration*, edited by Pierrette Hondagneu-Sotelo. University of California Press.

Phillips, Julie A., and Douglas S. Massey. 1999. "The New Labor Market: Immigrants and Wages after IRCA." *Demography* 36(2): 233. https://doi.org/10.2307 /2648111.

Pinedo, Miguel, José Luis Burgos, and Victoria D. Ojeda. 2014. "A Critical Review of Social and Structural Conditions That Influence HIV Risk among Mexican Deportees." *Microbes and Infection* 16(5, May): 379–90. https://doi.org/10.1016 /j.micinf.2014.02.006.

Pinedo, Miguel, José Luis Burgos, María Luisa Zúñiga, Ramona Perez, Caroline A. Macera, and Victoria D. Ojeda. 2018. "Deportation and Mental Health among Migrants Who Inject Drugs along the U.S.-Mexico Border." *Global Public Health* 13(2): 211–26. https://doi.org/10.1080/17441692.2016.1170183.

Pinillos Quintero, Gabriela Irina. 2023. "Re-encontrarse con el Estado: Visibilización e invisibilización de los procesos de retorno y post-retorno en la Ciudad de México." *Norteamérica, Revista Académica del CISAN-UNAM* 18(2). https:// doi.org/10.22201/cisan.24487228e.2023.2.630.

Pinillos Quintero, Gabriela Irina, and Francisco Flores Peña. 2020. "Migración de retorno y separación familiar: Un estudio de caso en la Ciudad de México." *Coyuntura Demográfica* 18(July): 93–97.

Pinillos Quintero, Gabriela Irina, and Laura Velasco Ortiz. 2021. "Recuperar la ciudadanía post-deportación en la frontera México-Estados Unidos." *Frontera Norte* 33. https://doi.org/10.33679/rfn.v1i1.2107.

Portes, Alejandro, and Min Zhou. 1993. "The New Second Generation: Segmented Assimilation and Its Variants." *Annals of the American Academy of Political and Social Science* 530: 74–96.

Prieto, Greg. 2018. *Immigrants under Threat: Risk and Resistance in Deportation Nation*, vol. 5. New York University Press.

Prieto, Victoria, and Martín Koolhaas. 2013. "Retorno reciente y empleo: Los casos de Ecuador, México y Uruguay." In *Población y trabajo en América Latina y el Caribe: Abordajes teórico-conceptuales y tendencias empíricas recientes*, vol. 14, edited by Luciana Gandini and Mauricio Padrón Innamorato. UNFPA, ALAP, UNAM.

Pugh, Allison J. 2013. "What Good Are Interviews for Thinking about Culture? Demystifying Interpretive Analysis." *American Journal of Cultural Sociology* 1(February 12): 42–68. https://doi.org/10.1057/ajcs.2012.4.

Ramírez Armas, Guillermo. 2018. "La reinserción sociocultural y laboral de los migrantes de retorno en Tabasco." *Revista Iberoamericana de Producción Académica y Gestión Educativa* 5(10).

Reich, Jennifer A. 2021. "Power, Positionality, and the Ethic of Care in Qualitative Research." *Qualitative Sociology* 44: 575–81.

Reichert, Joshua S. 1981. "The Migrant Syndrome: Seasonal U.S. Wage Labor and Rural Development in Central Mexico." *Human Organization* 40(1, Spring): 56–66. https://doi.org/10.17730/humo.40.1.c6148p5743512768.

Rendall, Michael S., and Susan W. Parker. 2014. "Two Decades of Negative Educational Selectivity of Mexican Migrants to the United States." *Population and Development Review* 40(3, September): 421–46. https://doi.org/10.1111/j.1728-4457.2014.00692.x.

Reyes, Victoria. 2020. "Ethnographic Toolkit: Strategic Positionality and Researchers' Visible and Invisible Tools in Field Research." *Ethnography* 21(2, June): 220–40. https://doi.org/10.1177/1466138118805121.

Riosmena, Fernando. 2009. "Socioeconomic Context and the Association between Marriage and Mexico–U.S. Migration." *Social Science Research* 38(2, June): 324–37. https://doi.org/10.1016/j.ssresearch.2008.12.001.

———. 2010. "Policy Shocks: On the Legal Auspices of Latin American Migration to the United States." *Annals of the American Academy of Political and Social Science* 630(1): 270–93. https://doi.org/10.1177/0002716210368113.

———. 2024. "Worlds in Motion *Redux?* Expanding Migration Theories and Their Interconnections." *Population and Development Review*, July 12 (online). https://doi.org/10.1111/padr.12630.

Riosmena, Fernando, César González González, and Rebeca Wong. 2012. "El retorno reciente de Estados Unidos: Salud, bienestar, y vulnerabilidad de los adultos mayores." *Coyuntura Demográfica* 2: 63–67.

Riosmena, Fernando, and Douglas S. Massey. 2012. "Pathways to El Norte: Origins, Destinations, and Characteristics of Mexican Migrants to the United States." *International Migration Review* 46(1, March): 3–36. https://doi.org/10.1111/j.1747-7379.2012.00879.x.

Riosmena, Fernando, Raphael Nawrotzki, and Lori Hunter. 2018. "Climate Migration at the Height and End of the Great Mexican Emigration Era." *Population and Development Review* 44(3, September): 455–88. https://doi.org/10.1111/padr.12158.

Rivera Sánchez, Liliana. 2013a. "Migración de retorno y experiencias de reinserción en la zona metropolitana de la Ciudad de México." *REMHU: Revista*

Interdisciplinar da Mobilidade Humana 21(December): 55–76. https://doi.org
/10.1590/S1980-85852013000200004.

——. 2013b. "Reinserción social y laboral de inmigrantes retornados de Estados
Unidos en un contexto urbano." *Iztapalapa: Revista de Ciencias Sociales y
Humanidades* 34(75): 29–56. https://doi.org/10.28928/ri/752013/atc2
/riverasanchezl.

——. 2015a. "Entre la incertidumbre y la esperanza: Narrativas de migrantes
retornados." *Migración y Desarrollo* 13(24): 185–99.

——. 2015b. "Movilidades, circulaciones, y localidades: Desafíos analíticos del
retorno y la reinserción en la ciudad." *Alteridades* 25(50): 51–63.

——. 2015c. "Narrativas de retorno y movilidad: Entre prácticas de involucramiento
y espacialidades múltiples en la ciudad." *Estudios Políticos* 47: 243–64.

——. 2016. "¿Volver a casa? Desafíos y rutas divergentes de migrantes de retorno."
In *Continuidades y cambios en las migraciones de México a Estados Unidos:
Tendencias en la circulación, experiencias, y resignificaciones de la migración y el
retorno en el Estado de México*, edited by Jorge Olvera García and Norma Baca
Tavira. Universidad Autónoma del Estado de México.

Roberts, Bryan R., Reanne Frank, and Fernando Lozano-Ascencio. 1999. "Transnational Migrant Communities and Mexican Migration to the U.S." *Ethnic and
Racial Studies* 22(2): 238–66. https://doi.org/10.1080/014198799329477.

Roberts, Bryan R., and Erin R. Hamilton. 2007. "La nueva geografía de la emigración: Zonas emergentes de atracción y expulsión, continuidad y cambio."
In *El país transnacional: Migración mexicana y cambio social a través de la frontera*,
edited by Marina Ariza and Alejandro Portes. Instituto de Investigaciones
Sociales–UNAM.

Roberts, Bryan R., Cecilia Menjívar, and Néstor P. Rodríguez. 2017. "Voluntary
and Involuntary Return Migration." In *Deportation and Return in a Border-
Restricted World: Experiences in Mexico, El Salvador, Guatemala, and Honduras*,
edited by Bryan Roberts, Cecilia Menjívar, and Néstor P. Rodríguez. Springer.

Rodríguez Chávez, Oscar. 2021. "Violence Effects on Municipal Internal Emigration
Rates in Mexico: 1995–2015." *Migraciones Internacionales* 12. https://doi.org
/10.33679/rmi.v1i1.2045.

Rodríguez Pérez, Reyna Elizabeth. 2019. "Diferencial salarial por género entre
el sector público y privado formal-informal en México." *Revista de Economía*
36(93): 62–89. https://doi.org/10.33937/reveco.2019.108.

Román González, Betsabé, and Eduardo Carrillo Cantú. 2017. "'Bienvenido a la
escuela': Experiencias escolares de alumnos transnacionales en Morelos, México."
Sinéctica 48: 1–19.

Rosenbloom, Raquel, and Jeanne Batalova. 2022. "Mexican Immigrants in the
United States." Migration Policy Institute, October 13. https://www.migration
policy.org/article/mexican-immigrants-united-states.

Ruehs, Emily M. 2017. "Adventures in *El Norte*: The Identities and Immigration of
Unaccompanied Youth." *Men and Masculinities* 20(3, August): 364–84.
https://doi.org/10.1177/1097184X16634796.

Ruiz Peralta, Liza Fabiola, and Gloria Ciria Valdéz Gardea. 2012. "Menores de retorno: El proceso administrativo de inscripción en las escuelas sonorenses." In *Movilización, migración, y retorno de la niñez migrante: Una mirada antropológica*, edited by Gloria Ciria Valdéz Gardea. El Colegio de Sonora, Universidad Autónoma de Sinaloa.

Ruiz Soto, Ariel G., Rodrigo Dominguez-Villegas, Luis Argueta, and Randy Capps. 2019. "Sustainable Reintegration: Strategies to Support Migrants Returning to Mexico and Central America." Migration Policy Institute, January.

Saadi, Altaf, Maria-Elena De Trinidad Young, Caitlin Patler, Jeremias Leonel Estrada, and Homer Venters. 2020. "Understanding U.S. Immigration Detention: Reaffirming Rights and Addressing Social- Structural Determinants of Health." *Health and Human Rights Journal* 22(1, June): 187–97.

Saadi, Altaf, Caitlin Patler, and Maria-Elena De Trinidad Young. 2022. "Cumulative Risk of Immigration Prison Conditions on Health Outcomes among Detained Immigrants in California." *Journal of Racial and Ethnic Health Disparities* 9(6): 2518–32. https://doi.org/10.1007/s40615-021-01187-1.

Sabates, Ricardo, and Fabio Pettirino. 2007. "The Identity of Emigrants from Mexico City." *Papeles de Población* 13(52): 211–29.

Salas Alfaro, Renato. 2013. "Actividades productivas y migración internacional de retorno: Los panaderos de San Miguel Coatlán, Oaxaca." *Desacatos* 41: 107–22.

Salas Alfaro, Renato, Norma Baca Tavira, and Maripaz Alcántara Quintana. 2013. "Motivaciones para migrar y repercusiones en la estructura familiar de migrantes retornadas en el Estado de México: Una aproximación desde el género." In *La investigación social en México*, edited by Asael Ortiz Lazcano. Universidad Autónoma del Estado de Hidalgo.

Salas Alfaro, Renato, and Miguel Cruz Vázquez. 2013. *Migrantes retornados, actividades laborales, y nuevas habilidades adquiridas en San Miguel Ocotlán*. Universidad Popular Autónoma del Estado del Estado de Puebla, Universidad Autónoma del Estado de México, Consejo Nacional de Ciencia y Tecnología.

Salas Alfaro, Renato, and Patricia Román Reyes. 2017. "Investment in Small Business among International Migrants in the Estado de México." *International Journal of Business and Social Science* 8(10): 25–33.

Sánchez, Juan. 2007. "El retorno de menores migrantes a escuela de Nuevo León: Trayectorias escolares, identidades transnacionales, dinámicas de inclusión-exclusión y trabajo docente." Universidad Autónoma de Nuevo León.

Sandoval-Cervantes, Iván. 2022. *Oaxaca in Motion*. University of Texas Press.

Sarsfield, Rodolfo. 2012. "The Bribe Game: Microfoundations of Corruption in Mexico." *Justice System Journal* 33(2): 215–34. https://doi.org/10.1080/0098261X.2012.10768012.

Sassen, Saskia. 2000. *Guests and Aliens*. New Press.

Secretaría de Gobernación, Instituto Nacional de Migración. 2022a. "Guía el programa héroes: Brinda atención, orientación e información a los mexicanos que viven en otros países y visitan México." https://www.gob.mx/inm/acciones-y-programas/programa-heroes-paisanos.

————. 2022b. "Guía Procedimiento de Repatriación al interior de México." https://www.inm.gob.mx/static/repatriacion_h/Repatriacion_H.pdf.

Secretaría de Movilidad. 2020. *Programa integral de movilidad de la Ciudad de México 2020–2024: Diagnóstico Técnico.* SEMOVI. https://semovi.cdmx.gob.mx/storage/app/media/diagnostico-tecnico-de-movilidad-pim.pdf.

Secretaría de Turismo. 2019. "Actividad turística de la Ciudad de México: Enero–diciembre 2009–2019." Actividad Turística de la Ciudad de México. https://www.turismo.cdmx.gob.mx/storage/app/media/Estadisticas/est_2019/Enero%20a%20diciembre%202009%20-%202019.pdf.

Secretaría del Trabajo y Previsión Social. 2017. "Programa de Apoyo al Empleo/Repatriados trabajando: Datos y recursos." October 20. https://datos.gob.mx/busca/dataset/programa-de-apoyo-al-empleo-repatriados-trabajando.

Sheehan, Connor M., and Fernando Riosmena. 2013. "Migration, Business Formation, and the Informal Economy in Urban Mexico." *Social Science Research* 4 (4, July): 1092–1108. https://doi.org/10.1016/j.ssresearch.2013.01.006.

Silver, Alexis M. 2018. "Displaced at 'Home': 1.5-Generation Immigrants Navigating Membership after Returning to Mexico." *Ethnicities* 18(2, April): 208–24. https://doi.org/10.1177/1468796817752560.

Silver, Alexis M., and Melissa A. Manzanares. 2023. "Transnational Ambivalence: Incorporation after Forced and Compelled Return to Mexico." *Ethnic and Racial Studies* 46(12): 1–21. https://doi.org/10.1080/01419870.2023.2172354.

Slack, Jeremy. 2019. *Deported to Death: How Drug Violence Is Changing Migration on the U.S.–Mexico Border*, vol. 45. University of California Press.

Slack, Jeremy, and Howard Campbell. 2016. "On Narco-coyotaje: Illicit Regimes and Their Impacts on the U.S.–Mexico Border." *Antipode* 48(5, November): 1380–99. https://doi.org/10.1111/anti.12242.

Slack, Jeremy, Daniel E. Martínez, Scott Whiteford, and Emily Peiffer. 2015. "In Harm's Way: Family Separation, Immigration Enforcement Programs, and Security on the U.S.-Mexico Border." *Journal on Migration and Human Security* 3(2, June): 109–28. https://doi.org/10.1177/233150241500300201.

Slack, Jeremy, and Scott Whiteford. 2011. "Violence and Migration on the Arizona-Sonora Border." *Human Organization* 70(1, Spring): 11–21. https://doi.org/10.17730/humo.70.1.k34n00130470113w.

Smith, Robert. 2006. *Mexican New York: Transnational Lives of New Immigrants.* University of California Press.

Sobrino, Luis Jaime. 2008. "Diversidad y especialización económica en el subsistema de ciudades de la Región Centro." In *La urbanización difusa de la Ciudad de México: Otras miradas sobre un espacio antiguo*, edited by Javier Delgado. Instituto de Geografía-UNAM.

————. 2020. "Crecimiento económico y dinámica demográfica en ciudades de México, 1980–2020." *Papeles de Población* 26(104, April–June).

————. 2022. *Migración interna y desarrollo en México.* El Colegio de México.

Solís Lizama, Mirian. 2018. "Labor Reintegration of Return Migrants in Two Rural Communities of Yucatán, Mexico." *Migraciones Internacionales* 9(35): 185–212.

Solís Martínez, Yovana de la Luz. 2019. "Migración de retorno y reinserción laboral en Guanajuato: Entre la reemigración y el mercado local." Universidad Nacional Autónoma de México. https://ru.atheneadigital.filos.unam.mx/jspui/handle /FFYL_UNAM/3112.

Stark, Oded, and David E. Bloom. 1985. "The New Economics of Labor Migration." *American Economic Review* 75(2): 173–78.

Stecklov, Guy, Paul Winters, Marco Stampini, and Benjamin Davis. 2005. "Do Conditional Cash Transfers Influence Migration? A Study Using Experimental Data from the Mexican Progresa Program." *Demography* 42(4): 769–90. https://doi.org/10.1353/dem.2005.0037.

Suárez-Orozco, Carola, Hirokazu Yoshikawa, Robert Teranishi, and Marcelo Suárez-Orozco. 2011. "Growing Up in the Shadows: The Developmental Implications of Unauthorized Status." *Harvard Educational Review* 81(3, Autumn): 438–73. https://doi.org/10.17763/haer.81.3.g23x203763783m75.

Sue, Christina A., Fernando Riosmena, and Edward Telles. 2024. "Black Disadvantage or Advantage? Misalignment between State and Popular Understandings of Blackness in Mexico." *Socius* 10(January): 23780231231217821. https://doi.org /10.1177/23780231231217821.

Sweetman, Arthur, James Ted McDonald, and Lesleyanne Hawthorne. 2015. "Occupational Regulation and Foreign Qualification Recognition: An Overview." *Canadian Public Policy* 41 (supplement 1) (August): S1–13. https:// doi.org/10.3138/cpp.41.s1.s1.

Taylor, J. Edward, Joaquín Arango, Graeme Hugo, Ali Kouaouci, Douglas S. Massey, and Adela Pellegrino. 1996. "International Migration and National Development." *Population Index* 62(2, Summer): 181–212. https://doi.org /10.2307/3646297.

Timmermans, Stefan, and Iddo Tavory. 2012. "Theory Construction in Qualitative Research: From Grounded Theory to Abductive Analysis." *Sociological Theory* 30(3, September): 167–86. https://doi.org/10.1177/0735275112457914.

Tinajero Vega, Anya. 2015. *Mujeres de retorno a la zona de Morelos y municipios aledaños: Escolaridad e inserción laboral frente a las no migrantes, 2010.* FLACSO México.

Tinoco, Elizabeth. 2014. "Informal Employment in Mexico: Current Situation, Policies, and Challenges." International Labour Organization. https://www.ilo.org /wcmsp5/groups/public/—-americas/—-ro-lima/documents/publication /wcms_245889.pdf.

Torche, Florencia, and Catherine Sirois. 2019. "Restrictive Immigration Law and Birth Outcomes of Immigrant Women." *American Journal of Epidemiology* 188(1, January): 24–33. https://doi.org/10.1093/aje/kwy218.

Torre Cantalapiedra, Eduardo, and Luis Enrique Calva Sánchez. 2021. "Criminalización, separación familiar, y reemigración a Estados Unidos de varones mexicanos deportados." *Estudios Demográficos y Urbanos* 36(2): 637–72. https://doi.org/10.24201/edu.v36i2.1971.

Townsend, Camilla. 2019. *Fifth Sun: A New History of the Aztecs.* Oxford University Press.

Tuirán, Rodolfo. 2002. "Transición demográfica, trayectorias de vida, y desigualdad social en México: Lecciones y opciones." *Papeles de Población* 8(31): 25–66.

UN-Habitat. n.d. "Urbanization in Mexico: Building Inclusive and Sustainable Cities." https://unhabitat.org/mexico.

———. 2023. *Mexico.* https://unhabitat.org/mexico.

U.S. Citizenship and Immigration Services (USCIS). 2021. "Number of Form I-821D: Consideration of Deferred Action for Childhood Arrivals Requests by Intake and Case Status, by Fiscal Year Aug. 15, 2012–Dec. 31, 2020." U.S. Department of Homeland Security, USCIS. https://www.uscis.gov/sites /default/files/document/data/DACA_performancedata_fy2021_qtr1.pdf.

U.S. Customs and Border Protection. 2024. "Stats and Summaries." Last modified May 16, 2024. https://www.cbp.gov/newsroom/stats.

U.S. Department of Homeland Security (DHS). 2009. *Yearbook of Immigration Statistics 2008.* Office of Immigration Statistics, August.

———. 2022. *Yearbook of Immigration Statistics 2021.* Office of Homeland Security Statistics, Washington, D.C.

Valdéz Gardea, Gloria Ciria, Liza Fabiola Ruiz Peralta, Oscar Bernardo Rivera García, and Ramiro Antonio López. 2018. "Menores migrantes de retorno: Problemática académica y proceso administrativo en el sistema escolar sonorense." *Región y Sociedad* 30(72). https://doi.org/10.22198/rys.2018.72.a904.

Valdivia, Carolina. 2019. "Expanding Geographies of Deportability: How Immigration Enforcement at the Local Level Affects Undocumented and Mixed-Status Families." *Law and Policy* 41(1, January): 103–19. https://doi.org /10.1111/lapo.12119.

———. 2021. "'I Became a Mom Overnight': How Parental Detentions and Deportations Impact Young Adults' Role." *Harvard Educational Review* 91(1, Spring): 62–82. https://doi.org/10.17763/1943-5045-91.1.62.

Valenzuela Camacho, Blas, and Ashley Kamille Medina. 2015. "Jóvenes migrantes de retorno e incorporación al mercado laboral: El caso de los profesores de inglés en Sinaloa." In *Migración de retorno en América Latina: Una visión multidisciplinaria,* edited by Cecilia Montoya Zavala and Miriam Nava Zazueta. Universidad Autónoma de Sinaloa, Juan Pablos Editor.

Van Hook, Jennifer, Julia Gelatt, and Ariel G. Ruiz Soto. 2023. "A Turning Point for the Unauthorized Immigrant Population in the United States." Migration Policy Institute, September 13. https://www.migrationpolicy.org/news/turning -point-us-unauthorized-immigrant-population.

Varela Llamas, Rogelio, Juan Manuel Oceguera Hernández, Ramón A. Castillo Ponce, and Gerardo Huber Bernal. 2010. "Determinantes de los ingresos salariales en México: Una perspectiva de capital humano." *Región y Sociedad* 22(49): 117–42.

Vargas-Valle, Eunice D., and Elizabeth Camacho Rojas. 2015. "¿Cambiarse de escuela? Inasistencia y rezago escolar de los niños de migración reciente de Estados Unidos a México." *Norteamérica* 10(2): 157–86. https://doi.org /10.20999/nam.2015.b006.

Vargas-Valle, Eunice D., and Jennifer E. Glick. 2021. "Educational and Migration Aspirations among Children of Mexican Migrant Returnees in a Border Context." *Migration Studies* 9(3, September): 677–701. https://doi.org/10.1093/migration/mnab014.

Vargas-Valle, Eunice D., Jennifer Elyse Glick, and Pedro P. Orraca-Romano. 2022. "U.S. Citizenship for Our Mexican Children! U.S.-Born Children of Non-Migrant Mothers in Northern Mexico." *Journal of Borderlands Studies* 39(2): 1–21.

Vargas Valle, Eunice D., Erin R. Hamilton, and Pedro P. Orraca Romano. 2022. "Family Separation and Remigration Intentions to the USA among Mexican Deportees." *International Migration* 60(3, June): 139–53. https://doi.org/10.1111/imig.12905.

Vázquez Vázquez, José Dionicio. 2011. "Problemas de reinserción educativa en niños con experiencia migratoria: Tlaxcala." *Migración y Desarrollo* 9(17): 113–37. https://doi.org/10.35533/myd.0917.jdvv.

Vega Briones, Germán. 2004. "Migración de retorno en Ciudad Juárez: Un Enfoque cualitativo." In *Nuevas tendencias y nuevos desafíos de la migración internacional: Memorias del seminario permanente sobre migración internacional*, edited by Jorge Santibañez and Manuel Ángel Castillo. COLEF, SOMEDE, COLMEX.

Velázquez Gutiérrez, María Elisa. 2011. "Africanos y afrodescendientes en México: Premisas que obstaculizan entender su pasado y presente." *Cuicuilco* 18(51): 11–22.

Viera, Janelle Ashley. 2020. "Intergenerational Mobility among Return Migrants and Their Families: A Case Study in Mexico." *Ethnic and Migration Studies* 46(19): 4104–23. https://doi.org/10.1080/1369183X.2018.1515621.

Villarreal, Andrés. 2010. "Stratification by Skin Color in Contemporary Mexico." *American Sociological Review* 75(5, October): 652–78. https://doi.org/10.1177/0003122410378232.

———. 2014. "Explaining the Decline in Mexico-U.S. Migration: The Effect of the Great Recession." *Demography* 51(6): 2203–28. https://doi.org/10.1007/s13524-014-0351-4.

Villarreal, Andrés, and Erin R. Hamilton. 2009. "Residential Segregation in the Mexico City Metropolitan Area, 1990–2000." In *Urban Segregation and Governance in the Americas*, edited by Bryan R. Roberts and Robert H. Wilson. Palgrave Macmillan US.

———. 2012. "Rush to the Border? Market Liberalization and Urban- and Rural-Origin Internal Migration in Mexico." *Social Science Research* 41(5, September): 1275–91. https://doi.org/10.1016/j.ssresearch.2012.02.007.

Waldinger, Roger. 2023. "After the Transnational Turn: Looking across Borders to See the Hard Face of the Nation-State." *International Migration* 61(1, February): 92–104. https://doi.org/10.1111/imig.12868.

Ward, Colleen, Stephen Bochner, and Adrian Furnham. 2020. *The Psychology of Culture Shock*. Routledge.

Ward, Peter M. 1998. *Mexico City*. John Wiley and Sons.

Warren, Robert. 2021. "In 2019, the U.S. Undocumented Population Continued a Decade-Long Decline and the Foreign-Born Population Neared Zero Growth." *Journal on Migration and Human Security* 9(1, March): 31–43. https://doi.org/10.1177/2331502421993746.

Warren, Robert, and Donald Kerwin. 2017. "The 2,000 Mile Wall in Search of a Purpose: Since 2007 Visa Overstays Have Outnumbered Undocumented Border Crossers by a Half Million." *Journal on Migration and Human Security* 5(1, March): 124–36. https://doi.org/10.1177/233150241700500107.

Wassink, Joshua, and Jacqueline Hagan. 2018. "A Dynamic Model of Self-Employment and Socioeconomic Mobility among Return Migrants: The Case of Urban Mexico." *Social Forces* 96(3, March): 1069–96. https://doi.org/10.1093/sf/sox095.

———. 2022. "How Local Community Context Shapes Labour Market Re-Entry and Resource Mobilisation among Return Migrants: An Examination of Rural and Urban Communities in Mexico." *Journal of Ethnic and Migration Studies* 48(13): 3301–22. https://doi.org/10.1080/1369183X.2020.1758552.

Wassink, Joshua, and Douglas S. Massey. 2022. "The New System of Mexican Migration: The Role of Entry Mode–Specific Human and Social Capital." *Demography* 59(3): 1071–92. https://doi.org/10.1215/00703370-9938548.

Weiss, Robert S. 1995. *Learning from Strangers: The Art and Method of Qualitative Interview Studies*. Simon & Schuster.

Woo Morales, Ofelia. 2019. "Experiencias de mujeres migrantes retornadas de Estados Unidos a la zona metropolitana de Guadalajara." In *¿Volver a casa? Migrantes de retorno en América Latina: Debates, tendencias y experiencias divergentes*, edited by Liliana Rivera Sánchez. El Colegio de México.

Woo Morales, Ofelia, and Marcela Alejandra Ortiz Rangel. 2015. "La diversidad de la migración de retorno en Jalisco, estado de tradición migratoria." In *Migración y violencia: Dos caras del dolor social*, edited by José Dionicio Vázquez Vázquez. CONACYT, El Colegio de Tlaxcala.

———. 2019. "Reinserción escolar de menores migrantes: Experiencias de familias migrantes de retorno en la Zona Metropolitana de Guadalajara." In *Experiencias de retorno de migrantes mexicanos en contextos urbanos*, edited by María Dolores París Pombo, Alfredo Hualde Alfaro, and Ofelia Woo Morales. El Colegio de la Frontera Norte.

World Bank. 2023. "GDP per Capita (Constant 2015 US$)—Mexico." https://data.worldbank.org/indicator/NY.GDP.PCAP.KD?end=2021&locations=MX&start=1960.

———. 2024. "Labor Force Participation Rate, Female (% of Female Population Ages 15+) (Modeled ILO Estimate)." World Bank Databank, accessed February 6, 2024, from International Labour Organization, "ILO Modelled Estimates and Projections database (ILOEST)." https://data.worldbank.org/indicator/SL.TLF.CACT.FE.ZS.

Yoshikawa, Hirokazu. 2011. *Immigrants Raising Citizens: Undocumented Parents and Their Children*. Russell Sage Foundation.

Yoshikawa, Hirokazu, Carola Suárez-Orozco, and Roberto G. Gonzales. 2017. "Unauthorized Status and Youth Development in the United States: Consensus

Statement of the Society for Research on Adolescence." *Journal of Research on Adolescence* 27(1): 4–19. https://doi.org/10.1111/jora.12272.

Zárate Gutiérrez, Iliana. 2017. "Evaluación del subprograma Repatriados Trabajando desde una visión de gobernanza para resultados." Master's thesis, El Colegio de la Frontera Norte. https://www.colef.mx/posgrado/tesis/uec2016222/.

Zavala, Maria Eugenia. 1993. "La transición demográfica en América Latina y en Europa." *Notas de Población* 20(56): 11–32.

———. 2014. "La transición demográfica de 1895–2010: ¿Una transición original?" In *Los mexicanos: un balance del cambio demográfico*, edited by Cecilia Rabell Romero. Fondo de Cultura Económica.

Zayas, Luis H. 2015. *Forgotten Citizens: Deportation, Children, and the Making of American Exiles and Orphans*. Oxford University Press.

Zúñiga, Víctor, and Eduardo Carrillo Cantú. 2020. "Migration and School Exclusion: Interrupted School Trajectories among Migrant Minors Moving from the United States to Mexico." *Estudios Sociológicos* 38(114): 655–88. https://doi.org/10.24201/es.2020v38n114.1907.

Zúñiga, Víctor, and Silvia Giorguli-Saucedo. 2020. *Niñas y niños en la migración de Estados Unidos a México: La generación 0.5*. El Colegio de México.

Zúñiga, Víctor, and Edmund T. Hamann. 2014. "Going to a Home You Have Never Been To: The Return Migration of Mexican and American-Mexican Children." *Children's Geographies* 13(6): 643–55. https://doi.org/10.1080/14733285.2014.936364.

———. 2020. "Children's Voices about 'Return' Migration from the United States to Mexico: The 0.5 Generation." *Children's Geographies* 19(1): 1–13. https://doi.org/10.1080/14733285.2020.1743818.

INDEX

Tables and figures are listed in **boldface**.

children of Mexican migrants, 92–93,
99. *See also* Deferred Action for
Childhood Arrivals program;
U.S.-citizen children of Mexican
migrants
cholos, 41–42, 137
circular migration patterns, 10, 12,
50–51, 59, 90
Clinton, Bill, 5
Comunidad en Retorno (Community
in Return), 84, 147
Congress and immigration reform, 52,
67. *See also specific acts*
construction employment, 143
corruption, 78–79, 82–83, 104, 119, 138
Covid-19 pandemic: interviews during,
148, 165; U.S. border protocols
during, 50, 149
crime: deportable criminal offenses,
51–52, 60–61, 73, 97, 100; and violence
in Mexico City, 78–83

Deferred Action for Childhood Arrivals
(DACA) program: and deserving
access to U.S. residency, 137; and
family separations, 57–58, 61, 98, 158;
interview subjects and eligibility for,
55, **56**; program details, 48, 50, 53–54,
57, 58
Deferred Action for Parents of
Americans and Lawful Permanent
Residents (DAPA), 54
Department of Homeland Security
(DHS), 52–53
Deportados Unidos en la Lucha (DUL,
Deportees United in Struggle), 84,
147
deportations: activist organizations in
Mexico City for returnees, 84–85,
98–99, 122; and binational mixed-
status families, 101–2; border regions,
returned migrants settling in, 13,
15–17; and de facto deported family
members, 91, 99–102, 152, 157–58;
deferrals of, 47–48; deportable

criminal offenses, 51–52, 60–61, 73,
97, 100; and family separations, 98,
140–41; immigration raids leading
to, 47, 62; lack of preparation for
returnees, 15–16, 110–11, 114–15;
Mexican census data on, 187*n*1;
Mexican response to, 85–86, 131,
133–36; during Obama presidency,
5, 151; and Policy Trap era, 5;
repatriation vs., 136–37; and "Show
Me Your Papers" law in Arizona,
47; treatment of detainees in United
States, 48–49, 131–32, 145–46; Trump's
2024 presidential campaign on, 150
depression, 47, 132, 146
disability status, 73–76, 147
discrimination, 76, 110, 120, 121–22, 154.
See also race and racism
disorientation and disconnection. *See*
norteado of return migrants
DREAM (Development, Relief, and
Education for Alien Minors) Act,
proposed, 52, 136–37
"Dreamers," 136–37, 158, 176–77
drug cartels, 79–82
drug smuggling, 13
Durand, Jorge, 10–11

earthquakes, 31, 149
Eduardo (interview subject): on culture
of United States, 63; on migrant spirit,
42–43; return to Mexico City, 75
education: advantages of migration
experiences, 126–29; crossing U.S.
border for, 105; English language
skills and, 93, 101; in Mexico, average
attainment levels, 117; for returned
migrants in Mexico City, 101, 103–4,
111, 117; validating U.S. credentials,
127–28
employment of returned migrants,
109–30; and activist networks, 122–25;
advantages of migration experiences,
126–29; barriers to, 110–11, 118–19,
156; current vs. premigration

stigma of return migration: and deportation, 167; and Policy Trap, 154; and repatriation, 137, 177; and stereotypes of Mexican migrants, 41–42, 70, 139; successful migration stories and avoidance of, 176

Supreme Court, U.S., on DACA, 54

Tenochtitlan, 3, 29. *See also* Mexico City

Title 42, 149

transnationalism, 91, 94, 101–6, 153. *See also* U.S.-citizen children of Mexican migrants

trauma, 146

Trump, Donald J.: DACA, attempt to terminate, 54; deportations under, 5; immigration policy, 48, 50, 66; presidential campaign of 2024, 150; threatening rhetoric toward Mexican migrants, 85

undocumented immigrants: agency collaborations to capture, 52–53; DREAM Act proposed for, 52, 136–37; estimated number of, 156; fear of deportation, 79, 150; overstaying visas, 58–59, 95, 188*n*25; Policy Trap era and extended stays of, 51, 53; successful navigation of social spaces, 59–60; U.S. demand for labor from, 50; U.S. reentry restrictions for, 52, 58, 61, 66, 141. *See also* Deferred Action for Childhood Arrivals program; deportations

United Nations High Commissioner for Refugees (UNHCR), 152

Universidad Autónoma de la Ciudad de México (Autonomous University of Mexico City, UACM), 138

upward mobility, 111, 114–15, 156

urban migrants, 3–4, 15, 31, 35–37

U.S. border. *See* Mexico-U.S. border region

U.S. immigration laws. *See* Bracero Accord; Policy Trap era; *specific laws*

U.S.-citizen children of Mexican migrants: binational families, 91; and family separation, 140–41; Policy Trap and increase in, 51; returning to Mexico with parents, 9, 15, 100–106, 157

violence: crossing Mexico-U.S. border region, dangers of, 51, 59, 66, 81–82; migrating to escape family abuse, 96–97; and return to Mexico City, 78–83

visas: family sponsorship for, 55–57, 100, 102; obtaining after deportation, 86; overstaying, 58–59, 95, 188*n*25

Wassink, Joshua, 116

Wieczorek, Agnieszka, 109

Yazmín (interview subject): and Covid-19 pandemic, 148; DACA status of children, 57–58; family separation, 88–91, 95, 98, 106, 140; return to Mexico City, 1

Zúñiga, Víctor, 15, 157